T0304435

DOWN WITH THE SYSTEM

DOWN WITH THE SYSTEM

A MEMOIR
(OF SORTS)

SERJ TANKIAN

HEADLINE

First published in the US in 2024 by
HACHETTE BOOK GROUP, INC.

First published in the UK in 2024 by
HEADLINE PUBLISHING GROUP.

1

Note: "Down with the System" was originally published in Serj Tankian's *Glaring
Through Oblivion* (HarperCollins, 2011).

Cataloguing in Publication Data is available from the British Library

Hardback ISBN: 978 1 0354 0362 2
Trade paperback ISBN: 978 1 0354 0363 9

Print book interior design by Sheryl Kober

Offset in 12.48/18.72 pt Minion Pro by Jouve (UK), Milton Keynes

Printed and bound in Great Britain by Clays Ltd, Elcograf S.p.A.

HEADLINE PUBLISHING GROUP
An Hachette UK Company
Carmelite House
50 Victoria Embankment
London EC4Y 0DZ

www.headline.co.uk
www.hachette.co.uk

DOWN WITH THE SYSTEM

When the doors of hope open
To an illuminating silence,
We plead to the gods of industry
To release us from our lives.
Casual neckties embrace phantom
    genes,
Possessing cellular catastrophes,
As sex scandals dictate
The winding road of Re'al Poli'tic
The bully runs out of his corner,
Images rule through the media,
The hungry hunger further during
    Thanksgiving,
Where the landowner
Turned urban corporate,
Thanks the native population
For their lands and lives.
"Thank you for letting us fuck you!"
Dormant doorknobs professing
    decisions
Behind closed doors,
Behind closed minds,
Attractive feudalism,
Commercial Orwellianism,
Global pacification proclamations
Bought for a dollar increase in the
    minimum wage.
Devaluating nationalism against
    the dollar.
Repeating the mistakes of former
    empires.
Security is the deadliest and most
    misused word
Of the 20th century.
Under the auspices of security,
We murder, loot, and incarcerate.
We fight over the dismantling of
    others'
Weapons of mass destruction,
While building our sinister influ-
    encing programs.
We can feel the End near,
As we lay helpless against the global
Corporate, elitist machine.
Open your eyes,
Open your mouths,
Close your hands,
And make a fist.
Down with the System!

CONTENTS

INTRODUCTION

I t was only 5 a.m. and I already felt like I'd been run over by a truck. Sitting on the edge of my hotel bed in Denver with the phone pressed to my ear, I was wondering how it had come to this. On the other end of the line was Howard Stern—well, not just Howard but his whole motley radio show crew—and they were *grilling* me.

Two weeks earlier, System Of A Down had released our second album, *Toxicity*, and it was now the number-one album in the country. I think it's safe to say we were as unlikely a chart-topper as had ever existed in modern music history: a band of Armenian-Americans playing a practically unclassifiable clash of wildly aggressive metal riffs, unconventional tempo-twisting rhythms, and Armenian folk melodies, with me alternately growling, screaming, and crooning lyrics that could pivot from avant-garde silliness to raging socio-political rants in the space of a single line. I'd be the first to admit it: it's not easy listening. But the news of our surprise chart triumph was drowned out a little by another unexpected event.

The day we hit number one was September 11, 2001.

I was staring at my TV that clear, sunny, horrible Tuesday morning as I watched the second airplane hit the World Trade Center. Like most other people, I was in absolute shock. *How did this happen? Who would do such a thing? And why?* Politicians and many in the media quickly offered pat explanations like "they hate our freedoms." But I understood the history of the Middle East, I read the *New York Times*, I read *The Economist*, and that kind of oversimplification didn't sit quite right with me. Ultimately, I hunkered down and did what I always do when I'm trying to get my head around something I can't quite figure out: I wrote. Two days after the attacks, I posted my thoughts in the form of an essay titled "Understanding Oil" on the band's website.

"Terror is not a spontaneous human action without credence," I wrote. "People just don't hijack planes and commit harakiri without any weight of thought to the action." In the subsequent paragraphs, I dove deep into US foreign policy, particularly the steep price of our oil consumption. I explained that the 9/11 attacks were "a reaction to existing injustices around the world, generally unseen to most Americans." There was a long, sordid history to consider. The US government had secured oil concessions from Turkey through secret deals after World War I in return for ignoring the Armenian Genocide, which was perpetrated by the Turks. It had also overthrown a democratically elected leader in Iran and replaced him with a king in order to get access to that country's resources. The American government even allied with both Saddam Hussein and the Taliban when it suited their perceived interests. The sanctions in Iraq were contributing to mass suffering there, because they usually hurt the poor disproportionately.

The closer you looked, the less shocking the 9/11 attacks actually were. I could already sense the gathering thirst for vengeance throughout the country and was worried about the consequences of acting on it. "If we carry out bombings in Afghanistan or elsewhere to appease public demand and very likely kill innocent civilians along the way," I wrote, "we'll be creating many more martyrs going to their deaths in retaliation against the retaliation." Instead, I suggested a multilateral approach, one that would bring the terrorists responsible to international justice.

Most everything in that essay would be echoed by many others in the months and years to come. A lot of it has become conventional wisdom now. But at the time it was posted, two days after 9/11, it did not go over well. *At all.* The way a lot of people viewed it was like this: the whole nation is in shock and mourning, and the lead singer of one of the most popular bands in the country is suggesting that we might have brought this upon ourselves. That it's *our* fault. That's an overly reductive way to interpret what I was saying, but I get it.

This was the pre-social-media era, so the backlash didn't come as the all-consuming digital tidal wave you might get today, but it came all the same. I was condemned in newspapers, on music websites, and all over the radio, including by Howard Stern, who was arguably the country's most popular and influential media personality in those days. Our record label insisted that we take the essay down off our website and for the first and only time in my life, I acquiesced to such a request. The pressure was *that* intense. Notably, a lot of the anger at me and at the band had a xenophobic tinge. We were pilloried as immigrants from the Middle East who had the nerve to criticize the country that had taken us in and given us opportunities.

(Although Armenia is not actually in the Middle East, no one was getting hung up splitting geographical hairs.)

The night before I got on the phone for Howard's show, I'd had a meeting with my bandmates at that same hotel. They weren't much happier with me than everyone else was. They'd all dreamed of what we'd just achieved—a number-one album—and that success was being drowned out by death threats and accusations that we were all traitors. This was the band's big moment, and my essay was threatening to ruin it for us all. At that meeting, the first thing our guitarist Daron said to me was, "Are you trying to get us all *killed*?" I remember telling him that what I wrote was the truth, that it was all verifiable.

"Who *cares* that it's the truth?!" Now it was John, our drummer, going at me. He later compared it to giving a eulogy at a funeral and calling the dead guy an asshole in front of his grieving family and friends. It may be the truth, but it's not a very smart (or sensitive) thing to do.

"It's not a good time to talk about this," he said.

I was very apologetic to the guys. I had naively thought that in a democracy you could always tell the truth.

Going on Stern's radio show the morning that our tour was kicking off was seen as necessary damage control. I knew my job was to go on the air and calm everyone down. Rick Rubin, who'd produced both of our first two albums and was also the head of our record label, knew Stern and had helped set up the call. He also gave me some key advice: "Don't try to challenge Howard. It won't go over well if you do. Just try to pivot him into talking about government abuses and things like that. He understands that the US government has done some bad shit in the past."

So that's how I found myself, sweating it out on the phone before the sun even came up in Denver. The odd thing about all the criticism I'd been getting was that because the essay had been taken down off the website, very few people had actually *read* it. This included Howard, Robin, and everyone else in Howard's studio that morning. All they'd read was someone else's skewed report summarizing what I'd written.

I could tell from the minute I got on the phone that Howard and his crew were ginned up for a rip-roaring argument. I didn't take the bait. I declined to try to summarize my three-page essay into a tight soundbite for them. Every time they lobbed an accusation at me, I'd calmly pivot, just like Rick suggested. Rather than elaborate on the US government's mistakes, I explained that "all governments commit injustices." When I was asked about the dire human consequences of the no-fly zone and the embargo against Iraq, I merely pointed to the *New York Times'* reporting on the subject. I admitted that posting my essay when I did was, if nothing else, certainly a case of bad timing.

No matter what I did or didn't say, it seemed like Howard was fired up with righteous indignation, and his whole cohort acted like it was their patriotic duty to put me in my place. I can vividly recall staring out the window of my hotel room during that phone call and seeing the Denver Coliseum across the street. We were set to perform there that same night. Massive American flags were displayed on screens outside the arena, with "God Bless America" playing on a loop from the speakers. That kind of stuff was *everywhere* in those days. Politicians, newscasters, journalists, hell, even the front-desk staff at our hotel were wearing flag pins on their lapels. It was as if the flag itself had become some sort of universal marker to delineate what had become an all-consuming question in those weeks after 9/11: *Are you* with *us or* against *us?* Later that same day, George W. Bush framed it that way in an address to Congress: "Either you are with us, or you are with the terrorists." And that's kind of what that call with Howard was; it was his way of sussing out whether I—and by extension, our whole band—was with the US or against it. There was no middle ground, no room for nuance.

At one point, Howard asked flat out whether we hated America.

"No, we love America!" I responded.

It was true. I did and do love America. But I don't think I'd ever felt less a part of it than I did in that moment.

All four of my grandparents survived the Armenian Genocide. My parents met in Beirut, where I was born. We lived there until I was seven, when we fled the civil war in Lebanon and emigrated to California. I couldn't speak English well, didn't understand the culture, and grew up in a community near Los Angeles that was heavily populated with Armenian-Americans. But I don't think I've ever felt more like an immigrant, an outsider, than I did that day on the phone with Howard Stern.

That said, I guess the interview helped put the pin back in the grenade, so to speak. I'm sure some crisis PR firm could point to it as a masterclass in deflection. But I didn't feel great about it. To this day, it still bothers me. I'm not angry at Howard or anyone else; I'm disappointed with myself. I have no regrets about writing the essay, but I have lots of regrets about not defending it more vigorously. I pulled my punches. It was a difficult moment to stand up for the truth, and though I'd initially done so by writing that essay, when the heat got turned up, I wilted a little.

Look, it was an intense moment. People were freaked out. When you'd turn on the TV, there was a rolling ticker along the bottom of the screen tracking the death toll from the attacks and offering up context-free quotes from experts and public officials predicting where the next targets might be—water treatment plants, nuclear facilities, public gatherings. Our tour—which was called, I shit you not, "The Pledge of Allegiance Tour" (a title that, it should be noted, had been chosen *months* earlier)—had to be delayed because travel was completely shut down across the country. We were one of the first bands back out on the road, and just the idea of getting thousands of people together in an arena seemed wildly risky. In the case of our tour, the danger was further ramped up based on the domestic threats and hate being directed at us.

Our first single, "Chop Suey!," had essentially been banned from the radio. The song's chorus—"I don't think you trust in my self-righteous suicide / I cry when angels deserve to die"—did feel like a surreal reference to the disturbing events of 9/11, though obviously it was written long before that. But the ban itself was just a misguided knee-jerk effort by the country's largest radio conglomerate, Clear Channel, to prohibit songs they felt might upset listeners already distraught by the attacks. I suppose "Chop Suey!" was an obvious candidate for this list of banned songs, certainly more obvious than some of the others (which included John Lennon's "Imagine," Louis Armstrong's "What a Wonderful World," and Simon and Garfunkel's "Bridge over Troubled Water").

Amid all this tension and paranoia, maybe it's understandable that I backed down. I can look back on it now and see that if I had really tried to speak my mind at the time, to challenge the jingoistic fervor that had taken a hold of the country, it almost certainly would've fallen on deaf ears. No one wanted to hear that shit, and they *definitely* didn't want to hear it on "The Howard Stern Show." As Edward S. Herman and Noam Chomsky put it in their book, *Manufacturing Consent,* if you try to question the premise of the system in a thirty-second soundbite, you'll come off looking like a madman. I was there to defuse a bomb, to quiet the death threats, to make sure more radio stations didn't drop us from their playlists, to keep our tour on track, to convince my bandmates I was still part of the team.

There had always been a feeling within System that I cared more about our message and our political activism than I cared about the band itself. Ultimately, this was probably more true than I realized or was willing to admit at the time. My bandmates had all grown up with dreams of being rock stars. I hadn't. I loved music, but my artistic journey was still very much in its infancy; in fact, I'd never studied or even really played music growing up, and it wasn't until college when this passion really took off. I had a whole *life*—interesting, multilayered, diverse—before music became my everything. I was an activist long before I was an artist and I have never wanted to be one of those vacant souls who speaks to millions but talks to no one. In that moment, though, the most important thing seemed to be not fucking up everything for my friends—or worse.

People sometimes ask me how excited I was when *Toxicity* came out and hit number one, but all I remember is being unbelievably stressed out. The fact is I had just turned thirty-four and didn't really have the emotional and spiritual tools to deal with that kind of anxiety back then. I'd recently started meditating, but in the early days of my spiritual practice, I mistook passivity for nonaggression. When Howard was coming for me, I knew how to defuse his hostility, but not how to answer it. I hadn't learned the virtues of compassionate confrontation. This wasn't something I could simply read about or take a class on. It would take years, much experience, and the near collapse of System Of A Down for me to fully understand it. Even today, it's an ongoing process.

Just before I got off the phone with Howard, he wrapped up the segment by saying, "Serj came in here and he said the right things." If anything drives home the shortcomings of my appearance on his show, it's that sentence. I've *never* wanted to be the guy who says all the right things to make everyone feel better. That's not to say I'm trying to upset people, but rather, my life's work has always been about learning how to deliver hard truths at difficult moments in ways people will hear them. That was kind of the whole point of System Of A Down. Or at least, it was for me.

There is no doubt that morning on Howard Stern's show was an opportunity lost. I had a lot to say about American foreign policy, about our country's history of intervention in the Middle East, about how freedom of speech itself is always the first casualty of war—but I didn't. I let my actions be dictated by fear. Fear of ridicule. Fear of ostracism. Fear of violence. Fear, frankly, that my bandmates would never forgive me. But I like to think that the lesson I took from that failure was more important than the failure itself. It's at those moments when no one wants to hear the truth that it's so important to tell it.

Now I knew what it felt like to hold my tongue when it most needed to be unleashed. And I vowed that I would never let it happen again.

CHAPTER 1

My story starts in a small village I've never been to, nearly sixty years before I was born. Efkere was a quiet hamlet of stone houses that sat nestled on a modest hillside in what is now central Turkey. A brook ran through the center of the village, not far from an ornate domed church that was built into the hill behind it. When my grandfather, Stepan, was born in Efkere in 1909, it was a predominantly Armenian enclave. Today, much of the village has been reduced to rubble by time and neglect, and there are no Armenians among the remaining inhabitants. It's a place that no longer even exists on modern maps.

Stepan was my mother's father, and when I was younger, I knew him as a gentle, steady presence in my life. He was a doting grandpa who would buy me toys, make me towers of toasted bologna sandwiches, and spend hours working in his garden. He didn't talk much about his childhood and the life he'd lived, but at times I'd catch glimpses of a quiet willpower that his life's trials had forged in him. I can remember once, when he was well into his seventies, a conversation I had with him about the virtues of exercise. He mentioned to me that even at his age, he could still do twenty push-ups, no problem. He wasn't a big guy, and I shrugged a little, not wanting to disrespect him but clearly dubious of his claim. In a flash, my elderly grandfather was on the floor, cranking out twenty push-ups like he was a Marine recruit.

When he put his mind to something, nothing could get in his way. For years, like many men of his generation, Stepan constantly smoked cigarettes. One day when he was in his late sixties, my uncle was giving him a hard time about smoking, so Stepan told him, "Fine. I'll quit smoking right now." And he did. Right then, after more than fifty years of smoking two packs a day, he went cold turkey simply because my uncle had insinuated that he couldn't.

My grandfather lived well into his nineties, by which time his body was beginning to break down. He could no longer walk and was bedridden. Despite this, not much else was wrong with him. He didn't have any sort of life-threatening condition—no cancer, no heart ailment, nothing that had him yet marked for the great beyond. But in his bones, he felt like his time had come.

His first wife, my grandmother Varsenig, had died decades before, and his contentious relationship with his second wife had mercifully ended in divorce. He was living in a nursing home. To this day, I still feel terrible that he was placed there, but realistically, everyone in the family worked at the time, so no one was available to look after him. He hated being in a convalescent home, and I have no doubt it contributed to his sense of exasperation. At a certain point, he decided it was his time to go, so he stopped eating and drinking.

As you can imagine, this was tremendously distressing for my family, but there was nothing any of us could do to convince him to change his mind. I was in my thirties then, and I can remember sitting by his bed, begging him, "Grandpa, come on, you've *got* to eat!" He looked up at me from his bed and smiled. "Eat, and then what?" he asked. I had no real answer for him. Neither did anyone else. Less than a week later, he was gone. He'd essentially starved himself to death.

On one level, it was an incredibly difficult time for our family, but on another level, I couldn't help but admire the supernatural strength of this man's resolve. He chose the exact moment when he was ready to go, and in doing so, he showed that it was possible to override hunger, discomfort, and our innate survival instinct if you were committed enough. Who does that? What creates that sort of willpower in a person? To understand that—and to understand my life, my work, and the things that drive me—you need to understand what happened in Efkere.

——————

The village of Efkere dates to at least the thirteenth century. It formed in the shadow of the Surp Garabed Vank—a stately, walled monastery that was perched on top of a nearby hill. The monastery reportedly housed some of the remains of Saint John the Baptist.

There are two competing theories behind the origin of the village's name. The first is that it's an adaptation of the Greek word *yevkaria*, which can translate as "sacred place," a nod to the saint's remains. The second and altogether more delightful theory—and the one to which my grandfather subscribed—is that it's derived from the Armenian phrase *hevk arav*, which means "He took a breath" or "He panted." As the story goes, in the fourth century, Saint Gregory the Illuminator was carrying John the Baptist's remains up and down the steep hills through the region. *Hevk Arav*, or later, "Efkere," is right where he stopped to take a breath.

Despite such colorful origin stories, Efkere was in many ways an unremarkable place. It was a picturesque, little village that attracted pilgrims from around the region who made their way to the monastery on holy days, but it was by no means special. It was a way station. And what happened to the Armenians there, happened to them most everywhere.

By the time Stepan was born in 1909, there were about five hundred Armenian families living in Efkere, as well as a smaller number of Turkish families. Stepan lived on the second floor of a house in the *verin tagh*, or "upper neighborhood," on the hill that led up to the monastery. There was a workbench in his house where his mother, Vartouhi, made carpets. This was time-consuming and painstaking work. To weave one whole carpet would take an entire year.

Many in the town were artisans and tradesmen, but by the early 1900s, the local economy was floundering, and lots of families were relying on remittances from Efkerens living abroad, mostly in America, to pay for staples like food.

A grim specter seemed to be looming over Efkere in those days. In the years when my grandfather was a young boy, the town endured a cholera epidemic, a drought, a serious outbreak of typhoid fever, and the near-total collapse of the local economy. When the cholera hit in 1912, a crew of Turkish gendarmes set up a blockade around the town, and for a month, no one was allowed in or out. In retrospect, it was a disturbing harbinger of what was to come. When the epidemic abated, it had killed approximately thirty people in Efkere and accelerated an exodus of villagers already fueled by the drought and economic woes.

Stepan's father, Garabed, made and sold ink, and like many townsfolk, he moved to the US for a spell, when Stepan was young. At the time, Stepan did not know Garabed was his father. Even after Garabed returned from the US, he didn't live in the same house with Stepan, his mother, and his younger brothers, David and Harutyun, even though he was a frequent presence there. Everyone was instructed to refer to him only as "the Turkish man." If anyone asked who was at home, the reply would always be that "the Turkish man is there."

One day, at dinner, Stepan took his spoon and started eating, carelessly spilling some food onto the kitchen floor. Vartouhi raised her arm to slap her son when the Turkish man intervened, catching her hand.

"Don't you *dare* do that to the boy!" the man told his mother.

Later, Stepan confronted his mother, demanding to know who the man was who'd saved him from being slapped.

"That's your father," she finally admitted. "We called him the Turkish man so you didn't get used to calling him by his name, and he wouldn't get arrested."

Garabed was Armenian, not Turkish, but to be an Armenian man in those days was to invite unwanted attention from the Turkish authorities. As my grandfather put it many years later when he told me this story, "No one wanted the Turks to know about their Armenian origins. We lived keeping secrets."

It was the unraveling of these secrets that would eventually lead to unfathomable tragedy for my family—and many families just like my own. And it was this tragedy that would come to define the lives of its survivors for generations.

———

If you look at a modern map, Armenia is a small, landlocked country sandwiched between Turkey, Iran, Azerbaijan, and Georgia. But that country didn't exist during the time Stepan and my three other Armenian grandparents were children. The areas they lived in were hundreds of miles from the Armenia of today.

Armenians often trace their primeval beginnings to the biblical figure of Noah, the forebearer of the nation's legendary founding patriarch, Hayk, and there are written references to Armenia going back to the fifth century BC. It was the first country to adopt Christianity, just after 300 AD, a fact that would prove incredibly significant in its history, particularly after Islam became dominant in the region, beginning in the seventh century. After successive waves of invasions by Mongols, Turkmens, and other Central Asian tribes, what had been historically known as Armenia was swallowed more or less whole by the Ottoman Empire in the fifteenth century.

Although the Ottoman Empire was generally ruled by ethnic Turks, it was initially a sprawling, multinational empire that included Arabs, Kurds, Assyrians, Armenians, and many other peoples among its citizens. Islam was the state religion, but the burdens of non-Muslim citizenship for the empire's Jews, Christians, and other non-Muslims were not necessarily unwieldy. As such, Armenians lived, largely peaceably, under the rule of the Ottoman Turks for centuries. However, as the empire began to fray at the edges in the middle part of the nineteenth century, it began consolidating into a more explicitly Turkish, more explicitly Muslim empire, and the position of the Armenians within its borders grew increasingly fraught.

The Armenians were a Christian minority in an Islamic empire, but their marginalization grew, at least initially, more from economic and social factors, which were only later framed in religious terms. Like my great-grandparents, many Armenians had a long history as successful merchants and tradesmen, and the cultural emphasis they placed on education put them in an advantageous position within the Ottoman Empire. Many of them began to fill the ranks of a respected professional class as doctors, lawyers, pharmacists, bankers, and other well-paying vocations. But their visible upward mobility engendered resentment.

Then, in the late nineteenth century, a series of military defeats for the Ottoman Turks rapidly shrunk the empire's territory. The Armenians were portrayed as a restive alien population within the empire's borders and became a scapegoat for its inexorable decline. This phenomenon—in which a minority becomes a target of blame during a time of national hardship—is not necessarily uncommon throughout human history, as I'd learn later on, but it had a profound impact on the sequence of events that followed. As time progressed, the dynamic between the Armenians and their neighbors became a vexing issue. What were the Ottoman authorities going to do about this Armenian minority within their borders? Within and outside the empire, this became known, rather ominously, as "the Armenian Question."

When European powers pushed for better treatment for the Armenians, it was seen as proof of where the Armenians' real loyalties lay—namely, with Europe, instead of with the Ottoman Empire. When Armenian political leaders agitated for civil reforms and legal protections within the dying empire, it was presented to their anxious neighbors as evidence of a rising rebellion. Such efforts were then answered with widespread, state-sanctioned repression and violence.

In the mid-1890s, between one hundred thousand and three hundred thousand Armenians were brutally killed by Ottoman soldiers, Kurdish brigands, and a host of irregular militias and mobs in what became known as the Hamidian Massacres. The year my grandfather Stepan was born, in 1909, an additional twenty thousand to thirty thousand Armenians were massacred by Ottoman forces and local mobs in Adana, about one hundred miles from Efkere. This was the perilous world he and the rest of my grandparents were born into, where keeping your Armenian heritage secret could be the difference between life and death.

The Ottomans lost nearly all their European territory in the Balkan War of 1912–1913. When World War I broke out in 1914 and they threw their lot in with the Germans, most of the Ottoman Armenian soldiers fought *for* the Ottomans, yet they were still not trusted. Armenian military units were demobilized and converted into labor battalions. Most of those soldiers were then systematically slaughtered by the Ottoman Army.

Word of what was happening spread quickly. Back in the small town of Efkere, Stepan recalled Turkish gendarmes coming to a house that belonged to his grandmother. The woman who lived there had a seventeen-year-old son whom the Turks insisted should be fighting in the war. She knew that enlistment in the Ottoman

Army would be a death sentence for her son, so every time the gendarmes came, she told him to hide. Finally, the gendarmes beat the woman so severely that the boy emerged from a back room, where he'd been buried in blankets. "Take me, but please don't touch my mother," he cried. He left with them and was never seen nor heard from again.

All across the empire, early in the war, deportations of Armenians were carried out in the name of state security, and sporadic local massacres were justified as a military necessity. When the deportations began in Efkere, the authorities told people not to take food or heavy things with them because they'd be able to return in fifteen days. But those deported never returned. People were advised to take Turkish names and convert to Islam.

There were small pockets of Armenian resistance. As the noose began to tighten around Efkere, Stepan's uncle, then a teenager, eluded Turkish gendarmes and fled the village along with a dozen or so friends, intent on joining Murad of Sebastia, a legendary military leader who was conducting guerilla warfare with a small band of Armenian rebels. But the uncle and his would-be compatriots were intercepted in Ankara, besieged by Turks, and killed. Murad himself survived until 1918, when he died in battle.

Throughout the empire, there were mass arrests of Armenian men followed by summary executions. Stepan recalled watching his father and two older male relatives being hauled away in chains by gendarmes. His mother insisted Stepan bear witness to the arrests, even though Stepan was only five at the time. Recounting the story more than eighty years later, he grew agitated as he admitted that he didn't get a good look at his father. "His head was bent back, so I didn't see his entire face. I said, 'I didn't see him, Mom. I didn't see him.'"

The family was allowed to bring Garabed food at the local prison shortly thereafter. When they arrived, Stepan could see his father caged behind iron bars. He handed the food to a policeman who handed it to his father and then told Stepan to "go away!" As Stepan tried to give his father a kiss through the bars, his father strained to reach him but failed.

"Stepanik, don't go! I'm coming!" his father yelled after him.

But the police wouldn't allow it. It was the last time he'd ever see his father.

By the spring of 1915, the widespread violence and forced migration had coalesced into a systematic campaign to eliminate the Armenians from the Ottoman Empire. It was clear the state saw the First World War as their chance to settle "the Armenian Question" once and for all.

With most of the men already disappeared, hordes of women and children were then emptied out of villages, towns, and cities, and forced by the Turks and their allies to walk en masse hundreds of miles into the Syrian desert. The details of these death-haunted human caravans are almost too gruesome to bear. On the road, the Armenians faced widespread attacks, looting, rape, murder, torture, disease, and starvation.

Stepan was marched out of Efkere with his grandmother, his younger brother David, and his mother carrying his youngest brother, Harutyun, in her arms. They were part of a group of about fifty—all women, children under ten, or very old, infirm men—who left the village and joined a convoy of roughly a thousand other

Armenians. They walked through mountains, valleys, deserts, and forests, under the watch of the gendarmes, who steered the caravan to avoid population centers where outside observers might be able to witness the abject horror for themselves. Those who lagged behind were brutally beaten and whipped.

One night, the group stopped in a forest to sleep and was attacked by armed bandits. Vartouhi had her clothes torn off her body by knife-wielding assailants. In an effort to shield her baby son Harutyun from the violence and mayhem, she tried to toss him out of the way, to safety. It didn't work. He choked to death in the ensuing melee.

The Armenians walked for months with little access to food and water. Stepan's other brother David was a wily, clever boy who had a talent for finding scraps of food or, if that failed, snatching them out of other people's hands and not getting caught. He always shared whatever he found with his older brother. Stepan recalled David scurrying up to him and pressing a piece of bread or some figs into his hand with simple instructions. "Eat this. If you don't eat anything, you'll die." But there just wasn't enough food to go around for everyone. Shortly after the death of Harutyun, Stepan's aunt gave birth to a baby. Within two weeks, the infant starved to death.

The conditions bred an almost unimaginable desperation among those enduring the death march. Stepan recalled parents so wracked by hunger that when their son died, they cut him into pieces and cooked him to eat. Others on the caravan were appalled but did nothing in response. As Stepan put it simply, "They understood."

Death was a constant, and the macabre became distressingly common. On the edge of a forest, near the town of Jarabulus, Stepan wandered into the aftermath of a ghastly scene: eight dead Armenian women, stripped naked, their breasts cut off, with two dead children by their side. Eighty years later, as he began to tell me this story, he stopped himself. "I don't want to talk about this," he said, shutting down. It was still too painful.

These sorts of grisly stories spread among the caravans, creating an ever-present shadow of terror and dread. At a town along the Euphrates River, Stepan and others were given permission to go to a public bath, but doing so required crossing the mighty Euphrates, the biggest river in the Middle East, on a small ferry. On the boat with him was a group of teenage Armenian girls. When some Turkish sailors noticed the girls, they approached menacingly and cornered them. Fearing rape or worse, the girls, one after another, threw themselves over the side of the ferry into the rushing waters of the Euphrates, choosing death by drowning over leaving their fates to the Turks.

After walking for close to a year, Stepan and what was left of his family reached the city of Raqqa, in Syria, nearly four hundred miles from where they'd begun their forced trek. Of the thousand or so who'd been part of the caravan when they left Efkere, roughly half were already dead. The march would then continue on for another hundred miles or so to large, open-air concentration camps in the desert near Deir ez-Zor. Hundreds of thousands of Armenians ended up in these camps in Deir ez-Zor, where they were subject to further starvation and other assorted atrocities. That same desert in current-day Syria recently bore witness to another massacre, this time of Yazidis at the hands of ISIS.

History repeats itself, sometimes in the exact same places.

For Stepan and Vartouhi, malnutrition would cause them to go blind for two years before their eyesight began to return. When Stepan's grandmother died, the Turks would not allow her to be buried, so his mother and another woman wrapped her in a shroud and tossed her into the Euphrates.

Perhaps the most horrific part of Stepan's story is how ordinary it actually was. For Ottoman Armenians in 1915, forced displacement, brutalization, rape, starvation, disease, and widespread slaughter were the norm. I grew up listening to my grandfather's testimony, so much so that his story became inextricably woven into the fabric of my own lived experience. Later on, I learned more details about his story because I was able to record him on camera in a series of interviews conducted by an organization gathering stories from survivors of the Armenian Genocide. And his wasn't the only story passed down to me during my childhood. I also heard occasional appalling snippets of the manifold miseries endured by my three other grandparents—my mom's mother was denied an opportunity to kiss her father's hand as he was hauled away by the Turks to his death; my dad's mother saw her parents and brothers murdered in front of her house by Turkish gendarmes, and was then sold with her sisters to Kurdish tribesmen—but all of their stories are just another thread in this nightmarish human tapestry.

———

It's important to recognize that the Armenian survivors of this campaign of annihilation were not necessarily stronger, smarter, or made of sterner stuff than those who became its victims. As Auschwitz survivor Primo Levi wrote of the Holocaust's human and moral toll in *The Drowned and the Saved*:

> In the space of a few weeks or months the deprivations to which they were subjected led them to a condition of pure survival, a daily struggle against hunger, cold, fatigue, and blows in which the room for choices (especially moral choices) was reduced to zero. Among these, very few survived the test, and this thanks to the conjunction of many improbable events. In short, they were saved by luck, and there is not much sense in trying to find something common to all their destinies, beyond perhaps their initial good health.

Levi was writing about the Nazi concentration camps, but his words are no less true of the Turkish pogroms against the Armenians that preceded them. My father's grandfather, an orange farmer who would also deliver mail around his region of the Ottoman Empire when crops were out of season, was out on one of these long-haul postal deliveries when soldiers came to empty out his home village. So, he miraculously escaped the slaughter. My mother's grandfather also managed to elude the Turkish Army, hiding in the rugged hills outside Tokat in what is now central Turkey. But when he tried to return home, he was captured, taken to a prison camp, and then never heard from again. One was lucky, one was not.

So why open this book with this catalog of horrors? Am I just trying to throw cold water on all those readers who picked it up hoping to find behind-the-scenes stories of tour hijinks or to discover why System Of A Down hasn't made an album in more than fifteen years? I swear it's not that. (And I promise I will tell those tales, too.) But to understand anything about me, my life, or even System Of A Down, you need to understand the Armenian Genocide, which is the rough, rocky river that runs through it. It's the original sin that's nearly always being reckoned with, even when it seems far out of sight.

For my grandparents, these were traumas absorbed at a fatefully impressionable age. There have been studies that show how trauma is actually passed down across generations, literally imprinted onto your DNA. I have no doubt that this happened for millions of Armenians in the diaspora like me, but that's only part of what I'm talking about.

In very real ways, the Armenian Genocide has never been fully reckoned with and has continued to reverberate in people's lives for more than a century, right up until today. Despite the suffering that my family, and millions of other families, endured, what is perhaps even more painful is the fact that entire nations—most notably, Turkey, the perpetrators of the Genocide itself—deny to this day that it ever happened in the first place, sweeping my people's history under the rug. Throughout modern-day Turkey, remnants of Armenian life and culture, like my grandfather's village of Efkere, have been destroyed, discarded, and allowed to disintegrate into nothingness. If genocide is ultimately an act of erasure, denial is its final, comprehensive deed.

For Stepan, the horrific trauma he endured certainly didn't melt away with the defeat of the Ottoman Empire. After surviving the epic death march, he and his brother David were separated from their mother and became homeless, often sleeping on the streets wrapped in cardboard, hugging each other for warmth. They were discovered by missionaries who sent them to live in an orphanage in Istanbul, then later to similar facilities in Aleppo, Adana, and Corinth. But after both grew ill, they were separated from each other. Stepan was living in an orphanage in Cyprus when he received a letter informing him that his brother David had died. He was so distraught that he tried to hurl himself into the sea. When he was ten, Stepan was reunited with his mother, who took him to see David's grave. He was still so overcome with grief that on successive Sundays, he tried to dig up his brother to see him again before his mother finally convinced him to let David rest in peace.

A few years later, Stepan and his mother, Vartouhi, were separated again, as she was unable to take care of him. He landed in Beirut in 1924 at the age of thirteen, where he began working as a carpenter, a blacksmith, and a stone carver. Unbeknownst to Stepan, Vartouhi was also in Beirut for a while and, after a time, got remarried, albeit without informing her son of the wedding. When he learned of his mother's nuptials, he was furious, and went searching for the wedding party with anger in his heart. Fortunately, he never found them, but for years afterward, the two were mostly estranged.

Stepan and his mother eventually reconciled and spent time with each other's families. Vartouhi emigrated to Soviet Armenia, the country that had been incorporated into the Soviet Union in 1922 and would later morph into modern-day Armenia. When they connected for the last time in the days before her death, it had been years since they'd seen each other. Vartouhi held her son tightly, her hands roving across his skin. Stepan was momentarily confused.

"What are you looking for?" he asked her.

"There must be a scar here," she replied. "Do you remember the day when I threw the wooden clog at you? You were injured." Finally, she found the scar and was satisfied. "Now I know that you're Stepan."

Although they ended in a good place, the tumultuous nature of Stepan's relationship with his mother is emblematic of the way trauma quietly reverberates across multiple generations, in ways that are not always fully grasped. Did Stepan blame his mother on some level for not protecting him from the Turks? For not protecting his two brothers? For trying to move on after the death of his father? Even if Stepan were still here today, could he answer any of these questions? I doubt it. But knowing even a small part of his history undoubtedly helps explain a guy who took pride in being able to crank out push-ups as a septuagenarian and who'd seen enough death to know when it was time for his own.

There's also a direct line to be drawn from all these seemingly distant tales to the squalls and storms of my own life. Certainly, the story of Stepan's suffering, and that of all my relatives and the Armenian people in general, now lives on in me, his descendant—it runs through my veins, breathes within my lungs, beats as one with my heart. And as a recipient of this testimony, I feel a duty—and an honor—to continue fighting for recognition of the Genocide that my people lived through. In my early days with System Of A Down as I began to see the impact we were having, I made a promise to my grandfather that I'd keep telling his story, for as long as it took for the world to acknowledge and account for these atrocities. I also connected his struggle to a wider fight against injustice and inequality, not just for Armenians but for everyone and everything. You could say that activism has always been in my blood. But I think there's something a little more ineffable that I've inherited from Stepan too.

My bandmate John, who is also my brother-in-law, says I'm a stubborn bastard who will always do what I think is right regardless of what anyone else thinks. I've always taken that as a compliment—whether John means it that way or not. In my personal quest for truth, justice, and the path of righteousness, I tend to listen to everyone but ultimately stick to my gut. That's a quality that has probably cost me friends, certainly cost me fans, and maybe even cost me my band, but I wouldn't change it. I couldn't even if I wanted to.

For better or worse, I like to think that's my grandfather's legacy too.

Stepan moved to California in 1974 and lived a full and often happy life. But I don't think he ever made peace with what he'd lived through as a child. In his eighties, when he was asked about whether the psychic wounds of the Genocide had ever healed, he was unequivocal.

"No, they haven't," he said. "On the contrary, they seem quite fresh. At my age, it's dangerous, but that's God's will."

CHAPTER 2

I n 2011, I traveled to Lebanon to play a show backed by the Lebanese Symphony Orchestra at Zouk Mikael, this beautiful Roman amphitheater perched on a hill, looking out on the Mediterranean Sea, outside Beirut. My family came with me for the trip, which made it especially meaningful for all of us.

My parents first met back in Beirut, and I was born there in 1967. We lived on the first floor of a three-story apartment building in the Achrafieh neighborhood for the first seven years of my life. My memories of that time in Beirut are gauzy but visceral: the deep blue of the Mediterranean; the low rumble of my dad's Chevy Nova; the bright, white stucco of my grandparents' house; the sweet, fragrant smell of the jasmine tree in the yard behind our apartment. To this day, the faintest whiff of jasmine immediately whips me back to our little backyard and that tree.

Of course, life was more complicated than that, even for a small child—by the time we left, we were fleeing a civil war that had engulfed the country—but I have undeniably warm memories of my early years in Beirut. Despite this, it never really felt like *home*.

I remember getting ready to do an interview with the Lebanese equivalent of MTV before that show at Zouk Mikael. By 2011, I was nearly as well-known for advocating loudly and persistently for Armenian causes as I was for fronting System Of A Down. Before we went on the air, the producer of the segment was giving me a rundown of what they wanted to cover—my background, my plans for what I'd do while visiting Beirut, that sort of thing. When I started to tell him about my Armenian heritage, he gently cut me off.

"Can we tone down the Armenia stuff?" he asked. "I mean, aren't you from Lebanon?"

He wasn't trying to be rude, but that was definitely the first time anyone had ever asked me *not* to talk about Armenia. It really angered me. I understood the desire for Lebanese media to portray me as a Lebanese diaspora artist but asking me not to talk about being Armenian was outright offensive. I did so anyway.

As much as that producer's questions bothered me, he did hit on a salient point: *Where was I from?* I mean, in a very technical sense, yes, I was born in Lebanon. But it never felt like where I was *from*. When I visited in 2011, I felt little connection to the place, except as a family ethnologist. The people were friendly, the food was incredible, but the disparity between different ruling factions there, the weapons visible everywhere in the hands of soldiers on the streets, it all made me uneasy with the thought that the rest of the world would one day look a lot like Lebanon. No, this definitely wasn't "home" for me. But if not Lebanon, then where?

My father, Khatchadour, was born in the sanjak of Alexandretta in 1937. Sanjaks were administrative units of the Ottoman Empire, sort of like counties or provinces. Today, what was once the city of Alexandretta is called İskenderun, an industrial port on the Turkish Mediterranean. At the time my dad came along though, Alexandretta was still part of Syria. Until 1936, it had been controlled by the French, who'd occupied it since the region was carved up by the victorious Entente powers after World War I. But a local political crisis that began in 1936 passed ruling authority of the sanjak from France to Turkey over the course of the next few years. In 1938, columns of Turkish soldiers entered Alexandretta in an ominous show of force, and the following year, the region officially became part of Turkey.

Unsurprisingly, the local Armenian minority were unnerved by these developments. Most packed up and left. That included my father and his family, who soon landed in Aleppo.

Khatchadour's parents had met working on a road that was being built by the French military after World War I. Interestingly, his mother, Vartouhi, was doing hard manual labor, while his father, Nazaret, was charged with distributing water to the workers—by virtue of the fact that he owned two horses and a horse-cart. After they met and decided to marry, their French employers were so charmed by the couple that they offered to construct a special tent for them to spend their honeymoon in. The wedding night itself played out like the dark opening scene in a twisted fable: there was a deluge that washed away that special tent, and Nazaret's hand was bitten by a snake. I'm not sure in which order those two things happened, but because of the snakebite, Nazaret's arm was only partly functional for the rest of his life.

If you believe in omens, that snakebite may have been an allegorical curse. Nazaret had a heart attack and died when my father was only in second grade. Vartouhi, however, lived to be 102. She honored her beloved husband by never remarrying and wearing black until the day she died.

Khatchadour was one of six siblings—he had four brothers and a sister—and had to quit school after his father died so he could work and bring in money for the family. It was a hard life in Aleppo. The family lived in a neighborhood mainly populated by Kurds, Jews, Armenians, and other foreigners. To be a Christian in Aleppo marked you as an outsider, as it had for Armenians all over the Ottoman Empire. Armenians were also seen as being in league with the French, who'd only recently given up their status as the occupying power.

My dad found work assisting an Arab cobbler with whatever odd jobs needed doing—running errands, fetching supplies, that sort of thing—but he was essentially a street kid. He learned how to fight, literally and figuratively, for the things he needed, and to not take shit from *anyone*. One day, his boss told him to go fetch some water, so my dad ran to the local well with a jar. When he got there, some Arab kids started harassing him and knocked the full jar out of his hands. Recognizing him as a Christian, one of them got close to Khatchadour's face and snarled, "Fuck Jesus."

Never one to back down, my dad looked back at this kid and offered a similarly ill-mannered affront to the prophet Mohammed.

At this point, his tormentor turned to the crowd of people around him and pointed at my dad. "He just cursed the Prophet! He's an infidel!"

As the bystanders began to get riled up, Khatchadour realized that he may have misplayed his hand and did the only smart thing he could do: he ran. The crowd followed him as he dashed through the streets and alleyways of Aleppo back toward the shop where he worked. When he arrived back there, out of breath, an angry mob close on his tail, his boss naturally asked what was happening. His chief tormentor spoke first.

"He cursed the Prophet Mohammed!"

Khatchadour's boss, a devout Muslim, was disturbed to hear this.

"Is it true?" he asked my dad.

"It is," my father admitted, "but only after he'd cursed Jesus."

He looked at Khatchadour, raised his arm, and swiftly slapped him across the face. Then he asked my dad's tormentor to step forward. When he did, the other boy got slapped, too.

"Okay, that's it! It's all over! Now, everyone get the *hell* out of my shop. And you," he said looking at my dad, "get back to work."

———

I'm pretty sure I get my musical inclinations from my dad's side of the family. Throughout my childhood, I heard many stories about his great-uncle, who was a traveling minstrel. He moved from village to village sharing songs and learning new ones. In those days without modern telecommunications, that's how music spread around from region to region and became folklore.

Growing up in Aleppo, my father's family didn't have a radio or any sort of phonograph, so the way he'd listen to music would be to stand near other people's houses whenever he heard music coming from inside. It could be a radio or someone playing the piano, a violin, or a guitar, and there my dad would be—a kid, outside in the street, straining to listen to the melody.

Dad bought his first instrument, an Arabic drum made from clay called a *doumbek*, when he was still pretty young. When he'd play it, he'd sing, too, and people would gather around and sing along. Apparently, he made a lot of his friends this way. He eventually started playing the guitar and the oud, a short-necked, Middle Eastern stringed instrument, as well, but he was always a great singer. He'd occasionally get hired to sing at weddings and other big events.

By the time he was a teenager, he'd begun to ask himself: If he really committed to it, could he make a life for himself with music? With this in mind, he heard that a master oud player would be teaching a class several towns away. To get there would require taking a few different buses, but it seemed like an opportunity too good to pass up, so he grabbed his oud and bought a bus ticket. While he was on one of the buses, he noticed an interesting-looking older man eying his oud.

"That yours?" the man asked.

They quickly fell into conversation. The man seemed to know a lot about ouds. He knew the person who'd made my dad's instrument and he'd also heard of the oud master who my dad was headed to see. This man was a professional musician himself, which immediately sparked my father's interest.

"Wow. How is it? I want to hear all about your life."

The man paused and looked hard at my father. "You really want to know?"

"Please."

The man gave it to him straight. He told my father tales of endless traveling, of relationships that fell apart because he was never around, of money struggles, of lonely nights tossing and turning in strange beds, of watching fellow musicians numbing themselves with alcohol and drugs.

My father took it all in. Then he made a decision. At the next stop, he got off the bus, walked across the road, and got on another one headed back in the direction he'd come from.

He never made it to that oud class.

———

My mother was born in Beirut. She grew up in a white house that sat alongside a long, wide public staircase that was flanked on both sides by similar-looking homes. I knew the house well because my grandparents continued to live there until they moved to the US in 1974. I spent a lot of time there when I was younger. My Uncle Shant, who was just a teenager back then, still lived with my grandparents, and I loved hanging out with him.

My grandpa, Stepan, had lots of jobs after moving to Beirut—he worked as a carpenter, a stone carver, a screen printer, and eventually a shoe salesman in downtown Beirut—and although none of it made him wealthy, my mother's childhood was a fair bit more financially stable than my dad's. Whereas my father's young life felt unmoored, my mother was relatively content in Beirut.

When we went back to Lebanon in 2011, we knocked on the door of that white house where she had lived with my grandparents. There was an Arab family living there, and when someone answered the door, we explained that our family used to live there. To their great credit—especially in a region where the words "we used to live here" tend to be charged with political grievance and incendiary emotion—the family invited us in for coffee. As we settled in, I could see a tender mix of nostalgia and yearning wash over my mother's face. This was a special place for her.

She and my father first met in that very house. She was only fourteen then, and my dad was a couple of years older. At the time, her family lived on the first floor, but rented out the second floor of the house to another family. That family, as it turned out, was my dad's older brother Misag, his wife, and their kids. That year, my father moved to Beirut and stayed with his older brother while looking for work. Every night, my mother would hear my father playing the guitar before bed and was slowly enchanted. One day, she went upstairs with two apricots, coupled on one branch, and showed it to my dad.

"This is you and me," she told him.

They were both still teenagers then, and before any relationship could blossom, my father left on a boat bound for France. He was young back then and not ready to settle down just yet.

My father bought the cheapest ticket for this journey, which meant he didn't have a room and slept each night on the boat's deck. During the days, he'd frequently play his guitar and sing, drawing a crowd of onlookers. One day, the boat's chef heard him playing and asked if he knew any Turkish songs. As it so happened, he did. In fact, because my father's parents had been born in what is now central Turkey, they both spoke the language well and passed it along to him. So, upon the chef's request, he started playing a Turkish song, and the man's eyes welled up with tears, overcome with emotion.

"I'm Turkish," the chef revealed. "Hearing that song reminds me of home."

"I'm Armenian," my father told him.

After that, the chef would come by every day to hear my father play. He'd offer him food from the kitchen, and even a room below deck, but my dad always waved away these kind overtures.

"Thank you but no, I'm fine," he'd say. When he told me this story years later, he explained that he just didn't want to be in this man's—or *any* man's—debt. Nonetheless, when they arrived in France, the chef gave him a phone number to call so that when he was ready to return to Beirut, he could do so on the same boat.

Three months later, after an unsuccessful work venture, my father was back on the boat with the Turkish chef, headed for Beirut. The same pattern repeated itself again—my father playing music, the chef listening, reminiscing, and offering my father food he'd refuse. When they landed back in Lebanon, the chef asked if he could come visit him at his home someday. My father gave him the address.

One day not too long after, a taxi pulled up to the house where my father was living with his mother and his younger brother. The chef got out, opened the trunk, and lifted out a gigantic basket of food and drink that he'd brought for the family. He came in and they all ate and talked for hours. When he was getting ready to leave, he hugged my grandmother tightly.

"I'm so glad to have met you," he smiled at her, then turned to my father. "My mother is actually Armenian, but she never tells anyone that in Turkey. No one knows."

This kind of story was actually fairly common amongst Armenians. During the Genocide, many Armenian families converted to

Islam and took Turkish names to save themselves from slaughter. As such, millions of Turks today have Armenian roots. This man was one of them, but it was never something he could speak about freely in Turkey, which is why he'd moved west to Europe. It was as if my father, an Armenian man playing Turkish songs, unlocked a part of his heritage within him, allowing him to embrace his true self. Despite successive Turkish governments abusing and murdering Armenians and other ethnicities for their own political gains in the nineteenth and twentieth centuries, Turks and Armenians share a six-hundred-year-old history together: neighbors sharing food, shelter, stories, and music. My dad and this chef were embodiments of that shared history. And music was the bridge between them.

While my father was still in France, his older brother had a falling out with my mom's family and moved out of the second-floor apartment he'd been renting in her family's house. But my father stayed friendly with my mom's older brother, my Uncle Garo, so he'd still be around that white house occasionally. It wasn't until he broke his nose a year or so later and my mom visited him in the hospital that he finally asked her out on an actual date. In 2011, we visited the restaurant where he took her on that first date. It was a little ways out of the city, in an open area in the hills, where they had once sat down and ate kebabs together. They knew there was a real connection, but soon afterward, tragedy struck: my father's younger brother Setrak, who'd recently moved to Liberia to work as an engineer for General Electric, died in a house fire.

My father was overcome with grief. He was naturally protective of his younger brother and felt as if he'd somehow failed him. He sank into a deep depression. Ironically, this is what cemented his relationship with my mother. She stuck by him through this low point in his life, and that was proof, I suppose, to both of them that their relationship was for keeps.

When I was born, a few years later, I'm told that I was the spitting image of Setrak. My father initially wanted to give me his name, but my grandmother, Varsenig, talked him out of it. She figured that with Setrak's name *and* his looks, I'd be a constant reminder of a defining tragedy in the family's life, which felt like an unreasonably heavy burden for an infant to carry.

I think she was probably right.

———

Once I was born, my grandmother often took on the role of my protector. In Beirut, we lived in an apartment on a cul-de-sac, but my mother's parents lived close by, and we saw them frequently. Whenever I misbehaved as a kid and my mother would come looking for me, I'd in turn go looking for my grandmother, to try to hide behind her. She would *never* let my mother spank me—even when I'm sure I deserved it.

Those early years we lived in Beirut often come back to me as a fragrant bouquet of exotic smells. Besides the jasmine tree in our backyard, there was also the aroma of nearly burnt Armenian coffee that was forever emanating from our kitchen as my parents, grandparents, or whichever other adults passed through the house were fervently discussing one thing or another. When I started my own coffee company, Kavat, a few years ago, part of what I was trying to capture was not just that smell, but that *feeling*. It's an opulent memory rooted in the senses: passionate conversation and roasted coffee wafting in from the kitchen while my little brother Sevag and I ran around our apartment back in Beirut.

Then there was the sweet smell of the food. Besides typical Middle Eastern and Lebanese fare like tabbouleh and hummus, there were traditional Armenian dishes like *manti*, which are meat dumplings filled with onions and spices. Maybe my favorite treat of all was something that felt very exotic to me back then, but obviously less so now: French fries.

Occasionally, we'd pile into my dad's car and drive to the beach, which like all beaches, had its own unique scent—a mix of sand, sea, sweat, fish, and the smoky open grills at tiny restaurants and pop-up cafés by the waterfront. The real treat at the beach was that my dad would buy us burgers and fries. The burgers didn't do much for me, but Sevag and I would luxuriate in those crispy fries. I can remember enjoying them while riding in the back seat of my dad's car on the way home, with the slivers of late afternoon sun streaking in through the car's smudgy windows. During those rides, it was as if I was suspended in some liminal space between being asleep and awake. If it was early evening, I'd silently count the orange street lights as they whipped by, hypnotizing myself into a warm state of reassuring calm. Years later, when I took up meditation, I realized that the serenity I was trying to achieve was in many ways a version of what I'd felt in that back seat.

———

Not all the smells of Beirut come with happy memories. On my very first day of school, the building *reeked* of wet paint. They must've just repainted the place a day or two earlier and that acrid stench pervaded every corner.

I always hated school, even though I was a straight-A student. It wasn't the academics that bothered me, though; it was the environment. There was something about the way it was organized—a teacher standing in front of a group of students, supposedly imparting knowledge—that always felt to me more like indoctrination than learning. I couldn't understand why I had to sit there for hours on end—days, weeks, months, *years* on end, really—to get an education. I'm sure I couldn't have verbalized that at age five, but on some level, I think I felt it in my bones. At any rate, whenever I smell wet paint now, I get a pit in my stomach. It reminds me of the anxiety I felt on that first day of school, and how much I dreaded all the days of school that I knew would come after it.

Chatalbashian was a local Armenian school where most of the teachers were, unsurprisingly, Armenian. My favorite, though, was a Lebanese woman who was our Arabic-language teacher. I can't really remember what I liked about her. It may have just been that by virtue of not being Armenian, she seemed somehow exotic and different.

I grew up speaking Armenian as my first language, and Arabic as my second. It was always Armenian at home but out in the streets of Beirut, Arabic was the lingua franca. In school, we also learned French, which was the language of the most recent colonial occupiers and was still the preferred tongue of the upper classes. Street signs and official government documents often employed French right alongside Arabic.

Lebanon itself was a volatile mishmash of religious and ethnic groups at the time, much like it still is today. Armenians were a small minority who generally tried their best to avoid wading into the various sectarian disagreements and skirmishes that tended to roil the country. I lived among a community of *kilic artiklari*, or "leftovers of the sword," a pointed term that Turks sometimes used for Armenians who had either personally survived the Genocide or were among their descendants. (It's worth mentioning that Turkey's fascist president, Recep Tayyip Erdoğan, recently used the term after aiding Azerbaijan in attacking Armenians, presumably to remind Armenians of his lack of genocidal regret.) Having so recently paid such a devastating price for being a visible, upwardly mobile minority, the impulse in Lebanon to keep our collective heads down was understandable. We were visitors and we knew it.

This tangible feeling of displacement is something that can last generations in any community forced to flee their homeland. It's something I think about every time war, famine, poverty, or some other sort of disaster creates a new wave of refugees anywhere. Once the immediate emergency passes, once people secure housing, work, and some sort of stability, that feeling of otherness can still haunt these families for decades, if not longer.

In the case of my own family, my mother had grown up in Beirut, but my father never felt an enduring connection to Lebanon, nor to Syria—no matter what he did. Eventually, he built up a successful shoe manufacturing business in Beirut, but he was always ready to ditch it to find a place where he felt like we belonged. Some aunts and uncles of mine had moved to the US in the 1960s, and in 1972, my father went to New York—where his brother Hagop lived—to try to make arrangements so that we could move to the US as well.

Once he left, his absence from our life in Beirut was acute, and I didn't react well to it. I started behaving strangely. I was anxious all the time. I couldn't concentrate or follow directions. I became willful and disobedient. I'd do crazy shit like climb on top of the refrigerator or other furniture and then hurl myself off of it.

Perhaps the strangest aspect of this reaction was that before my father left for the US, he wasn't exactly a stay-at-home dad. He was gone most of the day, working almost constantly. But when he *was* at home, he brought a joy and vitality to the place. He told jokes. He shared stories. He was always playing vinyl records of Armenian, Arabic, or European music. He'd walk around the apartment singing and I'd harmonize with him. We'd often sing this Armenian folk song, "Bari Arakeel," about a stork that returns to the beauty of its home each year. My conception of home back then was pretty shaky, and without my father there in that first-floor apartment, it seemed to fall apart completely.

My mother was growing increasingly concerned, so after a few months, she started taking me to doctors. Modern psychology hadn't come very far by 1972, certainly not in Lebanon, but eventually one of the doctors looked at my mom and said simply, "There's nothing wrong with him. He just misses his dad."

Diagnosing the problem didn't solve it, though. My acting out got so bad that eventually my father had to cut the trip short and come back to Beirut, at which point my behavior quickly returned to normal. But the plans to emigrate to the US were delayed. It was because of me, it seems, that my family didn't leave Beirut for another three years.

By that time, the situation had changed considerably. In the spring of 1975, the Lebanese Civil War began. The war was a confusing, multifaceted conflict that involved a shifting array of ethnic and religious factions within Lebanon, as well as several from outside the country. When I say it was confusing, I don't mean that it was confusing to me as a seven-year-old experiencing it (though, obviously it was), but that it was confusing even to geopolitical experts, diplomats, and others whose job it was to understand this sort of stuff.

For the most part, the conflict didn't really involve the Armenian minority, who tried to stay neutral throughout—though that soon proved difficult. Christian partisans took the Armenians' neutrality as an affront and began attacking Armenian neighborhoods. There were Armenian militias who mainly stuck to the task of defending those neighborhoods, but there was even a split among Armenian groups over whose side to take.

I tend to think about this war using an Armenian word, *grvakhentsor*, which translates literally as "battle apple." It refers to places like Lebanon, Vietnam, and Armenia itself, which at various times in their histories became fighting grounds for global powers and ideological forces largely beyond their control. These places get chewed up and spit out, often suffering for years or decades, even after most of the actual fighting has ended. In the case of Beirut, the place was completely leveled. I remember looking at a book, years later, that showed side-by-side photos of the city before and after the war, and it was shocking to witness the scale of destruction capable by conventional arms: towering apartment complexes and office buildings reduced to piles of rubble, bustling city squares and picturesque boulevards turned into empty, dust-strewn wastelands.

For a child growing up in the city, the war represented a sudden and immediate end to my life as I knew it. School was closed. There were checkpoints on the street. There was no going to the beach and eating French fries. Electricity was only available intermittently. I was no longer allowed to go play in the big field at the end of our cul-de-sac, where I'd previously ran around playing tag or soccer with other neighborhood kids. My mother would no longer let me walk to the store or go visit friends, for fear I'd never come back.

Achrafieh, where we lived, was high on a hill, and bullets would occasionally strafe the neighborhood coming up from the valley. Mom would go shopping for food not knowing if the street was being scoped by snipers that day. One day, when my father was in the street talking to a militia member from the neighborhood, he realized the danger of being out in the open, so he suggested moving the conversation to the foyer of a nearby building. Just after they walked away, a bomb struck the very place they'd been standing.

Survival, as it so often does, came down to luck.

The war was all around us, and my world became very small, almost completely contained within our first-floor apartment. My most tangible memory of that time was hugging my younger brother as we crouched in our bedroom while bombs dropped outside, rattling our apartment walls. At those moments, the whole world seemed to be shaking. The feeling reverberated into my bones and in some ways, I feel like it's still there.

As a seven-year-old kid who was part of an ethnic minority that never really had a dog in this fight, I have nothing particularly insightful to impart about the political and historical cross-currents that fueled the civil war in Lebanon. But the experience of being caught in the middle of a war that seems to have nothing to do with you is, in fact, the experience of most people in war zones, and something that left a deep, indelible impression on my psyche.

Once you've had the experience of bombs raining down on you, it's impossible to think of military campaigns the same way. For most people on the ground, war is not an academic or geopolitical exercise. It's a deeply personal one. Once you've lived with the random, indifferent specter of death hanging over you, it's an everyday terror you never totally relinquish. Whenever I hear about some village in Myanmar or Artsakh or Afghanistan being bombed, I can feel that terror somewhere deep in my core plucked like a tuning fork.

It's that very feeling that's informed a lot of the work I've done as an activist. When I wrote and published that essay, "Understanding Oil," two days after 9/11, I was thinking not only about the terror of all those who perished on that Tuesday morning, but also all those who'd been bombed before and would be bombed after that event. It was called a War on Terror, but the one thing war is most effective at producing *is* terror. The phrase "collateral damage," used so often during war, is a cold euphemism for the killing of innocent people. Having that imprinted on me as a child, I can never be flippant about one country launching an attack on another, or worse, a government doing it in my name. So, when I talk about a desire for peace—in the Middle East, in Artsakh and Armenia, in Ukraine, wherever—I talk about it as someone who knows what it's like to live with the opposite.

I relay all this knowing that my experience in war, my family's experience, was—comparatively speaking—not that bad. In the years after we left, one of my cousins was framed as a spy, then abducted from his apartment by a militia; he was never heard from again. Another relative, my mom's first cousin, was injured in a bombing and permanently disabled. But other than that, for the most part, the rest of my extended family was pretty lucky. My mom's parents, Stepan and Varsenig, had moved to California the year before the war started, and we already had our paperwork in motion to leave, too. It took us a few months, but by the summer of 1975, my mom, my brother, and I were on a bumpy Pan Am flight out of Beirut, headed straight to Los Angeles. My father, however, was a Syrian citizen, which made his emigration much more complicated. We had to leave him behind initially and start our new life in the US without him.

CHAPTER 3

The landing at LAX was rough. I'd never been on an airplane before, so I was initially very excited, but by the time I arrived in the United States for the first time there was no mistaking the feeling that overwhelmed me—and it was definitely nausea.

It may have been more than just the turbulent flight. For me as a young kid, arriving in Los Angeles from war-torn Beirut felt like slipping through the looking glass into another world. It was more than a new home; it was a complete paradigm shift.

The change was palpable practically from the moment we walked out of the airport terminal. The sun itself felt different in California. Beaming in through layers of smog and automobile exhaust, it seemed more diffused, painting Los Angeles with an ethereal orange hue. Air pollution was a real problem in Southern California, and not one that many had woken up to by the mid-1970s. Still, I suppose it had its aesthetic upsides, too, which were the eerily beautiful sunsets that descended upon LA, closing out nearly every day like the last frames of a Sergio Leone film.

California had that kind of feel back then. In fact, it still does. Its beauty and its ugliness feel inextricably linked, two sides of the same coin, so to speak—glamour and grit woven together in mutual codependence.

My Uncle Shant shared an apartment with my grandparents on Bronson Avenue in Hollywood, and when we arrived, we moved in with them. It was just down the block from the Château Élysée, a luxe, white, seven-story hotel and apartment house built in the 1920s that's since become an LA landmark. In the 1930s and 1940s, the Château's residents included a who's who of movie stars and famous faces: Clark Gable, Errol Flynn, Bette Davis, Humphrey Bogart, Ginger Rogers, George Burns, Katharine Hepburn, George Gershwin, Cary Grant, Ed Sullivan. A few years before we arrived, the Church of Scientology bought the building and turned it, somewhat fittingly, into their infamous "Celebrity Centre." It was the glittery façade of old Hollywood in service of the seamy hucksterism of new religion. I was, of course, oblivious to that dichotomy as an eight-year-old who barely spoke beginner's English, but the place nonetheless freaked me out.

Right next to Uncle Shant's apartment, on Franklin, was the space-age-looking Mayfair Market, which itself became such a well-known spot for spotting stars doing their grocery shopping that it was called the "Celebrity Mayfair." And it wasn't just the rich and famous; all sorts of strange characters would mill around the Mayfair. I remember once seeing a guy wearing a slick sixties-style jacket eating a large stick of Philadelphia cream cheese right out of its wrapper as he strolled across the parking lot.

The whole neighborhood seemed like something from another planet. In the coming years, my little brother and I would walk to school in the mornings hand in hand down Alexandria Avenue, past disheveled drunks sleeping in doorways and friendly, if haggard-looking, prostitutes making their way home after a long night's work. No one ever really bothered us, though. It seems crazy now to think about it, but Hollywood actually felt much safer back then.

Coming from the chaos and strife of what Beirut had become, America felt like a dramatic cultural whiplash. I was bemused by the bright yellow-orange slices of Kraft American cheese that my grandfather brought home from the supermarket—I'd never known that cheese came in such an otherworldly shade—and the similarly vivid technicolor of American television. I remember sitting with my uncle and watching *SWAT*, this highly stylized, action-heavy cop show, and thinking how different it was from the dull, soapy Arabic television I'd watched in Lebanon. The contrast between the high-gloss, glorified violence that people tuned in to watch for fun in America and the misery of the actual violence we'd just fled from was stark.

In the living room of his apartment, my Uncle Shant had a stereo with a bad-ass vinyl collection. Up until that point in my life, most of the music I'd heard had been from the records my dad played back in Beirut, which were predominantly Armenian and Arabic music. My uncle, though, was really into soul and R&B, so he had records by Stevie Wonder, the Jackson Five, Marvin Gaye, and Earth, Wind & Fire, as well as some 1970s time-capsule stuff like Chuck Mangione. This was my first real introduction to American music.

When I think about my first few months in the US, songs like "I Want You Back," "Superstition," and "Mercy Mercy Me" provide the score. I can recall afternoons passed sitting on the floor in front of that stereo, enthralled by the energy coming from the speakers. My dad's records didn't sound lesser in comparison, they just sounded like they belonged in a different universe altogether.

———

Late one night, only a few weeks after we'd moved into my uncle's ground-floor apartment, my mother woke up to see the silhouette of a male figure standing in the hallway near her. She sat up in her bed, confused.

"Is that you, Shant?" she asked the silhouette.

No response. Now, she was even more confused. She wondered if maybe it was her father, Stepan. "*Hayrig*?" she called out, using the Armenian word for "father."

Again, no response. Then the figure started walking toward her. She screamed. Loudly. The figure in the hallway stopped, turned around, walked back down the hall toward the window, then nimbly climbed out.

My mother was still yelling when Shant and my grandparents ran into the room and flicked on the lights. She was shaking. At this point, Sevag and I were sitting up in our beds, clutching our blankets, looking at each other nervously. A quick scan of the apartment revealed only one thing missing: my grandfather's wallet, which one of our neighbors would find the next day, tossed on their lawn, empty.

We'd moved to the US, at least in part, because Lebanon was no longer safe. Navigating a war in Beirut, my mother—in particular—had grown into a fearful person, worrying every time she or anyone else left the house. Moving to California was supposed to change all that, so having a burglar tiptoeing around the apartment only a few weeks after our arrival did not exactly settle her nerves. In fact, fearfulness became something of a permanent fixture of my mom's personality. To this day, she's insisted on having bars on the windows in every place she and my father have lived in. After System Of A Down signed our major-label deal, I bought my parents a small house in a nice neighborhood in Valley Village, California, before heading out on tour. When I came home, she'd had steel cages installed on every window and door. It looked like a prison.

Ironically, all those bars haven't really helped—not to alleviate her fears, nor to even keep her home secured. In pretty much every home they've lived, at some point, there's been a break-in. So maybe it's not surprising that this anxiety has never fully receded for her. She still has nightmares filled with burglars and thieves; not too long ago, she even fell off her bed mid-sleep because of one. I think about this now and wonder whether there's anything more to all this than just bad luck. Does fear invite negative outcomes? Isn't fearful thinking just a form of negative visualization?

I certainly absorbed my fair share of this fear as a kid. I sometimes think of that fearfulness as an inheritance from my mother, but having lived through the same foundational traumas, I may have simply come by it naturally. At any rate, I was kind of a worrywart back then. Life felt unsettled. I walked around with a sense that everything could turn bad at any minute, which, as you can imagine, could be a little exhausting.

The fact that my father was still back in Syria and Lebanon at the beginning of our American adventure definitely didn't help. My Uncle Shant did everything he could to be a fatherly figure for us—he bought me and my brother our first bikes, he took us to the movies and out for *lehmejunes*, which are these really amazing Armenian pizzas—but nothing could quite replace having my dad around.

It was six months before my father finally got his immigration paperwork in order and was able to join us in California. He showed up late one night, past my bedtime. I was allowed to stay up and give him a big hug before I went to sleep. The next morning, Sevag and I left for school before he woke up. The whole day, as I sat in class, I was distracted and fidgety. At one point, I just burst into tears. The teacher, a tall blonde woman named Ms. Hall, brought me outside to the porch where we sat down.

"What's wrong?" she asked.

Through tears, I blubbered that my father had finally arrived, but I barely got to see him before I had to come to school. Now, he was all I could think about.

I suppose the timing of my outburst was odd. All the time that my dad had been scrambling to get his visa, I'd managed to hold it together just fine. It hadn't been like it was when he was gone years earlier. But it was as if I'd repressed all that worry, all that emptiness, all that yearning for a home that felt settled and secure, and then at the slightest emotional provocation, the dam had broken.

Ms. Hall was sweet. She put her arm around my shoulders and reassured me that in just a couple of hours, I'd be back home with my dad for good. After a few minutes, I calmed down. I wiped the tears from my face and the snot from under my nose, took a deep breath, and walked back to class.

———

Once my father was in California, we moved out of Uncle Shant's apartment and into a small Craftsman bungalow a mile or so away. It was a little one-story rental with two bedrooms—my parents in one, Sevag and I in the other. There was a small backyard with what in my memory was a gigantic tree just a few paces from our back door. My father built a little treehouse up in it, but the yard was so tiny that my brother and I probably spent more time playing in the street in front of our house than we did in the back. We'd ride our bikes, we'd play basketball, and we had a few friends who lived nearby, too.

The neighborhood was certainly less volatile than the literal war zone we'd left behind in Beirut, but it wasn't exactly conflict-free. Growing up in our little house on Alexandria Avenue, street fights were not a completely uncommon occurrence. I remember once seeing two cars stopped in front of our house. One honked at the other, then the driver who'd been honked at got out of his car, walked over to the other car, dragged the other driver out, and just started beating the shit out of him. He had the poor guy's face pinned beneath his foot before he finally decided he'd made his point, returned to his car, and simply drove away. It was shocking and repulsive to witness. Coming from a civil war, being surrounded by violence that felt inescapable, the idea that people would engage in completely avoidable and unnecessary violence by choice seemed confusing and dumb.

My family did their best to insulate me from actual conflict. Still, sometimes conflict comes looking for you. One day, an older boy named Gary—a spoiled, popular Armenian kid who'd been born in the US—started picking on me at school. I'm still not sure why he chose me. I was mostly friends with the smart, nerdy kids who were good at math, so maybe he just saw me as an easy target. Whatever the reason, he seemed to be goading me to fight him.

And I wouldn't do it.

I'm not sure if it was a philosophical revulsion to violence or maybe the fearfulness that I carried with me, but as a kid, I simply couldn't, or *wouldn't,* fight. Maybe it's that very fact that made me an attractive target to this bully. I look back now and realize this kid was probably all of nine months older and not much bigger than I was. But back then, in my head, he might as well have been a hulking, twenty-year-old ex-con. I don't know if that cliché about the usefulness of fighting your bully is sound, but I can say that *not* fighting him didn't help at all. He'd torment me day after day, and no matter what he did, I'd just take it. It made me feel diminutive and even more like I didn't belong.

That feeling trailed me wherever I went. I can remember being with Sevag once, riding our bikes near my Uncle Garo's house in the Valley, when we were approached by five or six kids we didn't know. One of the kids came up to me and said something like "I want your bike."

"You mean you want to borrow it and try it out?" I asked innocently.

The kid shook his head.

"No, dumbass. I'm gonna take it from you."

At this point he got in my face, and his crew of pubescent ruffians began issuing a steady stream of insults and threats to both me and my brother. It finally dawned on me that we were being robbed.

We started yelling for our uncle and one of the kids punched me hard in the stomach. Shortly after, they took off running.

For a while, it really bothered me that I never hit that kid back. I mean, they didn't take our bikes in the end, and no one was seriously hurt, so in some ways, it was the best possible outcome. But I'm not immune to the testosterone-fueled sensitivities of the male ego. There is something almost prehistoric or animalistic in the male need to be able to handle conflict, to be able to protect himself and others. At the time and for a long time after, I was ashamed that when pressed, I'd failed to protect not just myself, but my little brother as well.

As an adult, I've thought a lot about how we react to provocation and how we deal with conflict and how all of that relates to justice and injustice. I think being an immigrant kid in the US gave me an appreciation of what it means to be the underdog, the outsider, which in turn seeded empathy within me for other underdogs and outsiders. I have the same revulsion to bullying on an international level between nations as I do between people. That said, my refusal to engage in what might be understood as a primary coming-of-age ritual of pre-adolescence was not because I was a budding eleven-year-old pacifist, but just that on some gut level, I've always found violence itself to be an abhorrent and stupid way to solve problems. However, avoiding violence and avoiding conflict are not the same thing. Even now, I think the former is probably healthy. The latter, not so much. But that can be a hard lesson to learn.

———

My brother and I attended the Rose and Alex Pilibos Armenian School, a K–12 private school that was just a couple of blocks from our house. We had a typical academic curriculum, but it was supplemented with classes on Armenian history, language, and culture. The school had been founded in the 1960s and it was still very small at the time when we started. Our classes all took place inside an old house, and the closest thing we had to a gym was a concrete slab next door where we'd run around and play. As schools go, I suppose it was okay, but I didn't like school any more in the US than I had in Lebanon. We had to wear ugly gray pants and a white button-down shirt every day, which felt like a fittingly drab symbol of everything I hated. The whole idea of a thirty-five-hour school week felt like a laboratory experiment on human indoctrination. I chafed against the hidebound traditions and parochial hierarchy that were part and parcel of institutionalized education.

At Pilibos, there weren't a lot of extracurricular activities—we didn't have the budget for that—but we did have a choir, which I joined. We practiced at St. Garabed Armenian Apostolic Church, across the street from the school, and we were directed by the head priest, an older man. We sang mostly liturgical hymns and occasionally some old Armenian folk songs, both of which I really liked. By the time I was a teenager, though, I'd grown pretty bored with the choir, so one day after practice, I approached the priest and told him I was quitting. He looked shocked. He tried to guilt me into staying.

"In my day, a student would never have had the gall to tell the head priest that he was just going to up and quit," he told me.

"Well, that was your day," I said with a shrug and a smile. "See you later."

I was very good at the academic part of school, but it always seemed as if the regurgitation of facts was prized over critical thinking. Authority was to be revered, not challenged. In high school, I had a world history teacher I really liked named Mr. Paulus, who was one of a few non-Armenian teachers there. One day, Mr. Paulus was teaching us about the Boston Massacre, explaining how a colonial-era protest over taxation escalated into a raucous demonstration, which the British soldiers dealt with by opening fire on the protestors. I raised my hand and Mr. Paulus called on me.

"How many people died in that massacre?" I asked.

"Five colonists were shot and killed," he replied.

I laughed out loud. I didn't mean to, but it just came out. So did most of my classmates. Mr. Paulus turned beet-red and told me to come talk to him in the hallway, so I followed him out the classroom door.

"Why would you laugh at something like that?" he asked me. "That was so disrespectful."

I apologized and told him I didn't mean to be disrespectful but that, as Armenians, to hear the word "massacre" applied to the killing of five people when the killing of 1.5 million Armenians was being largely ignored by the same country that used this so-called massacre as a pretext for the revolution that led to the country's founding—it was just hard to do anything but laugh. Sighing, Mr. Paulus told me he understood my point and let it go. I told him that I understood his, too, and we both walked back into the classroom.

———

Pilibos was part of a vibrant Armenian-American community in and around Hollywood. Although the neighborhood was a diverse

mix of Hispanics, African-Americans, Filipinos, and other minori-
ties, within that, there were a lot of Armenians. We had Armenian
neighbors, Armenian restaurants, Armenian shops, Armenian
churches, an Armenian school, and an Armenian community
center, all within a mile or two. Many years later, the city gave the
neighborhood the official moniker "Little Armenia," but people were
already calling it that back when we lived there.

The early 1980s were a volatile time for the Armenian diaspora
community in Southern California. The collective agitation for recognition of the Genocide had reached something of a fever pitch.
After decades of working largely peacefully and diplomatically to
persuade Turkey to acknowledge their crimes against humanity,
frustration and desperation led some within the community to go to
more extreme measures to draw attention to the cause.

On October 6, 1980, a member of a group calling itself the Justice Commandos of the Armenian Genocide hurled two Molotov
cocktails at the residence of Kemal Arıkan, the Turkish consul general in LA. The building was damaged, but fortunately, no one was
seriously injured. Several more bombings around Southern California
followed—a travel agency owned by a Turkish-American, an empty
convention center that was scheduled to host a Turkish cultural festival, and the Turkish consulate itself—all of which made headlines
without incurring casualties. Then, in early 1982, Arıkan, the same
Turkish consul general who was targeted two years earlier, was gunned
down in a hail of bullets while sitting at a stoplight in Beverly Hills.

A threshold had been crossed.

In October of 1982, five people from the Armenian-American
community in Southern California were arrested for plotting to

bomb the Turkish consulate in Philadelphia. One of them was someone a few years older than me who I vaguely knew. Another was the popular Armenian singer Karnig Sarkissian. Those arrested became known as the "Los Angeles Five."

Martin Luther King Jr. once called a riot "the language of the unheard." Political violence is often similarly the desperate cry of the frustrated and the ignored. Turkey's denial of the Genocide—and the US's collusion in it—had created a potent wellspring of anger and exasperation among Armenians. While some in the Armenian-American community around LA took issue with the violent tactics of this years-long campaign, there was nothing like widespread condemnation of those activists accused of employing them. In fact, many of those arrested became local heroes. As a teenager, I found myself increasingly engaged with these debates, and sympathetic to the larger cause.

It was during these teenage years that I joined the Armenian Youth Federation. The AYF is the youth arm of the Armenian Revolutionary Federation, a nationalist Armenian political party founded in 1890 that is particularly active among the Armenian diaspora. In practice, the AYF was sort of like a combination of the Boy Scouts and the YMCA for Armenian kids, but a lot more political. It was also very social. They organized after-school programs, camps, classes, dances, concerts, and lectures. So, we'd pass out flyers and protest the Turkish government's denial of the Genocide, but we'd also sneak booze into dances and scurry off into the woods to mess around. It was a huge part of my growing up.

My parents, while supportive, weren't necessarily thrilled that I'd joined the AYF. My grandparents, Stepan and Varsenig, had been extremely active for Armenian causes their whole lives, and Stepan was an active ARF member. But I think my mother came to resent how much time they devoted to the community and the impact it had on their family, so she steered clear of it. My father had arrived in the US with less than a thousand dollars to his name, and although he was politically astute, he'd focused his attention and time in America on working to support his family, not on activism.

This wasn't an unusual generational dynamic within the Armenian diaspora or within immigrant communities in general. The older generations arrive saddled with the responsibility of building a new life, so naturally their focus is more on economic concerns. Their successes enable future generations to start asking more complicated political, cultural, and social questions.

In the case of my parents, I have no doubt they also saw the campaign of bombings and assassinations often being carried out by young men only a few years older than I was, many of them current or former AYF members, and were concerned. Their fears were understandable. The FBI had begun investigating the AYF as a potential recruiting ground for the Justice Commandos of the Armenian Genocide (JCAG), the organization that claimed responsibility for many of the Southern California plots. The AYF also organized fundraisers for the legal defense of many of those arrested.

The very first concerts I ever attended were these kinds of AYF events at the Armenian Cultural Center in Hollywood. The artists at these gigs—which sometimes included Karnig Sarkissian, one of the LA Five, while he was out on bail—usually played what's called Armenian revolutionary music. These were dramatic rock, pop, and folk songs, mostly celebrating heroes of the resistance against the Turks, exhorting Armenians to stand up to their oppressors, or memorializing the blood spilled in defense of the nation and its people. Occasionally, there might be a love song mixed in, but this music and these shows were inherently political. People got worked up. The concerts were packed with teenagers and twenty-somethings, but also older people too, sometimes even those who'd survived the Genocide. They'd sing along, they'd dance, they'd pump their fists in the air, they'd sign petitions, they'd collect money. It was unifying.

Seeing those AYF shows was incredibly formative for me. When I say that I was an activist long before I was an artist, *this* is what initially brought me into the fold. As a teenager, I was going to protests, I was organizing, I was fundraising, I was passing out flyers, I was writing letters to political prisoners. I liked music back then, but I wasn't particularly rabid about it, and I certainly didn't think about making it myself. My parents had bought me an acoustic guitar when I was ten, perhaps thinking I might follow in my father's footsteps, but I was totally disinterested. That guitar sat lonely and unplayed in my closet for years before I finally gave it away to one of my cousins. My mom also offered to sign me up for piano lessons. Again, I had zero interest. But seeing music and activism together at those AYF shows made something click for me. I was suddenly more interested in *both*.

Throughout my childhood, I'd heard many stories of the atrocities my grandparents and our extended family had faced during the Genocide. The fact that we moved to "Little Armenia" also meant that even after arriving in the US, the community around me was filled with Armenian people—all of whom had either experienced or inherited trauma of their own from that same Genocide. And so the very idea that there were entire countries that refused to acknowledge that the Armenian Genocide had ever occurred was absolutely insane.

The more I learned about the history of the Genocide, as well as its perpetrators' continuous attempts at erasure, the more incensed I became. In May of 1915, the phrase "crimes against humanity" was invented to describe the Turks' treatment of the Armenians. An estimated 1.5 million Armenians perished during the Genocide, along with hundreds of thousands of Assyrians and Greeks. By 1920, ninety percent of the Armenians that had been living within the borders of the Ottoman Empire were gone. It was this calculated, wholesale destruction of a people and their culture that led the jurist Raphael Lemkin to coin the word "genocide" to describe the Turks' vicious and systematic campaign against the Armenians.

Although history books frequently date the Armenian Genocide to 1915–1916, there was not any neat and defined end date to the Armenians' suffering. Even after the war ended in 1918 with the defeat of the Central powers alliance that included the Ottoman Turks, violence and repression continued against the Armenians for decades. In September of 1918, the Turks' Azeri allies massacred twenty thousand Armenians. In February of 1920, the Turks murdered at least another five thousand Armenians in Cilicia.

The lack of accountability or even acknowledgment of the fact of the Armenian Genocide by the Turks was one of the main things that allowed these atrocities to continue. Despite thorough, indisputable documentation by historians, the Turkish government denies the Genocide ever happened. They repeatedly paint the events as just unfortunate results of a wide-ranging war rather than the sadistic, planned extermination of an entire ethnic group by a powerful nation-state.

What's more, the lack of accountability by the Turks has had tragic consequences that extended far beyond the Armenian people. It certainly did not go unnoticed by their World War I allies, the Germans. When Hitler was readying his invasion of Poland in 1939 and formulating plans for what he saw as a restive, alien population within the borders of so-called Greater Germany, he waved away concerns about his military acting humanely with a haunting rhetorical question: "Who, after all, speaks today of the annihilation of the Armenians?"

There will always be people who naively say we should focus more on the present and the future than the past. However, as I learned more about not just the history of the Armenian Genocide but also the history of war throughout human civilization, a new realization dawned on me: if we as humans do not acknowledge and account for our shared history, we will be doomed to repeat it ad nauseum. And *that's* why recognition of the Armenian Genocide is so essential.

Consider Germany post–World War II, whose government was obliged to acknowledge the abject horrors of the Holocaust. The Nuremberg Trials held specific officers to account. The German people were forced to face what had been carried out in their name and, for many, with their help. The difficult national reckoning continued for decades afterward. Anyone traveling to Germany would be hard pressed to miss the markers, the monuments, and the statues commemorating the Jewish community that was targeted for destruction by the Nazis. While pockets of Holocaust denial exist on the fringes of German society, it has never been government policy. In fact, displaying Nazi symbols or denying the Holocaust is a *crime* in Germany.

None of this is meant to minimize the trauma still felt by Jews, but only to note how much *worse* this trauma might be if the German authorities had tried to pretend the Holocaust never occurred in the first place. That has long been the policy of successive Turkish governments with regard to the Armenian Genocide. Turks who have publicly acknowledged the Genocide, including Nobel Prize–winning author Orhan Pamuk, were put on trial for "insulting Turkishness." The sole park in Istanbul that featured a memorial to victims of the genocide was dismantled and disappeared in 1922 during a resurgence of Turkish nationalism.

More recently, when Turkey joined Azerbaijan in attacking Armenians in Artsakh in 2020, the trauma of the Genocide was reawakened. Here we had two fascist dictatorial regimes—who, to this day, deny the Genocide that their ancestors perpetrated—targeting the descendants of that horrific crime with a promise to finish the job that had been started more than a century earlier. History does indeed repeat itself and "never again" is always yet again.

How many more deaths will it take before the Turks—and the rest of the world—finally acknowledge our suffering?

There were lots of good reasons why the issue of Genocide recognition would be the thing that would first fire me up as an activist. Some of those reasons were certainly personal, but initially, it wasn't really the facts of the Genocide or even my family's tale of surviving it that spurred me to want to do something to ensure it wasn't ignored. It was the *hypocrisy*. In school, I'd learn all about American history—or, as someone like Howard Zinn might point out, a whitewashed version of it—with its nods to high-minded ideals like liberty and justice for all. I'd watch the news and hear then president Ronald Reagan project a vision of America as this proverbial city on a hill, a beacon for democracy and human rights across the globe. So how could the country that helped liberate the Nazi concentration camps refuse to acknowledge the Armenian Genocide that preceded it?

The dirty little secret, of course, was that the US saw Turkey as a vital NATO ally in a turbulent geopolitical neighborhood. After a 1980 accord between the two countries, Turkey also became a voracious recipient of US military aid and arms sales, as well as home to multiple US military bases. *This* was the price of the US's continued silence on the Genocide.

As all of this came into focus in my teenage mind, I struggled with the cognitive dissonance. How could this nation that took me and my family in, that has always loudly trumpeted its bona fides as, in the words of Abraham Lincoln, "the last, best hope on Earth," be part of such a vile deal? And in a democracy, how could "we the people" consent to this? Furthermore, if the people in power were lying about this, what *else* were they lying about?

This slow-burning realization did more than just turn me into a teenage activist. It became a fundamental part of my worldview. I'd always had an almost inherent antipathy toward authority—my unhappiness at school was evidence of that—but this was my brain confirming what I'd long felt in my gut. I didn't yet know much of anything about punk rock, but I'd already become a stout believer in its guiding principle: those in power were suspect and needed to be challenged.

My political awakening wasn't that different from what a lot of teenagers go through. After all, the revelation that those in charge might not have your best interests in mind, that they might in fact be lying to you for their own greedy, selfish reasons, is—in some ways—the founding doctrine of rock 'n' roll.

It was a heady time. In many ways, the multi-year campaign of bombings and assassinations in the early 1980s had its intended effect, by bringing attention to the Turks' perpetration and subsequent denial of the Genocide. A 1984 CIA report on the JCAG that has since been declassified noted that the assassination of Arıkan, in particular, "focused US attention on Armenian grievances against Turkey." For an "older generation of Armenians, the assassination demonstrated that terrorism obtained results whereas the peaceable efforts of 69 years had failed. To the young, third-generation Armenian-Americans, the terrorists represented romantic figures who did more than talk about the Genocide." The report acknowledged that while most in the diaspora community recognized that terrorism alone wouldn't solve their problems, "many Armenians have become convinced that, if it had not been for the use of violence, no one would be aware of Armenian grievances." That old phrase, "one man's terrorist is another man's freedom fighter," feels particularly apt here.

As a teenager, there was something intoxicating about being around this mix of militancy, patriotism, idealism, and community.

For a kid who'd grown up afraid of getting in fights, the allure of banding together with like-minded peers to engage in the biggest fight I could imagine at the time felt empowering. There *is* undoubtedly a romantic appeal to aligning and allying yourself with dedicated, young revolutionaries. There is a reason why successive generations of would-be rebels have plastered their bedroom and dorm room walls with Che Guevara posters. But to be ensconced in this world meant being confronted with hard questions at a pretty tender age.

What does a realistic vision of justice look like?

What is permissible in the quest for it?

Is violence ever necessary to achieve political goals?

Can you support someone's goals without endorsing their means of achieving them?

At sixteen, I wasn't really ready to answer any of these questions, at least not definitively, but I think the fact that I was ready to ask them was a step in the right direction.

CHAPTER 4

I didn't realize this when I was leaving Beirut as a seven-year-old but, in retrospect, when you're born elsewhere, America isn't so much a *place* as it is an *idea*. To much of the world, moving to the United States is a golden ticket, a chance to alter the trajectory of your family's life. In the 250 years since the country's founding, America's most successful and significant export is this vision of itself as a land of opportunity. It doesn't hurt to have billion-dollar box office hits and American pop culture as the leading cultural flag of our times. No matter the country's political leadership, no matter its invasive foreign policy, no matter how inconsistent its treatment of its underprivileged, the so-called "American Dream," while nebulous and ill-defined, still flashes as a welcoming beacon to waves of ambitious would-be émigrés the world over. Of course, like any dream, it's often better in the abstract than it is when met with cold, hard reality.

My family didn't arrive in California with particularly unrealistic visions of what sort of opportunities the United States would hold for us. I mean, as far as I was concerned, I don't think I even really understood where we were moving, so I *definitely* didn't have any high-minded ideas about what it all meant. Before the war in Lebanon, my father had already been doing pretty well. He'd studied shoe design and pattern making in Milan and had parlayed that into his own successful shoe manufacturing business in Beirut. So, on one level, leaving meant forfeiting all he'd built there. On another level, though, there were bombs dropping on our heads, so I can't imagine it was a difficult choice.

When my father arrived in California, he couldn't speak much English; nonetheless, within days, he secured a job working as a designer for a shoe manufacturing company. He later opened a shoe repair shop in a mall in Sherman Oaks. A few years after that, he was introduced to an Armenian guy who owned a small chain of shoe stores and was looking to get into the manufacturing side of the business. He needed someone who could design shoes, open a factory, and hire employees. My father was that person. They partnered up and built a thriving business selling women's footwear. My father handled the manufacturing and design side, while his partner handled sales.

My dad worked his ass off. He worked six days a week and often fourteen to sixteen hours a day. In some ways, the idea of a person arriving in the US with a few hundred dollars to his name, a family to feed, and an inability to speak fluent English quickly going on to start his own successful business just a few years later feels almost superhuman. In fact, it's what immigrants do *all the time.* Perhaps the idea of America as a land of opportunity inherently attracts people who are entrepreneurial, who are risk-takers, but I also think there is an element of people arriving with so little that they've got nothing left to lose. The American Dream is often understood in a way that flatters America's conception of itself, but at best, that's only half the story. The other half are the immigrants who, generation after generation, take huge chances, work incredibly hard, and achieve things that those born here might be less likely to attempt.

In the case of my father, the hard work paid off. His company's success changed my family's life. Finally, there was money coming in. My parents each got nice cars—a Mercedes and a Cadillac. We moved from that little Craftsman bungalow in Hollywood to a nice, big home right off Laurel Canyon Boulevard near Mulholland Drive in Studio City. We'd bought the house from an Iranian family. It was bright and colorful with an airy, open feel to it, and a swimming pool in back. There was enough space that my brother and I both got our own bedrooms for the first time in our lives. The house was perched on a hill and offered beautiful views of the deep greens and sandy browns of the surrounding hillsides. It wasn't as drastic a shift as it had been to move from Lebanon to California, but it still felt like we'd traveled a whole lot farther than the seven or so miles from Hollywood to Studio City.

I have a lot of great memories at that house: summers in the pool, Dad using the intercom to make us laugh when he came home after work, the parties we threw as teenagers, our extended family visiting for long stays, hiking up the hill to play with BB guns. When I think of a lot of my best moments growing up, they're in and around that house.

My dad's business became something of a family affair. When they needed a bookkeeper they could trust, they hired my mother. When I was sixteen, I got my first real job at one of his partner's retail stores in the mall. Although peddling women's shoes doesn't sound like a great gig, it kind of was. The manager was really cool, and for a sixteen-year-old in Southern California in the 1980s, the mall was more or less the center of the known universe. Think of that opening scene in *Fast Times at Ridgemont High*, when the camera is zooming around the mall from the movie theater to the food court to the clothing stores, and everywhere you look you see teenagers living their best lives. My experience at the shoe store in the Sherman Oaks Galleria was kind of like that. During my breaks, I could hang out at the food court or flirt with the teenage girls who worked at the ice cream place across the hall from our shop.

My father and his partner eventually had a falling out over the direction of the company that they couldn't resolve, so they decided to go their separate ways. Each offered to buy the other out, but in the end, it was my father who relinquished his half of the company in return for a healthy buyout and signing an agreement with a non-compete clause that promised he wouldn't manufacture the exact same shoes as they'd made together previously.

Initially, our lifestyle didn't really change. My father used the money from the sale to buy a car wash and invest in some commercial real estate. But he was a bit of a workaholic, and after a spell, he grew antsy. He missed the grind and the day-to-day churn of running a business. He wanted to do it again, and the business he knew—the one he'd basically been in since he was working for a cobbler on the streets of Aleppo as a kid—was shoes. He was concerned about the noncompete clause he'd signed, so he consulted a lawyer who assured him that as long as he didn't manufacture the *exact* same shoes he'd made with his old company, he was in the clear. He followed that advice and opened his own shoe manufacturing firm.

This didn't go over too well with his former partner, who sued him for violating the noncompete clause.

My father felt like he'd done nothing wrong. He'd also come to believe in the fundamental fairness of the American system, so he did what he was supposed to do: he got himself a lawyer and fought this suit.

Defending yourself against an avaricious lawsuit can be a peculiarly frustrating experience. For my parents, it was almost Kafkaesque. In the same way that Gregor Samsa woke up transformed into a giant insect, unable to communicate with the rest of the world or do anything to stem the cascading misfortunes that follow from that inexplicable transformation, my parents—who didn't speak much English—were confounded by a lawsuit that seemingly turned on the definition of the word "exact." When they were soon swimming in legal briefs, subpoenas, and discovery documents, it fell upon me to translate for them. I was in my late teens at the time this all began, but the lawsuit dragged on for nearly a decade. It came to dominate my own life as well as theirs. Evidentiary hearings, court filings, meetings with attorneys and judges—I was intimately involved with pretty much all of it.

I spent days, months sometimes, sitting at our big kitchen table, poring over discoveries, answering questions, and doing my absolute best to guide my parents through all the legal jargon and decisions. They were my parents, but I felt responsible for them. So, I had to grow up fast.

Worse than having to undergo an involuntary crash course in the intricacies of the American legal system was seeing what this lawsuit did to my parents. It chipped away at them, at their self-confidence, at their belief in the country they'd made their home. My father was my hero—he'd lived a swashbuckling youth, he'd shepherded us out of a war zone, he'd built this beautiful life in America out of nothing. He'd seemed capable of handling *anything*.

Until this.

As I graduated high school and started to think about college, my initial plans to go to Stanford or another top-level university were shelved. Instead, I enrolled at Cal State–Northridge and continued to live at home, both to save money and so I could be around to assist with the ongoing legal situation. Whatever I did during those years, the lawsuit seemed to always be there, looming over me like a dark cloud. It was inescapable.

Suffice to say, I didn't have a typical college experience. I didn't live in a dorm, I didn't join a fraternity, I didn't go to a lot of parties. I was a serious student and I worked hard, not just at school, but also managing my father's car wash for a while. I was a business major, not because I had any great interest in business but because I was good at math, and my dad was in business. It seemed practical.

Having grown up in an Armenian-American community and attended an Armenian school, college was the first time I broke out of that insular world. I'm not suggesting that living among the Armenian diaspora was the equivalent of living among the Amish, but I went from a high school with a graduating class of thirty to a university with thirty thousand students, so it was quite a change.

Still, I made an effort to find my tribe at Northridge. I joined the Armenian Students Association and later became its president. We passed out flyers, we staged protests, and we made sure there were memorials on campus to the Armenian Genocide.

All in all, I made some good friends at Northridge but still felt like an outsider. To be fair, I think I'd always felt like that, even growing up around people with backgrounds pretty similar to my own. My worldview just didn't mesh with most everyone else's. I didn't fit into the mainstream. Maybe the throughlines in my family's story—the older generations were running from a genocide; the younger ones were running from a civil war—predisposed me to having issues with authority and a distrust of institutions. But it's hard to disentangle all that history from what may simply be my personality. Somewhere deep within me, I have always felt like a dissident. Following the conventional wisdom and going along with the crowd bother me on a gut level. I've never been a contrarian for its own sake—in fact, I have a somewhat countervailing instinct to avoid confrontation, to try to get along with people—but unquestioning obedience drives me nuts.

During my freshman year at Northridge, I was enrolled in a political science class that met in a big auditorium. There were probably one hundred students in the class, and the teacher was a guy named Professor Gorman. He was great because he'd lecture but he'd also pose hard questions that were designed to actually make us think for ourselves. One day, we were studying the US's acquisition of Hawaii. For non-history buffs, the basic story is that in the late nineteenth century, a regiment of American marines invaded what was then the sovereign kingdom of Hawaii and overthrew the government in a "bloodless" coup. They did so not at the order of the president and commander-in-chief but rather at the urging of a US diplomat to Hawaii, who was in turn acting on behalf of American sugar and pineapple interests on the islands. A lawyer and business-man named Sanford Dole declared himself to be the president of the Republic of Hawaii, at least until the US completed its annexation a few years later and Dole became its first governor. If that name, "Dole," sounds familiar, it's because his family used his political machinations as a springboard to build the giant, multinational fruit conglomerate of the same name.

At the end of this lecture about Hawaii, Professor Gorman asked a simple question: "How many of you think that America should not have gone into Hawaii?" Instantly, my hand shot straight up in the air, but when I looked around the cavernous room, there was only one other hand raised, a Jewish kid sitting a few rows behind me. It didn't take long for the ensuing discussion to get heated.

To me, Hawaii was a straightforward case of colonialism run amok in the service of capitalistic greed. The US government was an occupying power in a land whose people didn't want it to be there in the first place. To the square-jawed, blond frat dudes all around me, thinking, let alone *saying*, such things was traitorous and, judg-ing by their angry reactions, perhaps worthy of a post-class beat-down. It was wildly unsettling to be the target of all my classmates' ire, but I held my ground. The other kid who'd raised his hand did, too. Unlike me, he'd actually spent time in Hawaii with locals there. He talked about how the scars from the US's illegal annexation still resonated, how locals resented the presence and financial muscle of white settlers and tourists from the mainland, how it had created a structure of social and economic inequality that continued to persist there. But it didn't matter how much sense we made or how tight our arguments were; pretty much everyone else in the class thought we were anti-American turncoats.

I remember viscerally how it felt to take an unpopular opinion and not back down in the face of angry opposition. In that moment, it wasn't great. Seeing a whole roomful of people vehemently disagree with you can rattle your own beliefs. But the thing is, once I got through that discomfort, I was fine. In fact, I was *better* than fine. No one kicked my ass after class. My grades didn't suffer. And, best of all, I could take pride in the fact that I didn't buckle under the pressure or go along to get along. As George Orwell wrote in *1984*, "There was truth and there was untruth, and if you clung to truth even against the whole world, you were not mad." And I was not mad. The truth was worth standing up for. Confrontation might not be fun, but it could be endured for the greater good.

Despite these moments of clarity, college was a difficult time for me. It's hard to quantify exactly how much the lawsuit shaded my experience at Northridge and contributed to my disaffection with the supposed institutions of American democracy, but it was a lot. My parents were struggling, emotionally and financially. Every day, I'd wake up and there would be something else unpleasant to deal with—a meeting with an attorney, or a set of court documents that needed to be translated, filled out, and filed. While most of the other students at Northridge were partying and enjoying their newfound freedom, I was neck-deep in legal briefs. It *sucked*. Amid all this stress and uncertainty, the one place I found relief, the one thing that could reliably take my mind off all the depositions and the motions and the petitions and the writs, was something I hadn't paid that much attention to up until that point: music.

———

When I was seventeen, my first girlfriend, Lara, dragged me to go see Iron Maiden at the Irvine Meadows Amphitheatre. Other than those AYF benefits, that Maiden show was the first real concert I'd ever attended. A lot of people will probably read that and think that it makes total sense that the future lead singer of System Of A Down would be baptized into the world of big-time concertgoing by a theatrical heavy metal band like Iron Maiden, but I actually knew nothing about them at the time.

After all, I was a preppy kid with a 4.0 GPA who wasn't really into rock music. My tastes leaned more toward vaguely goth pop acts like the Cure and Depeche Mode. But, if I'm being honest, I wasn't really that into *any* kind of music. I mostly listened to bands I'd hear on the radio or at AYF events. I wasn't reading music magazines or flipping through vinyl at indie record stores. In fact, the very first albums I'd ever bought for myself were through the Columbia House Record Club. For those of you who didn't grow up in the seventies or eighties, this was probably the ultimate signifier of casual fandom in that era. Columbia House offered to send you twelve LPs of your choice for only a penny, a truly amazing deal as long as you didn't read the fine print—which obligated you to buy an *additional* twelve records at inflated prices. Nonetheless, I remember leafing through their catalog of hit records and picking out my first haul, which, if I recall correctly, included music from ABBA, Rick James, and the Saturday Night Fever soundtrack.

I was the antithesis of cool.

Fortunately for me, Lara was different. She insisted that we go to the Maiden show and I'm glad she did. I'd never seen anything like it. Irvine Meadows was packed with wild-eyed fans, headbanging and pressing toward the stage. But it wasn't menacing; it was joyous. The band was so tight, and they really put on a show, packed with frenetic energy and ghoulish larger-than-life visuals.

I was blown away.

It would be a convenient tale if I could claim that this Maiden show was the moment I suddenly woke up to the joys of heavy music, which set me on a course toward System Of A Down, but alas, that wasn't really the case. It would be another few years before that awakening happened for me, and even then, I was never a metal diehard like my System bandmates. Many years later, after System had toured with Maiden and I'd actually become friends with their lead singer, Bruce Dickinson, I got an email from Lara playfully reminding me that she was the one who introduced them to me first.

The Maiden show was great, but what I realize now is that for me to fundamentally change the way I thought about music, my life itself had to change—and, in this case, not for the better. As the lawsuit started to rule my and my family's lives, I sank into a deep depression. I needed something to occupy my mind. And it turned out that something was a little Casio keyboard.

I have no memory of how I ended up with it. I can only imagine that someone must've given that keyboard to me at some point—maybe as a gift, maybe because they just didn't want it anymore—but there it was, sitting in my bedroom, collecting dust. One day, I started to plonk around on it. I figured out how to pick out some simple melodies, and after that, I was hooked. I'd start playing and, the next thing I knew, three hours had passed.

It's not like I was a natural who just sat down at this keyboard and immediately could play. Friends would sometimes show me how to play chords or little flourishes, but I never took any lessons. To anyone else listening, I'm sure that's exactly what it sounded like. But it's not what it felt like.

For me, playing that keyboard, generating sound and music from nothing, felt almost spiritual. It used a part of my brain and a part of my soul that I didn't use in my classes or when reading through legal documents or working at the car wash. Growing up, I spent so much time and energy *thinking* and that little Casio was my invitation to *stop*. While my fingers were on those keys, the rest of the world faded away into a fuzzy background. All that mattered in that moment was the sound that came out of those chintzy speakers. It was like being cocooned in a warm netherworld, insulated from all the everyday shit that could drag me down. In a way, the feeling was almost akin to those hazy rides in the backseat of my dad's Chevy Nova on the way back from the beach in Beirut as late afternoon became early evening. Making music was meditative.

I wasn't very good at playing, but it didn't take me long to realize that the Casio wasn't all that great as an instrument, either. After a few months, I upgraded to a kickass Roland D-50 that I got at Guitar Center along with a keyboard amp. There was something significant about that Roland beyond just the fact that it wasn't an instrument made for children. It was a statement of intent. I wasn't someone fiddling around with a rinky-dink keyboard anymore; I was someone fiddling around with a damn *nice* keyboard! In all seriousness, I can look back now and see that as the moment when I crossed an invisible threshold. At the time, though, I had no delusions of artistic grandeur. All I wanted from music was a refuge from the rest of my life.

It was around this time that I also started filling notebooks with what I'd now call poetry but back then I just thought of as writing. Just about every night, before bed, I'd scribble down thoughts, feelings, ideas, sometimes just unmitigated bile. I suppose this was a way of processing my emotions—not just what was happening with my family and the lawsuit, but thoughts about politics, history, love, whatever. I'd just spew emotion onto the pages, stream of consciousness, often in a mix of Armenian and English. It wasn't about trying to write anything coherent or literary, it was simply about trying to make myself feel better.

Back in the real world, the lawsuit was gradually draining our family's finances as well as its spirit. My father had to sell the car wash and his other investment properties. We had to sell our cars. We moved out of that big house in Studio City and into a rental in North Hollywood. The new house was only ten or fifteen minutes away, but it felt like a profound metaphorical realignment—moving from the heights on top of that hill in Studio City to the depths of the Valley in this much smaller home.

The worst part of the whole ordeal was not the loss of income or the downgrade in our living situation. It was the daily drudgery and negativity. Watching my father have everything he'd worked for, everything he'd built, methodically stripped away was incredibly painful.

The case was going badly. The judge seemed to be against us from the beginning and was openly antagonistic toward our lawyer.

When it went to trial, the jury ruled against my father. There was a regular judgment and a punitive judgment. My father was advised to appeal, which he did. And so, the case dragged on and on. At one point, my Uncle Shant tried to broker a peace deal with my dad's ex-partner, but the whole situation was already too far gone.

Looking back on it now, I wish that the lawyers would've insisted from the beginning that he just settle the case out of court, which, at the time, was still in the cards. Even if he'd won at trial, it wouldn't have been worth the time, the expense, or the misery he'd have had to endure to get there. The fact that he was a successful businessman who didn't speak very good English didn't help either.

It was a dark time. One day during this period, someone shot out the window of my dad's car, right in front of our house. I'm not sure if it was related to the lawsuit, but it was frightening, nonetheless. I felt vulnerable for my family in a way that I hadn't really experienced since we'd left Beirut. I asked a friend of mine if I could borrow a handgun of his to keep at our house for protection and peace of mind. I stuck it in the side table right next to my bed.

Not too long after that incident, at 7 a.m. one morning, there was a loud knock on our front door. When we opened it, several police officers rushed in on us with guns drawn and pointed. At first, we had no idea what was happening. There was a lot of shouting and confusion. It gradually came out why they were there: my father's ex-partner had just been shot and killed.

I was stunned. To think that this person who once seemed to be the architect of my family's demise, who had been the subject of my own negative thoughts for so long, was now suddenly just *gone* was hard to wrap my head around.

The police questioned each of us. I can remember sitting at our dining room table when a detective asked if we had any weapons in the house. I tensed up. I hadn't even told my parents about the gun I'd borrowed, but I figured I'd better come clean to the police. They took the pistol into evidence and had a lot more questions for me. They also confiscated some of those notebooks of mine that were filled with my semi-poetic ramblings.

At one point, I had to answer questions in front of a grand jury about a few of those journal entries. One entry was written almost entirely in Armenian except for the word "KILL" scrawled right in the middle of it, in English. The poem was about how we need to kill our ego in order to succeed as a community, but to anyone who couldn't read Armenian, it looked like a bunch of mysterious squiggly marks surrounding an ominous directive. You can understand why it had initially been concerning. Once I explained it, everyone seemed satisfied, and, needless to say, the gun they'd pulled from my room didn't match whatever they were looking for. Still, the whole episode only added more stress to an already difficult time. In the end, I'm not sure they ever figured out what happened to my father's ex-partner.

As for the appeals process, it went nowhere. The judge in the original case had been rated as "not qualified" for his position by the Los Angeles County Bar Association due to his lack of "judicial temperament," but nonetheless, the judgment stood and he kept his job. My family was effectively ruined financially. We tried to declare bankruptcy but were prevented from doing so because of the nature of the punitive judgment. Not long afterward, the judge was investigated by the Commission on Judicial Performance following repeated complaints that he was rude to lawyers, playing favorites in the courtroom, and making up his mind about cases before they began. He was forced to retire, but it was too late to do anything to help my family.

The whole episode was massively disillusioning, not just for me, but for my whole family. We'd lived the American Dream, arriving here as poor, huddled masses, then working hard to build a fruitful life, only to see it snatched away from us. The American Dream is often portrayed as an upward climb—hard, for sure, but always ascending to greater heights. In fact, as I came to understand it, the American Dream is more like a rollercoaster, with towering peaks, deep valleys, and all sorts of sharp twists and turns in between. And like a rollercoaster, the ride itself could be disorienting enough to make you sick.

CHAPTER 5

During my AYF days, I'd spent quite a bit of time at the Armenian Cultural Center in Hollywood, but it looked very different from this angle. I was now twenty-three, onstage in the auditorium, sitting behind my beloved Roland D-50, surrounded by my bandmates in my first band, Forever Young. Well, nearly surrounded. Michael, our guitarist and main songwriter, was so nervous at the prospect of playing live in front of an audience that he refused to get onstage. We'd tried to coax him up there but the best we could get was a compromise: he'd play but not from the stage. Instead, he was set up in the industrial kitchen next to the auditorium, with his guitar around his neck, connected to his amp onstage by a long black cord.

It's not like I was filled with confidence right off the bat either; I was nervous, too. I'd never been onstage in my life, but I downed a few quick drinks beforehand to steady myself. As such, the performance itself was a bit of a blur. The venue could hold about 250 people and it was relatively full, which seems impressive for a band playing its first-ever gig until you consider that nearly everyone in the room was a friend or family member of someone in the band.

I'd been drafted into Forever Young as the band was forming just a few months earlier. Michael and the lead singer, Raffi, were friends with my younger brother. They already had a drummer and a bassist but needed a keyboard player. They'd seen me playing the keyboard at the house when they were hanging around with Sevag, and that was enough for them. Just like that, I was in a band.

I was a few years older than most of the other band members, and although I was still a novice as a musician, I was spending a lot of my free time playing, so I was getting better quickly. I'd started fiddling around on the guitar as well as the keyboard. Some of the other guys were more technically proficient on their instruments than I was, but the idea of playing in an actual band was new to all of us, and as such, everyone seemed mostly just happy to be there and enamored with the novelty of the whole thing.

Playing music had transformed me into a ravenous music fan almost overnight. I'd go through these intense binge-and-purge cycles, where I'd spend two or three months devouring everything I could find in a particular subgenre—trippy 1960s rock, classic punk rock, West Coast hip-hop, hardcore death metal—then move on to something completely different. Sevag was a great resource for these binges. Even though I was the older brother, he'd always been much more into music than I was, so he was frequently the one pointing me toward new musical rabbit holes to dive down. One week it might be Slayer or Metallica, the next it was Camel or Kyuss.

In Forever Young, the songs Michael wrote were sort of standard-issue alternative rock, which I don't mean as a dig. He was a good songwriter who had a knack for composing catchy hooks and melodies. Raffi wrote most of the lyrics in a mix of Armenian and English and then sang them in a soaring, dramatic voice. As first bands go, we weren't terrible. We actually made an album that a friend of ours who had a small Armenian record label released as a self-titled cassette.

I mostly stuck to playing the keyboards, but I did write the music and lyrics for one song on that cassette called "Prisoner of Faith." It was this melodramatic piano ballad about guys like the "LA Five" who were imprisoned for wanting to help their people fight for justice. I think it was probably the first of my songs that was ever released in any form—if you consider a few hundred cassettes put out by a tiny indie label as a "release"—but it was not the first I'd ever recorded. A year or so earlier, I'd made a brassy, triumphant anthem for my local AYF chapter, which, I suppose, was my stab at making the kind of Armenian revolutionary music I'd seen at those AYF shows as a teenager. The song was called "Musa Dagh," which was the name both of our chapter and of a mountain in Turkey that was the site of a famous Armenian resistance during the Genocide. The lyrics harked back to the formation of the AYF and touched on its history.

I was a serious guy in those days, and I took being in Forever Young as seriously as I took everything else in my life. I certainly didn't think of it as a potential career or a route to fame and fortune, but I guess I subscribed to the old adage, "Anything worth doing is worth doing well"—or at least trying hard to do well. For most of the other guys in that band, Forever Young was mainly just a reason to hang out, have fun, and meet girls. Not that there's anything wrong with that. Still, there was a division that slowly started to break us apart as time wore on: most of the other band members' interest in music itself seemed to be waning as mine was intensifying.

One day, Michael and I met up at our rehearsal space so that we could finish up a song called "Waco Jesus," for which I'd written the lyrics and he'd written most of the music. This wasn't long after the U.S. Bureau of Alcohol, Tobacco and Firearms had besieged and then razed the Branch Davidian compound outside Waco, Texas, where cult leader David Koresh was holed up with his followers and a lot of guns. I wrote the lyrics from the perspective of Koresh himself, the "Waco Jesus" of the title. Michael and I wanted to record it, but a few of our bandmates weren't around, including our singer Raffi.

"Why don't you just sing it yourself?" Michael asked me. "I mean, they're *your* lyrics."

I'd never really thought of myself as a singer up to that point but what the hell—I was willing to give it a shot. I still have that recording, and when I listen to it now, I can hear myself trying to channel all the singers I was really into at that exact moment in time. I sing in this low, deep, aggrieved voice that would be largely unrecognizable to System Of A Down fans but very recognizable to anyone who has heard the Doors, Danzig, or Pearl Jam. The song itself is pretty derivative, too, but it's got a lot of pure, youthful energy. Recording it also helped me realize something: I liked singing. *Really* liked singing. It gave me a physical, adrenalized rush that was so different from the feeling I got playing keyboards or guitar. I often wonder if Raffi hadn't been out of town, how long it would've taken me to figure that out.

"Waco Jesus" was an important milestone for me, and not just because it was the first time I'd sung on a recording. For all its flaws, the song itself is pretty ambitious. It explores a lot of the same thematic ground I'd spend much of my career focused on. Although Koresh has become something of a pop-culture punchline nowadays, he was a dissident who challenged a powerful, arrogant government and ultimately sacrificed himself in the search for some sort of spiritual salvation. I'm not saying I think he was somehow a righteous character—I mean, he was also a megalomaniac with a god complex who was having sex with most of his followers (which is why I alternated between singing "Waco" and "wacko" in the song)—but he was definitely an interesting one and the kind of conflicted figure I'd be drawn toward again and again as a writer.

The song was also a landmark for another reason. A second guitarist worked on "Waco Jesus" with us—a young, skinny, long-haired Armenian-American kid with dark, round, piercing eyes who played lead guitar and sang harmonies. His name was Daron Malakian. I'd first met him when he was practicing with another band in our shared rehearsal space. He was only sixteen at the time, but he could really play, and like me, he took the idea of making music seriously. In fact, he took it more seriously than anyone I'd ever met. He ate, drank, and slept music. I liked him immediately.

After I graduated from Northridge at twenty-two, I took a job working for my Uncle Shant, who had a jewelry business in downtown LA. I'd had a brief notion that I'd take my business degree and go work for a record company, but the fifteen or so major and indie record labels to whom I sent my resume quickly trashed that notion. Only one even responded, sending a polite note to inform me that they had no openings but would keep my resume on file.

My Uncle Shant lived just down the street from us, so he and I would drive to work together every morning. It would've been an altogether pleasurable way to start the day if he hadn't insisted on listening to smooth jazz the whole way. It didn't bother me so much at first, but every day, it'd be the same *exact* music, and after a while, I felt like those detainees at Guantanamo Bay who were played Barney the Dinosaur's theme song on perpetual loop until they slowly went insane.

My uncle's business was in LA's now-popular jewelry district. My desk was next to his in his large office with a massive bay window that looked out onto a sizable showroom. There was a manufacturing facility, too. In the early years, Shant specialized in yellow gold, heavy nugget jewelry, or chain links, charms, and pendants. Later on, the business transitioned into fine jewelry, diamond rings, earrings, and bracelets. I helped manage everything and kept very busy. I answered calls, handled sales, dealt with clients, did trade shows, learned about the manufacturing side of the jewelry business, and eventually worked with a computer programmer to create industry-specific software to help manage the business. Basically, we modified a fully modular accounting system that allowed source-code modifications to customize it specifically for wholesale jewelers with pricing by weight, digital scale integration, and daily price recalculations, followed by a program to conduct metal tracking for metal manufacturers and a retail point-of-sale system for retail jewelers. *Basically.* These were the early days of vertical industry software, and I have to say, mine worked pretty well.

As much as I wanted to support my uncle, if I'm being honest, my heart was never fully in this job—and I'm sure everyone around me knew it, too. I felt like I was just killing time, waiting for my real life to start. It was slowly grinding me down.

I'd been working in the jewelry business for about two years when one day, I found myself in the bathroom, standing at the urinal, taking a piss. Normally, my day was a blur of sales reports, client calls, visits with vendors, and the like. Often, the bathroom, with its plain white walls and its antiseptic smell, was the only respite from all that. For just a moment that day, my mind was quiet, and I was staring at the tile wall in front of me. Just then, a thought crept up on me: *How amazing would my life be if I could just be at home right now playing music?*

In a lot of ways, it was just an idle daydream. But it was a little more than that, too. It was as if my subconscious had taken that short break to remind me that the way I spent my time was not an obligation but a choice. I was working hard and being productive, which I enjoyed—but this seemingly forbidden fruit that I adored was waiting for me at home.

Once I gave oxygen to that thought, it refused to disappear. For weeks, at work, it kept recurring in my mind. I'd try to reason it away. After all, what was I going to do? Quit my job to focus on a music career when that music career amounts to nothing more than playing keyboards in a local band that's played one solitary show? It was a patently ridiculous idea. Still, I was desperate for something else—*anything* else—on my horizon.

One idea seemed to rear its head several times a week. By this point, I'd worked with my uncle's business for about two years. When I wasn't there, I was spending so much time helping my parents with the lawsuit that I felt like I had an understanding of civil litigation nearly equal to that of many young lawyers. So why not make lemonade out of lemons and just become a lawyer myself? If I did that, I'd be in a position to help people like my parents instead of so often feeling impotent in the face of their struggles. The more I thought about it, the more it seemed to make sense.

It was this completely reasonable line of thinking that explains how I ended up in a giant classroom in Long Beach one weeknight, surrounded by people who, like me, had signed up for a multi-week course to prepare themselves to take the LSAT. There was a palpable excitement among these students, who were embarking on the first step in a journey toward fulfilling what must've been for many of them a long-held dream: becoming a lawyer. I sat there, I listened to the instructor, I took notes, I chatted politely with my classmates, and I left.

I don't remember much else about the class itself, but the drive home is seared into my mind. It was raining, and I was steering my Jeep through the wet, winding curves along Laurel Canyon Boulevard, besieged by a sense of disquiet. Both hemispheres of my brain were on neural overdrive. I could smell the damp night air and seize upon the gentle trails of light left by passing cars as I zoomed in on the realization of my life situation: something wasn't right. While the idea of becoming a lawyer made logical sense, there was one substantial problem that was resting somewhere deep in the recesses of my cerebrum. The more I stared out that rainy windshield, the more clearly I could see it: *I didn't* want *to be a lawyer.* In fact, the prospect of going to law school—hell, the prospect of even going back to that LSAT class with those enthusiastic law student wannabes—filled me with unbearable dread. My overriding feeling about the entire legal profession at that time in my life was one of abject disgust. *Why in the world would I want to sign up to be part of that every day for the rest of my life?*

As the Jeep's headlights cut through the dark, pointing the way forward, my head was spinning. *If not law school, then what?* I couldn't envision spending my life in the jewelry business either. I wanted something that was mine. Maybe it was the fact that I was driving through Laurel Canyon, a place that's rich with LA music history—the Doors; Joni Mitchell; Crosby, Stills, and Nash; and Frank Zappa all called the place home in the 1970s—but at that moment, the only thing in my life that felt like it was *mine* was music. I'd started playing simply to distract myself from my real life, but it turned out, playing was one of the only times when I really felt *alive*. But what was I supposed to do with this feeling? What was the practical application?

My parents had risked everything to bring us to the United States. They'd built up a thriving business and then seen their ambitions crushed under the weight of legal briefs. They'd sacrificed everything for me and my younger brother. Now, because of the lawsuit, they were really struggling, financially and emotionally. I knew I should do something sensible, something that would put my college education to work, something that could help the whole family. But what did that really mean?

Then, in a flash, there was clarity. On another road, thousands of miles away and a generation earlier, my father had gotten a glimpse of what his future might look like if he decided to dedicate his life to music. An aging oud player told him about the heartache, the struggle, the impracticability of it all, and my father made the sensible choice to pivot his life in another direction. I didn't have to. He and my mother had sacrificed for me so that I wouldn't have to sacrifice for them. They didn't need me to spend my life in misery as a lawyer or a jeweler. How would my unhappiness honor their sacrifices?

I slammed on the brakes, and my Jeep skidded to a stop in the middle of the empty road. I pounded my palms on the steering wheel and said, at first quietly to myself and then shouting to the heavens, "I want to do music. I want to fucking do *music!*"

The next day, I went into work and knew I had to talk to my uncle. By this time, his business was thriving. I was his right-hand man, and he'd gradually given me more and more responsibility. I was managing our employees, helping run trade shows, and mixing gold with alloy for manufacturing. I told him how much I appreciated everything he'd done for me, how much I loved him for it, but that it just wasn't what I wanted to do with my life. My uncle listened carefully and nodded.

"So, what is it that you want to do instead?" he asked.

I looked down at the floor and then raised my eyes to meet my uncle's gaze. "I want to make music," I said quietly.

There was another long pause, and Uncle Shant, to his credit, did not laugh. He didn't quite understand either, though.

"Serj, what I think you need is to run your own business," he said. "You already run this one with me. I've been thinking of expanding into direct-to-consumer catalogs. What if I broke off a piece of this business, focused it on these catalogs, invested a little money in it to get it started, and then it would be your business to run?"

The more he talked about it, the more enthusiastic he seemed to grow about this idea. Finally, I cut him off.

"The thing is, nobody gave you this," I explained, motioning to his sprawling office complex, retail showroom, and manufacturing facility. "You came here, you opened it, you built it yourself. This is yours because you made the choice to do it. Nobody gave my dad his business. He did that himself. I need to do something for myself now, too. I need to do music."

Years later, I'd learn there's a term for this in music business circles: a lifer. It's not someone who necessarily makes a living from playing music but for whom playing music makes life itself *worth* living irrespective of its worldly rewards.

The deep-seated feeling in my gut was definitive, unmistakable.

I knew that was me.

———

Wanting to devote my life to music was a really beautiful concept in the abstract, but it was nowhere near a financially sustaining enterprise for me in those days. After I quit working for my uncle, I spent a few months burning through my savings before realizing I needed a source of income to keep me afloat and not be dependent on my parents, who had their own financial woes to worry about without me adding to them.

I had a college degree, lots of job experience, and a real work ethic, so finding a day job wasn't hard. Finding one that didn't suck was a little trickier. I lasted about two weeks at Guitar Center before the magic of being surrounded by musical instruments wore off and the drudgery of working at a retail chain set in. I then found part-time work as an accountant for a video company. That worked for me to generate some short-term cash, but it wasn't really enough.

One day, my uncle called me with a question about the software that I'd developed for his business. As we were talking, it hit me that my day job was staring me in the face. If I could just adapt the software a little, I could sell it to other jewelry businesses. I could be my own boss. I could make my own hours. The great thing about the software business is that you put in the work on the front end, but then each time you resell it, it costs you very little. It's like music that way. Plus, I already knew the ins and outs of the jewelry business and knew all the vendors, so once I got the business up and running, it would be easy. As it turned out, I was right about all that—except for the part about it being easy.

My company, which I gave the hilariously dry moniker "Ultimate Solutions I" (because "Ultimate Solutions" was already taken by another company), was more successful than I could've ever imagined. There was big demand for industry-specific software at that time, and for my software, in particular. Suddenly, I was flying to Arizona, to Florida, to Hawaii to help install it for out-of-state clients. I was making real money. And it was mine. The whole thing was hugely satisfying, although admittedly a bit of a distraction for someone who had so recently declared to the heavens—or at least to the shrubs and trees lining Laurel Canyon Boulevard—his intention to commit his life to music.

—

Forever Young plodded along for more than a year but that wasn't long enough for us to play a second gig. We didn't so much break up as much as we just sort of stopped playing. Somewhat shockingly, there was not much mainstream interest in a band who sang half their songs in Armenian. Go figure.

I wasn't losing a ton of sleep over the band's demise. Ever since working on "Waco Jesus," Daron and I had been spending a lot of time together. We'd meet up at his house in Glendale, and sometimes just sit around and listen to records. Daron had really diverse tastes even back then and turned me on to a lot of music I hadn't yet heard. We spent afternoons listening to the Clash, Tom Waits, Black Sabbath, NWA, whatever. Other times, I'd bring my keyboard, he'd play the guitar, and we'd sing together. Our voices seemed to mesh and complement each other in a really compelling way.

Daron went to Glendale High School at the time but he'd also attended Pilibos, the same Armenian school I'd graduated from. I was eight years older, though, so we'd never crossed paths there. For a twenty-four-year-old to be hanging around with a sixteen-year-old kid seems a little odd in retrospect, but back then, it didn't even occur to me. When it came to music, Daron carried himself with a confidence that belied his years. He gave the impression that he knew what he was doing even when he didn't. He lived and breathed music. More than anyone I was hanging around with back then, he seemed like a real artist.

Most importantly, though, he and I had an undeniable creative chemistry. It made sense that we'd start a band together.

First, we pulled in Dave Hakopyan, a friend who'd played bass in a late-era version of Forever Young. We needed a drummer, so we put an ad in *The Recycler*, this free weekly mag filled with classifieds selling used gear and want ads for musicians. I think the only person who answered our ad was a Hawaiian guy named Domingo Lariano. Domingo was a great thrash metal drummer who also had a real talent for arranging songs.

The four of us started getting together in a practice space in North Hollywood and making a lot of noise. The place was so small and insulated that it got really warm while we practiced. It also got pretty loud in there, so loud that I had to use an earplug (but only in one ear so I could still hear the melodies).

Eventually, all our noise began coalescing into songs—big, bruising, angry shards of progressive metal. It felt like we were onto something. We decided to call the band Soil.

Daron wrote most of the music, and I started channeling my rage and all the scribbling I'd done in those poetry notebooks into lyrics. There was so much angst in those early songs. I was exorcising a lot of demons, venting about the lawsuit, about injustice, about denial of the Genocide, about American politics, about whatever else it is that dudes in their twenties get worked up about, I guess. The music was wild and aggressive. We kind of sounded like a mishmash of a bunch of progressive death metal bands if they were trying to sing Armenian folk melodies. It wasn't very polished, but it was imaginative and had raw power. I can listen back to it now and recognize the seeds of what would eventually blossom into System Of A Down. Many of the ingredients were there, we just didn't quite know how to cook them yet.

Soil practiced a few times a week. Once we'd get going, those small rehearsal spaces would be so loud, and I'd just be screaming my head off to the point where I was starting to notice the effect it was having on my hearing. I was young though—or young-ish, anyway—and didn't really give a fuck. There was something cathartic about it all. Those rehearsals were probably the closest I ever came to primal scream therapy.

The songs themselves could be bleak. We'd named the band after one of our early songs, also called "Soil," which I'd written about one of my best friends from high school, Paul. A lot of people probably have had a friend like Paul: outgoing, tons of positive energy, a charismatic guy who was a lot of fun to be around but also with an essential darkness never too far from the surface. Paul had issues—among other things, he'd lost his dad at a young age—and being around him, you couldn't help but sense an edginess. He was the guy who drank a little too much, smoked a little too much, and pushed everything a little bit farther than it should probably go. Sometimes, it was harmless. Once, he borrowed our friend's car, and rather than treat it with the extra-special care one might when handling someone's else's valuables, he drove it like a stunt driver. I can remember sitting in the backseat as he was doing donuts in a parking lot and smoking the tires. Typical teenage guy shit.

As time wore on, Paul's energy got even darker. He and I had drifted apart a bit by the time he killed himself in his early twenties. It hit me hard then. It still does. I initially wrote about his death in my notebooks, just a collection of phrases—"shot the gun that startled my life," "friends for years, images in red," "confidence death insecurity," "for reasons undefined"—that I eventually coaxed into the song. "Soil" ended up as a pretty accurate reflection of my own emotions around his death. It's angry, embittered, confused, and grasping for understanding, or if not understanding, at least some sort of acceptance and serenity.

Paul was the first person close to me who took his own life but sadly not the last, and that one phrase—"for reasons undefined"—is the one that seems to run through and ring true for most suicides. You can think you know everything about a person, about their trials, about their pain, but ultimately, on some level, we're all enigmas to each other. Many years later, my friend Chris Cornell would take his own life, and that same sentiment returned with even more intensity. I was crushed. Chris was a really beautiful guy and a good friend. We had chatted just months earlier at Elton John's birthday event when we sat next to each other. So careful not to drink after years of recovery, he didn't even take a sip from his champagne glass to toast Elton. He had a myriad of plans, from tours—with Soundgarden and solo—to a covers record. I told him he needed to do a show and record with an orchestra, as his voice would be magical with them, and even offered to help with arrangements for it. From the outside looking in, he seemed to have everything, but at his core there was a hurt that was almost unknowable.

Sadly, the same could be said for Anthony Bourdain, who I also eventually met and befriended. His life seemed like a dream to most people, like he'd won a lottery, but to live it, for him, must have been some kind of incomprehensible nightmare. I don't judge my friends for the choices they made, but the void they left behind is real. There's a phrase that I scream at a break in that song "Soil," "Why the fuck did you take him away from us, you motherfucker!" that I think about as a sort of an interrogation of God for all the planet's sins and injustices. It's both an angry howl of mourning and an acknowledgment that some parts of life are hard to fully comprehend.

The way I crafted lyrics back then—and the way I suppose I still do—was peculiar, though not intentionally so. I had these notebooks full of my writing, and my strategy for working them into the framework of the songs was pretty much no strategy at all. I'd just sort of jam what I wanted to sing into the lines regardless of whether they fit or not. If that meant singing too fast and tripping over words, so be it. If that meant howling one syllable for an entire line, that was fine, too. Sometimes, I'd just toss in lyrics that were pure nonsense because they felt like they belonged there. It was a real punk-rock approach to writing, although I didn't really think of it like that at the time. I just didn't know what I didn't know.

I think the way I constructed lyrics also informed the way I'd learn to use my voice. Other than my short tenure in the school choir and singing around the house with my dad, I didn't really have much experience as a vocalist. I still sometimes sang in that deep Jim Morrison/Eddie Vedder baritone, but the more I sang, the more I realized that my vocal cords could also do a lot of other things. In Soil, I did a lot of growling, a lot of screaming, along with some actual singing, in large part because that's what the songs called for. I was discovering that my voice was a pretty dynamic instrument that could join other instruments in the cacophony of a song. If I'd ever taken a voice lesson back then, I'm sure the teacher would've wrung a lot of eccentricities out of my approach, but looking back now, my ignorance and naivete were a gift.

That said, apparently, the rest of the band wasn't completely sold on me as their singer. I found out years later that at one point, they secretly tried to replace me, and even auditioned a few different people. It turned out none of the folks they brought in could really sing along with the crazy, chaotic noise that the band churned out, so I kept the job by default.

After all the rehearsing, Soil finally booked a gig, a daytime show at a blues club in Los Angeles called Club Fais Do-Do. It was my first time being the frontman onstage and only the second time I'd ever even been onstage at all, so I was filled with anxiety and nervous energy. I think we all were. The best way we knew how to deal with pre-show jitters back then was alcohol and weed, so I'm pretty confident that by showtime, we were all filled with both of those too, which probably explains why I have very little memory of the show itself, and almost certainly explains the one memory I do have: Daron falling off the stage, three feet onto the floor during one of his guitar solos. It was all very *Spinal Tap.*

Like Forever Young, Soil lasted only long enough to play one show. Domingo was married with a kid, and when he got a job to support them, they moved back to Hawaii. He'd been such an integral part of the band that it didn't seem to make sense to carry on without him. Soil was dead and buried. I was disappointed but, to his credit, Daron was already plotting our next big move.

CHAPTER 6

The phone rang, and when I picked up, it was Daron.

"Yo, bro. I'm going to ask Shavo to come play bass with us." He was excited almost to the point of agitation. "I already have some new music I've been working on, and I think Shavo would be *perfect* for it."

Domingo had just told us a few weeks earlier that he was moving to Hawaii, effectively putting an end to Soil in the fall of 1994. There seemed to be an unspoken agreement that Daron and I would carry on playing music together, but this was the first real conversation I can recall having about it.

Shavo Odadjian had gone to Pilibos around the same time as Daron. I'd gotten to know him a little when he started occasionally hanging around at Soil's rehearsals. Shavo was tall and really skinny, and he had a hint of a nervous stutter when I first met him. He may have actually helped us book our one and only gig when we were in Soil. But as far as I knew, he was a guitar player, not a bassist. Plus, we already had a bassist.

"Wait, what about Dave?" I asked. Dave wasn't just a great bass player; he was also one of our closest friends. "I don't get it," I told Daron. "We lost a drummer. Shouldn't we be trying to find someone to replace him, instead of replacing the band members we've already got?"

But Daron had fixed his mind on Shavo. "I just think Shavo will fit better with the music I'm writing and the vision going forward," he insisted. "You like him, right?"

I did like Shavo. He was impossible to dislike. He was a skate-boarding metalhead who worked at a flower shop and got along with everybody. He was sweet and didn't take himself too seriously. I remember all of us joking that he was so thin that he had to run around in the shower to get wet. Even so, I still didn't understand why converting him into a bass player was better than the bass player we already had.

"Trust me," Daron said. "Shavo will be great."

Daron seemed so certain that I guess his confidence won me over, or at least convinced me that any resistance was futile. When Dave caught wind of the fact that he'd been eased out of the band, he was understandably angry—and I don't blame him. A few weeks later, we'd found a drummer, too, a guy named Andy Khachaturian, whom Daron had also known since grade school, and we started meeting up to play at a warehouse in an industrial section of North Hollywood.

I'd originally leased the warehouse space to run my software business, Ultimate Solutions I, out of, though—truth be told—it wasn't really a great setup for that. It was one thousand square feet of space with high black walls, a concrete floor, and big roll-up metal doors for truck deliveries. I'd dragged some office furniture and a couple of couches into the back so I could work there, but the place really worked better as a rehearsal space than it ever did as an office. Before we started meeting up there, I'd gone out and bought several buckets of house paint in all different colors, then together with the guys painted one of those black walls using an old Takamine acoustic guitar as a brush. I'd dip the guitar body into the paint and then scrape it against the wall, sort of like Julian Schnabel, but obviously not that good. Many years later, I'd start devoting a lot of time to painting, but that warehouse wall was really my first canvas.

Shavo picked up playing bass quickly but played very differently than Dave had. Dave was more of a traditional bassist, who would lock in with a drummer and create a groove. Shavo, however, more closely followed Daron's guitar lines. I'm not sure if that was a stylistic choice on Shavo's part, which is why Daron wanted him in the band to compliment his own playing, or if it was him just playing what Daron asked him to play, but whatever the reason, it sounded pretty thick. I don't know whether Daron's maneuvering to get Shavo into the band was to achieve exactly this goal or if it was a bonus. Either way it felt to me like Shavo was more malleable, musically and personally, for Daron.

It can often take a while before a band starts clicking, before it's clear that there's something special or transcendent happening, but in our case, it felt like that magic was there right from the beginning. Daron and I were developing a really unique musical language between us, especially when we jammed. I'd riff vocally off what he was doing on the guitar and then he'd react to my voice with a different guitar part. It was like a musical conversation. We already had a bunch of songs we'd worked on together in Soil, and a few of those songs started to take on new shapes as we continued to play them with Shavo and Andy.

A part of what eventually became the song "Sugar"—that outro where I sing "How do I feel? / What do I say? / Fuck you, it all goes away!"—had been floating around since the Soil days, but we never really figured out what to do with it until Shavo came into rehearsal one day with this oddly jazzy bass line. Daron started playing guitar riffs to go with it, and then said something like "Let me take this home and see what I can do." He came back with the basic architecture of the whole song. I raided my trusty poetry notebook for this weird phrase about "kombucha mushroom people." I'd heard someone somewhere talking about kombucha mushrooms and it was such an odd-sounding collection of words that it made me think of some sort of bizarro cult, so I added some verses that had that kind of feel. We tacked the outro onto that, and Daron added his vocal tagline—"*sugar!*"—which had nothing to do with anything but somehow elevated the song. To this day, I don't really have any idea what the song is about other than it being angsty and kind of our "Fuck you!" song—not unlike Rage Against the Machine's "Killing in the Name"—in large part, I'm sure, because of that outro.

My vocals on "Sugar" are kind of intentionally all over the place: there are parts where I'm doing this sort of fast, poetic rambling in a psychotic, schizophrenic voice that lends itself really well to my stream of consciousness style of writing. There's also a sort of megaphone effect on my voice that has a hint of cabaret to it and reminds me of that Wall of Voodoo song from the early eighties, "Mexican Radio."

All in all, it's a pretty good example of the kind of musical math you hope for with any song: the whole is much more than the sum of its parts.

The warehouse became the band's unofficial HQ. Some nights we'd all go out together and go see other bands at clubs on the Sunset Strip like the Roxy, the Whisky a Go Go, and Filthy McNasty's. Many of those nights, we'd end up back at the warehouse, drinking, smoking, and hanging out. For me, the warehouse also became a home away from home. In my late twenties, I was still living with my parents, so having a place I could crash after a long, rough night out was a real bonus. Because the place was a warehouse, many of those nights when I crashed there at two or three in the morning, I'd be rudely awakened just a few hours later by a giant eighteen-wheeler rolling into the complex. It was a hell of a wake-up call.

One of those nights, I remember all of us out drinking somewhere and then in the wee hours of the morning, hopping into Daron's Honda to go back to the warehouse. Daron usually drove like a bit of a madman, and however many drinks he'd had that night did not calm him down. As we got into the industrial area near the warehouse, he ran a red light. Immediately, we heard the sirens and saw the flashing lights of a police car behind us. Well, I did anyway. Daron just kept driving with the cops in hot pursuit for a couple of blocks, then sped through the warehouse parking lot all the way to our space. By the time he came to a stop, multiple police cars had pulled in behind us. We were all ordered out of the car, forced onto our knees at gunpoint, and handcuffed. It was terrifying.

The cops seemed to think we were gang members and called backup. I tried to explain that we were just harmless musicians, and eventually opened the warehouse for them so they could see our equipment. Daron had to take a roadside sobriety test, but he couldn't manage to walk in a straight line, so he flunked. I assumed for sure that he was going to jail, but when nerves cooled a little, I think the police were worried that they'd overreacted by cuffing all of us and pointing guns at our heads, so they just let Daron go into the warehouse and crash on the couch. The whole episode was harrowing. I used it as the basis for the lyrics to a song that was originally called "Bacon" but which Daron later incorporated into another song, "Mr. Jack." So, if you've ever wondered why I holler "Fuck you, pig!" over and over at the end of that song, well—now you know.

We'd rehearse three or four times a week at the warehouse, and once we had a bunch of songs in our arsenal, we started inviting friends to come listen to us play there. What began as fairly intimate gatherings of twenty or thirty friends quickly grew into full-on warehouse keg parties with three or four times that many.

Before we knew it, those warehouse parties became bona fide events. Because we were in an industrial section of town, there was no one around at night. We could play as loud as we wanted for as long as we wanted, and if things got a little out of hand, there wasn't anyone nearby to complain about it. We'd play the songs we were working on in whatever state they were in and also sometimes throw in some covers, generally chosen by Daron and based largely on whatever he seemed to be into that week. He used to like to play that Dire Straits song, "Sultans of Swing," which I wasn't crazy about. We'd also do Wham!'s "Careless Whisper," Berlin's "Metro," and at least one Madonna song that I can't remember the name of anymore.

Initially, we were just playing for our friends, but then over the course of six to nine months, it gradually became friends of friends, and then even some who had only the loosest of connections to our social circle. Our former bassist Dave, who'd been unceremoniously ousted from the band when Soil ended, started a new band called Friik, who rented rehearsal space from me in the warehouse, and sometimes they would play with us at parties. He had some lingering bitterness about the way things had shaken out, but fortunately, he remained a good friend and a part of the little community we were building around the band and the warehouse.

When it came time to choose a band name, Daron had this poem he'd written titled "Victims of a Down." I don't even really remember what the poem was about—it was something personal for Daron—but it just sounded like a cool phrase and almost like a mission statement for the band. But there was discomfort with having the word "victims" in the band name as it denotes a negative connotation, so we subbed in "system of a down." I liked the name because even though it doesn't have any literal meaning, it has a figurative one that you can sense just by reading or hearing the words. I think that ended up being true of a lot of our songs as well. Even though the name itself doesn't really mean anything, "System Of A Down" became this wonderfully empty vessel that took on the meaning we gave it: a brotherhood, a partnership, a band, a business, a concord taking us to the far edges of the world to experience it as the universe experiences itself through us.

In System's early days, Shavo wasn't just the bass player, he was also the de facto band manager. This was largely because he was a personable guy with a good marketing sense who was willing to make endless rounds of fruitless phone calls to clubs, promoters, and the like. He called the bookers at clubs on the Strip over and over and over to the point where he'd routinely just get hung up on. Finally, he wore down the guy at the Roxy enough that he offered us a gig—well, sort of. We had to sell at least seventy-five tickets in order to play. This kind of arrangement is a bit of a scam that clubs pull on young bands, but we didn't care. We'd built up such a following through our warehouse parties that we ended up selling about 150.

We hadn't so much as recorded our first demo tape at that time, so no one outside of our circle had any idea what we sounded like. It was the Sunday of Memorial Day weekend in 1995, and we were sharing the bill with an industrial group called Engines of Aggression and five or six ska bands. It wasn't exactly a natural fit for us, but it didn't matter. There weren't many people in the crowd for the bands that played before us, but as we were setting up our gear, all our fans rushed into the club. All those friends and friends of friends who'd been coming to get drunk with us at our warehouse were excited for our first real show.

The lights dimmed onstage, and we opened our set with this Armenian chant. While we were chanting, Andy held up a white cloth banner in front of his drum kit that he'd spray painted with the words:

1915

1.5 Million

Always Remembered

Andy hadn't even told us he was going to do that but I'm so glad he did. When the spotlight picked out that banner onstage, it really set the tone, not just for that show, but, really, for System's entire existence.

The show was exhilarating, though from a technical standpoint, a bit of a mess. I'd been using a distortion pedal on my main mic, and it was feeding back the whole time, so my vocals came out as a roaring, garbled mess. But you couldn't fake the energy in that room. I was still a little nervous before we went on, but my hair was long, dark, and curly back then, so I could kind of hide behind it until I got comfortable in front of the audience. I've never really been an extrovert or someone who wanted the spotlight on him, but I was finding that once I kind of gave myself over to the music, my fears would melt away. To this day, I can step onstage and play a concert in front of two hundred thousand people without much anxiety, but if you ask me to give a speech in front of twenty people, I'll be petrified.

As soon as we got off stage at the Roxy, our fans left with us, which I think left a lasting impression on the club. They knew that we brought a crowd. It was the last pay-to-play gig we ever did. Three weeks later, we had a show at the Whisky, and after that we played every three to four weeks, hopping between the clubs on the Strip—the Roxy, the Whisky, the Coconut Teaszer—and a few other spots in LA like the Troubadour, the Dragonfly, and the Anti-Club. The crowds gradually got bigger, and we gradually got better—or maybe it was the other way around.

By 1996, it seemed like we might need a real manager, or at least someone to handle some of the administrative tasks associated with being in a rock band who wasn't also the bassist. One day, a guy named David Benveniste came to the warehouse to watch us rehearse. Everybody called him Beno. Apparently, he'd heard about our club shows. He had little or no experience managing artists, but he had a lot of moxie and seemingly some potentially valuable connections. He'd grown up in Southern California and gone to Beverly Hills High School alongside a lot of rich kids whose parents either worked in the entertainment business, had the money to fund their kids' ambitions to do so, or quite often both. He told us that his closest friend from high school was Guy Oseary, who by that time was already running Madonna's label, Maverick Records, and who'd soon become her manager.

We didn't know if Beno was feeding us a whole bunch of bullshit, but seeing as how artist management often involves extravagant flattery coupled with hustle and bustle, that probably wouldn't have been disqualifying. More to the point, he was hugely enthusiastic about System. We didn't know how far to trust him at first but we definitely liked him. At any rate, Beno seemed eager to hustle and schmooze on System's behalf, and we couldn't think of any reason not to let him.

The band's timing was good, or at least lucky. Although we didn't really sound much like any other bands, there was a weird alternative metal scene springing up around LA which meant there was a pool of fans who were open to the kind of noise we were making. We frequently shared bills with bands like Coal Chamber, (hed) P.E., Downset, Human Waste Project, and Bad Acid Trip, but there was one that really took us under their wing: Snot.

The guys in Snot were from Santa Barbara but had a hardcore following all over the state. We were building up a fan base in Los Angeles, but our first out-of-town shows were mostly gigs that Snot asked us to play with them. Keep in mind, "out-of-town" for us in those days meant suburbs like Pomona, Fullerton, and Corona, or occasionally slightly more far-flung locales like San Diego and Santa

Barbara. For a young band, that was how you made progress: in tiny, incremental steps.

The guys in Snot were funny and generous. There was no sense that they viewed us as competition. Their singer, Lynn Strait, had a buzzcut, an eyebrow piercing, and arms sleeved with tattoos. He was an incredibly unique, charismatic guy, and someone who'd go to the mat for the people he liked. Fortunately, I was one of them.

I remember one night, we were playing with Snot, and I was at the front door of the club, trying to get in, but the bouncer wouldn't let me by. I tried to explain that I was the singer in the opening band. This guy either didn't believe me or didn't care. In the era before cell phones, this sort of misunderstanding could be intractable. I was resigned to basically just standing there passively by the front door until someone in charge happened by or came looking for me. That's when Lynn walked up and realized what was happening. He immediately got in this bouncer's face and threatened him. He was squaring up, absolutely ready to fight this very large man whose job it was to physically force his will upon others. Finally, the bouncer backed down and let me in. That was Lynn Strait.

Sadly, just a couple of years later, Lynn died when his car was broadsided by a pickup truck on Highway 101 near Santa Barbara. The accident also killed his beloved dog, a boxer named Dobbs, who's pictured on the cover of Snot's album, *Get Some*. Lynn and I had stayed pretty close even as both of our bands had grown in stature, and his death felt like a heavy blow. I often question why some people are taken from this place in their prime. Has their vision already been realized? Why do others who rot the chair they sit on and exude nothing but villainy seem to live forever? It all seems so unfair.

Beno did a good job of catalyzing a lot of the excitement around System. We were playing more often, our crowds were getting bigger, and we were gradually moving up the bill from opener to direct support to headliner. We made a series of demo tapes and started to hear about record companies sniffing around, interested in potentially signing us. Beno set up showcases to specifically invite label executives out to see us play.

One of these showcase gigs was at the Troubadour in 1996. A few minutes before we were slated to go on, Daron, Shavo, and I were backstage, and noticed something important was missing: our drummer. I went downstairs but couldn't find him. I asked the bartender—he hadn't seen him. I asked the sound guy—nothing. I put the word out among some of our friends at the club, but no one knew where Andy had gone. I went to the back door of the club and asked the security guard there if he'd seen him. He shrugged.

"Is it okay if I open this door and have a look around for him?" I asked.

"Be my guest."

I opened the heavy, metal door and there was Andy, covered head-to-toe in white powder. He seemed out of it and also pretty angry.

"Why the *fuck* didn't you open the door?" he yelled. "I've been out here pounding on it for twenty fucking minutes!"

"Bro, it's a rock club. No one can hear you knocking on the door." I paused. "Also, where the fuck have *you* been and why are you covered in powder?"

As rock 'n' roll as it would've been for him to have been covered head-to-toe, *Scarface*-style, in cocaine, I believe it was just baby powder. Apparently, Andy had decided that it would create a great visual effect for the show if the drummer looked like a powdered donut; unfortunately, he had gone off on his own without telling anyone to accomplish this feat. The show went off without any more hitches, but it was a harbinger of further instability to come.

A month or two later, we finished a set at the Dragonfly, and when we came off stage, several LAPD officers were waiting in the wings. Andy saw them, seemed to recognize they were there for him, and immediately took off running. Unsurprisingly, they caught him, and took him to jail. He got bailed out, and not too long after, he broke his arm punching a wall. His injury couldn't have come at a worse time as we were scheduled to play another showcase later that week. We were in a real bind, but to his credit, Andy suggested a solution: Why not ask the drummer from Friik, the band we shared our rehearsal space with, to fill in? So, we did.

The very first time we played with John Dolmayan it was obvious that we sounded like a different band with him than without him. Andy was a good drummer who played with a lot of swing and funk, but John was more of a straight, down-the-middle metronome with an iron core. He was powerful and steady, and it turned out that with so much other stuff going on in our songs, having that stability really anchored the music in a way that it needed. It also created a bit of a dilemma.

Well, not so much for Daron and Shavo, who immediately suggested that we ditch Andy and offer the drum stool to John permanently. Look, they had two good points: Andy was increasingly unreliable, and John's drumming fit the band better musically. They were thinking about this purely from a standpoint of "What is best for this band?" Daron, in particular, lived his entire life more or less by that philosophy. He believed that nothing in the world was more important than music. Everything else came a distant second. I think he still does. There is nothing he wouldn't do in service of that creative impulse. *Nothing.*

To me, hiring John seemed almost unconscionably cold-blooded. Andy may have been a bit of a mess, but he was our bandmate and our friend. If the whole story was that he'd broken his arm, suggested a substitute, and then we'd hired that substitute to replace him, that would be callous enough, though given his antics he likely deserved it. But it would also mean essentially taking John from Dave's band, the *same* Dave who we'd already pushed out of Soil under slightly unsavory circumstances. Could we really be that ruthless?

The answer, of course, was a resounding yes.

It's easy for me to blame this mercenary vision on Daron, and to a lesser extent Shavo, but I also have to own my part of it. The disloyalty may have made me uncomfortable, but I went along with it. I had ambition, too, and I knew John gave us the right combination to achieve what we wanted to achieve. It might've made me feel guilty but that didn't make it wrong.

It was a hard call, but artistically and intuitively, it was the right one.

———

With so much action and drama going on around the band, it's easy to lose sight of the fact that music wasn't even a full-time pursuit for me at the time. Although we were getting paid for our shows, it wasn't really enough money to live on—certainly not enough to live well on. For me, it was my software company, Ultimate Solutions

I, that was keeping the lights on, so to speak. In fact, it was doing more than that. It had become phenomenally successful to the point where I pulled in something like $85,000 in 1995.

But maintaining a business like that is not really a part-time job. If I really wanted to focus my life on music and the band, I knew that I couldn't keep running a company and handling all of the responsibilities that came with it. It just didn't work. For a while, I tried to find someone who could run the business for me, so I could essentially just own it from afar, but that proved more difficult than I'd hoped. I even hired a cousin of mine for a little while, but it ultimately didn't work out. I was making enough money to support two to three employees and thought maybe I could spend six months training them to take over and run it without me, but that would be both time-consuming and risky. I found myself with the strange problem of having this successful business that I'd built from scratch and now didn't want any part of anymore.

One day, around this time, I was sitting at the kitchen table in our rental house in North Hollywood, when my father walked in and saw me.

"What's wrong?" he asked.

I shrugged. "Nothing, really. I'm fine."

He sat down next to me at the round table. "No, something is wrong. What's going on?"

"I just don't know what to do about Ultimate Solutions," I sighed. He knew the story, but I laid it all out for him anyway, about how the company's success wasn't leaving me enough time to work on music, how I couldn't find anyone else to run it, how I felt like the only option was to essentially kill off my company even though

SERJ TANKIAN

doing so would be financially irresponsible. "I just feel stuck. I don't know what the right thing to do is."

He nodded and put a hand on my shoulder. "If I have to get a second damn job, you are going to do music. Just do what you want to do."

I get goosebumps thinking about that conversation now. Remember the context: at this point, our family had been *devastated* by the lawsuit. My father had lost his business and was back to being someone else's employee. We were living in a small rental house in the Valley. The family's economic situation was as precarious as it had ever been, and the money from Ultimate Solutions was helping to keep everything afloat. But my father knew what it meant to give up on a dream of making music. I don't think he regretted his own choice, but I think he would've seen it as a personal failure if his son had to make the same sacrifice. He wanted better for me than he had for himself.

I realize this isn't how these conversations with parents normally go, especially with Armenian parents who are generally laser-focused on their kids being working professionals. I have a theory that people who have suffered through the Holocaust or the Genocide—or those who have experienced real hunger, tragedy, and loss on an epic scale—tend to play it safe in their own lives, even if their genetics are predisposed toward art or music. Certainly, most parents want safety and financial security for their kids. But I think the lawsuit laid bare that that kind of safety and financial security is a mirage. It can be taken away just like *that*. It was for us. People often run toward what they imagine is pragmatic because it all seems so tangible—a good job, a steady income, a 401(k), health benefits. But when you've seen all that disappear, you realize those things are more ephemeral than they seem. They have no meaning beyond their economic worth.

Music or art, on the other hand, felt meaningful to me by virtue of their mere existence. Art doesn't need accountants or balance sheets to validate it. It just *is*. If I write a song or if I hear a song that makes me feel something, that's the whole fruit and its seed. It doesn't matter what else happens or doesn't happen with that song. It doesn't matter who buys it or who hears it. The way it makes me feel—or the way it makes someone else feel—is the whole fucking point. Coming to understand this changed my life. Music *liberated* me. And in the face of that, who really gave a shit what happened to my software company? That my father got this on a molecular level and passed it along to me is the greatest gift he could've ever given to me.

Shortly after that talk with my dad, I found someone who was willing to buy Ultimate Solutions I, albeit for what I considered to be a fraction of what it was worth. It was fine. I just wanted out. The money wasn't important. I knew that killing off my company was me making the biggest bet I could on music. I was all in now. It had to work. I didn't have room to fail.

———

It was the end of July in 1997 and System was onstage at the Viper Room, roaring through "War?"—an intense song about religion, the Crusades, foreign policy adventurism, and the debased sanctification of international conflict. The song had become a highlight of our early shows, at least in part because the shout-along chorus—"We will fight the heathens! We will fight the heathens!"—would send audiences into wild fits. At the back of the club, sitting on top of a booth, I could see Rick Rubin and his dark, shaggy beard. He was laughing.

Rick was already a legend in the music business, and even getting him to one of our gigs was a coup. He'd cofounded Def Jam when he was still in college and he'd produced the Beastie Boys, Run-DMC, Slayer, Red Hot Chili Peppers, Danzig, Johnny Cash, and many others. Rick was seen as something of a guru, an artist whisperer who could get things out of musicians that they may not have known they had in them. He had his own label, American Recordings, and we were beyond excited about the mere possibility of working with him.

By this point, System hadn't released any music and hadn't even played a show outside Southern California. We weren't making any real money, but it was clear we had something intangible and coveted: buzz. As someone who had already earned a business degree, managed a car wash, worked in his uncle's jewelry business, and run his own software company, I was highly skeptical about all the flattery that was being heaped on us. Its real value seemed dubious. We made music that was loud, heavy, political, artsy, and *weird*. It didn't sound like anything that had ever been on the radio or at the top of the Billboard charts. We'd already met with some record label execs, and the meetings had not always gone well. Everyone had a sense that there was something happening around System, but not many seemed to know what to do with it.

We met with Universal, but the team there seemed like they'd barely listened to our music. Their pitch to us was mostly marketing buzzwords. One woman there had ideas about molding us into something or other, and for a second, we went along with it. She took me to a hairdresser who gave me a crew cut and bleached my hair blond. When I saw my reflection in the mirror, it was kind of a wake-up call that maybe these people didn't know what they were doing. We also met with Monte Conner from Roadrunner Records, a big indie label that focuses on heavy music. We loved Monte, but even he admitted that he wasn't sure how to get a band like us on the radio. He could probably help make us big among metalheads, but maybe not much more than that. I was convinced that Rick Rubin was the person who would be able to take us to the next level.

Beno deserves credit for getting Rick to that Viper Room gig. It turned out that his original pitch to us hadn't been bullshit. He *was* good friends with Guy Oseary, who in turn was tight with Rick and convinced him to come see us. The Viper Room is a small club, and it was packed that night. Before we went on, we kept checking the crowd to see if Rick was there, and for a long while, he was not. We stalled and stalled, finally going on a good thirty minutes late to make sure Rick didn't miss a beat of our performance.

I wasn't the least bit put off when I saw Rick out in the crowd laughing hysterically, even at a song as serious as "War?" In fact, I took the fact that he laughed through most of our set as a sign that he *got* it. There's a strain of humor, a streak of Dada-esque absurdity, in almost all of System's music. Whether it's goofy lyrics, odd juxtapositions, or just the sort of unhinged spirit of the performances, we were always conscious that bringing this sort of lightness could make the darkness in the songs both more palatable and more powerful. That Rick could sense that on some level made me even more sure that he was the person we needed to introduce us to the rest of the world.

Behind the club, after the show, we met Rick for the first time. I'm a shy person, but I knew this might be my only chance, so I didn't hold back.

"We love what you do," I told him. "We'd be so honored if you'd produce us. Would you ever consider that?"

I could tell Rick wanted to be careful about making promises he couldn't keep. He answered slowly and deliberately.

"I would be really excited for something like that," he said.

The tricky part was that Rick was in the process of finalizing a deal to move American Recordings from Warner Bros. to Sony/ Columbia. It seemed like he was interested in signing us and producing our first album, but he couldn't make us an offer until that deal closed. For months, we were hanging in limbo, with several other offers on the table but the one we really wanted dangling somewhat uncertainly just out of reach.

As an activist and someone who had read Noam Chomsky and Howard Zinn, I had some trepidation about getting into business with massive multinational conglomerates that might find my activism, my politics, or my lyrics a problematic fit for their investors, their partners, or their overall corporate vision. Whether we ultimately made a deal with a division of Sony or Universal, these were mega-businesses with their hands in many, many pies, some of which I might find distasteful. We hadn't come up through the indie-punk underground worried about losing our street cred, but there was an argument to be made that System was too radical a proposition for the mainstream and belonged on an independent label, where we'd be freer to operate as we saw fit. But the rub with that is—or at least it *was* in the late nineties—that you're likely compromising your potential reach. If I wanted the world to know about Genocide denial or environmental degradation or whatever else I felt I had to say, I'd have a much better shot at getting that message out using the machinery of these titanic corporations. There is a line in that song "War?" that says, "You must enter a room to destroy it," and that's ultimately how I saw it. If we were going to make any real noise whatsoever, we had to get into the room first.

I also was confident that if Rick was running our label, he'd have the juice to be able to protect us from the slings and arrows of the corporate overlords. So, when he finally inked his deal to bring American Recordings to Columbia, I was proud that System Of A Down was the first band he signed under that partnership. It felt like we were exactly where we belonged.

CHAPTER 7

efore Rick Rubin took over the Shangri-La recording studios in Malibu, one of the studios he often worked out of was in the basement of a home he owned on Miller Drive—just off Sunset Boulevard, not far from the Strip. The house, which was built in the 1920s, felt old and kind of spooky, and Rick liked to keep it dimly lit, perhaps to enhance that effect.

We'd recorded the basic tracks for the first System album at Sound City, the iconic studio where classic albums, including Tom Petty and the Heartbreakers' *Damn the Torpedoes*, Nirvana's *Nevermind*, Rage Against the Machine's self-titled debut, and Tool's *Undertow*, were all recorded. But I have enduring memories of the months we spent in the basement of that Miller Drive house doing overdubs and vocals. There was no isolation booth, so we set up a small tent with strings of lights in it for me to record my vocals in, which felt more comfortable than the sterility of many colder and more impersonal studios.

Rick is not a traditional record producer. He's more of a musical curator than a knob-twiddler. His talent is listening closely and communicating back to you what he hears and what he doesn't hear. He'd often lie on a couch with his eyes closed, listening to the playback of what we'd just recorded. If you didn't know better, you'd think he'd fallen asleep until he opened his eyes and told you something about the song that you'd never even considered. Rick has such a Zen vibe that he could impart hard truths about your work in a way that made you grateful to hear them. He always pushed me to enunciate when I sang, even when he had no idea what I was singing about. Everything down in that basement felt so laid back that it made it easy to take even the most surreal moments in stride. Tom Petty even stopped by one day to have dinner with Rick, then popped downstairs, where Daron and I smoked a joint with him while he listened to what we'd been working on.

Yeah, just another Tuesday.

We were incredibly lucky to essentially have two producers on that first album. Sylvia Massy, who'd produced Tool's *Undertow*, and who we'd been considering working with before we hooked up with Rick and American Recordings, engineered the album. She was a huge part of the creative process.

I'd recently bought my first sampler, an Akai S1000, and Sylvia and I had a blast using it on the record. Reverse choirs? Check. Weird ethnic sounds popping in and out? Check. She pushed us to experiment. At one point, she suggested that I hang upside down from a pull-up bar in Rick's gym to record a vocal part. Never one to shirk a challenge, I climbed up and draped my legs over the bar. I made it through the first verse okay, but when I tried to take a deep breath for the chorus, I got light-headed and came crashing down off the bar. Fortunately, like a seasoned pro, Sylvia was there to catch me. When I got my bearings, I looked up at her quizzically.

"Why did you ask me to do that?"

"I don't know," she said. "I was just curious to see what would happen. I didn't think you'd actually do it."

The cliché is that you spend your whole life making your first album, and while that wasn't literally true for System, we'd spent *years* working on and playing these songs, so by the time it came to record them, we knew them backwards and forwards. Some, though, still had room to evolve. The original version of "P.L.U.C.K." is considerably longer than what we recorded for the album. That drum-heavy battle cry of a song is an angry denunciation of the perpetrators of the Armenian Genocide, and we found that culling the middle section of the song made it hit even harder. The title stands for "Politically Lying Unholy Cowardly Killers," and it's meant to evoke the phrase "pluck the Turkey," for obvious reasons. The lyrics, particularly the lines about "recognition, restoration, reparation," are essentially an extension of my AYF activism.

But not all the lyrics were so serious. Some songs, like "DDevil" and "CUBErt," wove in moments of humor, whimsy, and tongue-in-cheek absurdity. I wrote a poem a long time ago that had the lines "My words are hidden in the blanket folds of my mind / Tucked away, neatly, like an orphan, or a carcass / Beneath the shifting waves of neurological reality." That's the way I often think about writing lyrics; I sometimes have to go searching for them in those blanket folds of my mind, beneath the waves of reality.

———

Rick continued to be a creative guide even after we'd finished recording and mixing the album. When it came time to design the cover art, we brought him several ideas we were considering. He looked over what we had but wasn't sold on any of it.

"Some of this stuff is cool, but none of it feels timeless," he said. "I like album covers that I'm drawn back to again and again, that still resonate forty or fifty years down the road."

I think he was the one who suggested the eye-catching image of the hand with five outstretched fingers that eventually ended up on the cover of our self-titled debut. The artwork was created by a guy named John Heartfield, a German communist who used his art to oppose the Nazis during their rise to power. The more I learned about him, the more I recognized a kindred spirit.

Born Helmut Herzfeld, he changed his name to the more English-sounding "John Heartfield" during World War I to protest anti-British sentiment in Germany. He became part of the Dada movement and hung out with Bertolt Brecht. His artwork and cartoons lampooning Hitler, Göring, and the Nazis were often printed on the cover of a widely distributed weekly paper. When the Nazis came to power in 1933, the SS stormed his Berlin apartment, and he escaped by diving out the window and hiding in a garbage can before fleeing the country. At one point, he was number five on the Gestapo's most wanted list. If you can judge a person by the enemies they make, Heartfield made some good ones.

The image of "The Hand" was originally plastered up all over Berlin in 1928 with the text "The hand has five fingers! With these five, grab the enemy!" beneath it. It seemed like a perfect visual introduction to System Of A Down.

The power of protest,
John Heartfield.

The hand has five fingers,
Capable, powerful,
Asking for the revolt
Of the people
Against the fascist state,
And its western industrial/financial interests.
The hand has five fingers,
Upright, revolution.
Sideways it takes us to the present,
With the third eye open
Going down.
Upside down, the hand is help,
From a position of power.
You can create, feed, construct,
Count, and comfort with the hand.
It's a dare to the populace,
To stand, in unison,
With the power of protest.

I wrote that around the time when I was first learning about Heartfield. Back when he was confronting the Nazis, their nationalistic message was resonating across a country that was still reeling from a humiliating defeat in the First World War and a ravaged economy. His belief in wielding art as a political weapon, even when it came with a steep cost, was inspiring.

Not everyone was moved the same way. Rick was with us in a studio in Hollywood one day—I can't remember if we were recording or just rehearsing—when Gene Simmons stopped by. Daron and Shavo were *huge* Kiss fans, so Rick graciously introduced us all to Gene. We had the cover art for our album there and eagerly showed it to Gene.

"What you need to do," he said, nodding a little, "is make a t-shirt for women that you can sell with two of these hands, one on each of their tits."

I knew Gene was born in Israel and that his mother had survived the Holocaust, so I told him about John Heartfield and his artistic campaign against the Nazis. Gene listened closely.

"Yeah, that's all well and good, but I'm telling you, the merch would be *amazing*," he said, motioning with his hands as if he was cupping a woman's breasts. "You'll make a fortune."

As the guy who created the merchandising juggernaut that is Kiss, I don't doubt Gene's business savvy, but I have to say that I'm pretty comfortable with our decision not to reduce a profound artistic statement against the Nazis into a boob joke.

"Bumper to bumper, baby!"

Those were the immortal words of our first tour manager, Eddie Ortiz, when we asked him whether the RV he'd convinced us to spend $30,000 on had a warranty. The words were still ringing in my ears as they towed that RV away after it had an electrical meltdown at the side of the freeway in Utah, a week into our first national tour. As for that bumper-to-bumper warranty? Not so much. The RV was sold for parts. But that phrase became an inside joke and something of a slogan for that first tour.

We were opening for Slayer, which was a massive opportunity for a band who hadn't yet released their first album. But that tour was like going to rock 'n' roll boot camp. Slayer fans famously love Slayer and hate just about everything and everyone else. As their opening act, the crowd saw us as the one thing standing between them and Slayer. This was a group of fans for whom "homemade" knife-carved tattoos were not unusual, so when we'd turn up—me in tribal makeup, Daron sporting pink hair and a glammy little outfit—they were not necessarily predisposed to welcome us with open arms. In fact, when we'd take the stage, we'd often be facing a wall of crossed arms and extended middle fingers.

We learned to give as good as we got. Sometimes we'd finish our first song and be showered with boos, so I'd grab the microphone and smile.

"Oh, you *like* that song, do you? Okay, we'll play it again!" And with that, we'd launch into the song for the second time. Our moxie eventually started winning fans over.

Sometimes, though, shit just got out of hand. At a show in Utah, when it started to rain, the concert was canceled, much to the dismay of the fans who'd turned up there. Trash started flying, fights broke out all over the place, and I jumped behind our merch table to help our merch person pack up all our stuff. After a few minutes, I realized it was a lost cause.

"Fuck the merch," I told her. "Let's get out of here."

A small subset of Slayer fans had a disturbing practice of showing up to gigs in full Nazi regalia. I distinctly recall watching a team of African-American bouncers at a club in Detroit called Harpos brawling with these Slayer fans outside the club after we'd finished our set. Later that year, while we were touring with Slayer through Europe, we were onstage in Poland being pelted with coins by fans who were also raising Nazi salutes in our direction. At one point, I was hit in the face with a bagel and lost my shit. I told our lighting guy to point the lights into the audience and target the bagel-thrower. Then I launched into an angry tirade and threatened to start kicking people's asses. When I finished, the venue went dead silent. You could literally hear a pin drop in that place. Then we walked off.

Afterward, I realized that I'd just exercised a Stalinist trick on these people who'd only recently left their Soviet-dominated past behind them. It was almost Pavlovian the way this otherwise raucous crowd had immediately responded to my show of authority by falling in line. I had taken a rock audience out of their own context.

The whole tour was a real trial by fire. We came out of it tougher than we'd gone in. If there was one valuable lesson I learned, it was this: don't be neutral—it's boring. Everyone who saw us didn't necessarily like us. Some may have actively hated us. But very, *very* few were indifferent. We provoked a reaction. To me, that's really the mandate for any kind of art. Don't make neutral art and don't make neutral music—that's for elevators and malls. At the very least, make people feel *something*.

Through all the tumult, it helped enormously that Slayer had our backs. When we walked off that stage in Poland, the guys in the band were standing there at the side of the stage to tell us we'd handled the situation perfectly. Later on during that tour, we were scheduled to play in Istanbul. After talking about it with Daron, Shavo, and John, I told Tom Araya from Slayer that our grandparents had survived the Genocide, and as Armenian-Americans, we couldn't in good conscience play in a country whose government still denied that it ever even happened. For a young band who should've just been grateful for the opportunity to tour with Slayer, boycotting one of their tour dates for political reasons took some balls. Fortunately, the guys in Slayer understood and respected the stand we were taking.

———

I recall very little about the release of System's self-titled debut album in June 1998. We'd just finished the North American tour with Slayer and were about to go out to perform on the second stage at Ozzfest. I imagine we must've had some sort of release party or something, but if we did, I don't remember it. There is one landmark event from that era that I recall very clearly, though.

I was sitting in a car in Hollywood, not far from where we'd mixed the album, listening to KROQ. A DJ named Jed the Fish had a nighttime show during which he'd play up-and-coming artists and experimental music. Our album had just been released, but we hadn't had any expectations of churning out radio hits. We knew our music was probably too loud, too political, too strange, too *something*, to fit in neatly on any mainstream playlist. And that was fine. I hadn't grown up with dreams of being a rock star or imagining my songs blasting from car radios on summer nights. But I felt something undeniably transcendent when "Sugar" was suddenly blasting from this particular car radio on this particular summer night. Just a few years earlier, on a nearby stretch of road, I'd been shouting to the California sky about how I wanted to devote my life to making music. My voice coming out of that radio was like hearing the heavens answer back that I'd made the right choice.

That sublime moment notwithstanding, we understood that we weren't a band that was going to be able to rely on radio play. We'd have to earn fans the hard way, one at a time, out on the road. We were lucky that thanks to Rick's belief in us, our record label was willing to pony up for considerable tour support, which meant that we had luxuries many bands on their first national tours wouldn't have had. Our RV, however janky it was, was *much* better than driving around in a van, and the label would pony up for day rooms at hotels so we could take hot showers and relax on the day of shows. Even so, that didn't mean it was easy. We played 138 shows in 1998. We played nearly that many the following year too. We'd never played as many as thirty in any previous year. It was a *lot*.

On our early tours in RVs, John usually drove because he was the only one we all trusted behind the wheel—but it wasn't always a relaxing ride. One day, Daron and I were lounging around on the bed in the back of the RV when John slammed on the brakes. For a moment, time seemed to slow down as I was rocketed through the air, likely on a collision course with something hard and metallic, before Daron reached up his arm and snatched me out of the air. I took a deep breath, and Daron and I laughed, unable to do anything else as we quietly registered how close we'd just come to something tragic. Moments like that were both terrifying and a welcome break from the unrelenting tedium of life on the road.

Our audiences were growing steadily, and we graduated fairly quickly from an RV to a tour bus, which seems like a step up but wasn't really for me. Some musicians are able to turn their tour buses into a home away from home, but I had a specific, intractable problem: I simply could not sleep while the bus was on the road. No matter what I did, no matter what I drank or smoked, no matter if I was packed into one of the coffin-like bunks, laid out on a bed in the back, or collapsed on a bench with my head resting on a table, if that bus was moving, my brain wouldn't turn off. So, on overnight trips from Orlando to Atlanta, from Denver to Lawrence, from Peoria to Omaha, I'd read, I'd talk to the driver, I'd stare aimlessly out the window at the procession of mint-green highway signs breaking up the vast swaths of darkness. I'd do anything but sleep. We'd often arrive in the parking lot of the next gig's venue around six or seven in the morning, at which point, with the bus stopped and idling, I could finally close my eyes and get a couple hours of rest before people started waking up and contemplating visiting the catering tent for the daily Russian roulette of cuisine on offer: stale burgers, soggy meatloaf, badly burned bacon, runny eggs. It's no wonder I became a vegetarian during that tour.

We used to call John "Tarzan" because everything was simple, all or nothing, with him—and sleep was no different. One day, when I was having a hard time sleeping on the tour bus, I asked John how he was able to fall asleep so easily on the road. His response is engraved into my memory. He turned to me casually and said, "I just imagine large planes bombing the shit out of the whole planet to a point where there is nothing to think of, and then I gently go to sleep." My jaw dropped. *What the fuck, psycho?* That was John.

Most touring musicians will tell you that life on the road is like *Groundhog Day*. Each day is essentially the same as the one that came before it, with only minor details swapped out. "Hello, Cleveland!" becomes "Hello, Pittsburgh!" The radio promo interviews move from "Larry and the Hedgehog" on Rock 102 to "Sly, Toby, and Jammer in the Morning" on 97X. I-80 transforms into I-65. Burger King is traded for Taco Bell. But so much stays the same. Call time, load in, soundcheck. Deli trays that have been sitting out too long. Stale coffee in Styrofoam cups. The acrid locker-room stench of a bunch of dudes living together in close quarters.

And yet, for all the day-to-day tedium, the feeling of being onstage, as most artists will attest to, is unlike any other high you can experience in life. Imagine a whole city laser-focused on sending you loving energy, partying, and enjoying themselves. For me, the joy of being up there was also the transcendent bond it created among the band members themselves. While we were onstage, the target of most of my metal contrarian silliness was usually John. I'd scream, facing the audience, with death metal intensity, then turn around and look at John, who was hands down the most serious-looking guy onstage, and do something—pull a goofy face, make some gesture—to make him laugh. I'd feel like I won on the very rare occasions when it would cause him to miss a hit. The victory gleaned from such an episode would send Shavo and Daron into fits of laughter too because when the drummer messes up, there is really nothing else to do but laugh and ridicule in unity. Of course, I fucked up onstage all the time—sang the wrong lyrics, failed to hit a note—the difference was when that happened, all the guys would play on unperturbed.

Ultimately, the sixty minutes or so you'd spend onstage each night would pump you full of endorphins, but once they wore off, the comedown could be rough. If you've ever wondered why so many musicians end up with drug problems, it must have something to do with navigating the distance between that glorious natural high onstage and the other twenty-three hours of monotonous drudgery that make up each day.

My sleep deprivation served to make this already surrealistic blur into a dreary, interminable slog. In those early years on tour, I ate poorly. After a while, I became irritable. Look, there were *plenty* of good times. I made real friends crisscrossing this blue globe. Having lunch with one of them, or spending an afternoon wandering through a museum, visiting a cool music shop, or sitting with a good coffee and a mille-feuille made days feel well spent. But most days on tour managed to feel somehow both rigidly scheduled and largely formless. I was surrounded by friends but felt isolated. Traveling with this bustling carnival of souls, I'd dream of being in my car, driving somewhere, all alone, luxuriating in the quiet, the seclusion, the tranquility. My only escape was a quiet café serving a decent meal and good coffee, or an afternoon jaunt at a local gallery.

Growing up, I'd struggled with the concept of home, wrestling with how to pinpoint it on a map, but now, in its absence, I began to realize it wasn't so much a place as it was a feeling. To me, home is where your spirit feels unconstrained. In that regard, I had to find glimpses of comfort simply looking at various places from the window of the tour bus: a cozy living room with faded lighting, a grass-covered lawn with a large tree, a café playing jazz with the smell of coffee wafting from it, a wooded area brimming with pines. All eyes were on us onstage, but offstage, I seemed to be the voyeur, jealous of other people's casual daily normalcy. I once pitied all those who'd grown from ambitious, smiling children into disappointed, humdrum adult professionals, but as the miles whipped by on the road, I found that now I envied them.

Reflecting on the grinding whirlwind of spending the better part of three years on tour, some memories start to surface: Lemmy from

Motörhead wearing nothing but a Speedo and a cowboy hat as he lay around backstage at Ozzfest on a lounge chair outside his bus. A Ryder truck with all our instruments and gear being stolen in Philadelphia, then recovered as an empty, burned-out husk in New Jersey. The tense meeting with local police who wanted to arrest me for "causing a mayhem," after we'd played a free KROQ show in a Best Buy parking lot in Burbank. Telling Ozzy Osbourne how excited I was to sing "Snowblind" with him in his hometown of Birmingham, England, to which Ozzy snarled dismissively, "This fucking industrial dump?"

Some tours became more noteworthy simply because of the company we kept. Those first two Ozzfests gave us a chance to see that that community of alternative metal fans that we'd started to discover in Southern California extended farther than the state's borders. We also connected with bands like Incubus, Tool, Deftones, and Limp Bizkit, all of whom we'd play with again and again in the years to follow.

On the Sno-Core tour, back in 2000, I spent a lot of time with Mike Patton, the lead singer of Faith No More and Mr. Bungle. Mike had been a big influence on me. As a vocalist, he uses his voice as an instrument and can seemingly do anything with it. He can growl, shout, croon, hiccup, rap, whisper, scream, whatever. Artists like him, like Frank Zappa, like Tom Waits, show how musicians can be both instinctual and experimental, both thoughtful and unhinged.

Like me, Mike also couldn't sleep on a moving bus, so we'd stay up late into the night on his bus, just talking. It was just as well because the System bus had somehow become party central on that tour. At all hours of the night, every TV in the bus would be on, hip-hop would be blasting from the speakers, and everywhere you'd look there would be girls, booze, drugs, and all the rest of those wonderful rock 'n' roll cliches.

One night in the venue parking lot after a show, Mike told me he had an idea for how to clear our bus out. Once everyone on the bus was good and drunk, I turned the music down and Mike slipped a German *scheisse* video into the bus's VCR. If you're unaware of what a *scheisse* video is, I'm about to ruin your day. Suddenly, all the TVs lit up with images of Germans having sex while shitting. People couldn't get off that bus fast enough. I believe at least one person threw up. Even rock 'n' roll debauchery has its limits, I guess.

Mike loved twisting expectations of life on the road. At one show, somewhere in Utah, a couple of fans had snuck backstage and found Mike and I hanging out. These fans were ecstatic to meet him. After a few minutes, they asked if they could have some all-access backstage passes.

"You want backstage passes?" he asked. "Okay, but I have a request."

They made it clear they were down for anything.

"You see that hill over there?" Mike said, pointing to a steep, snowy embankment a few yards away. "You've got to get naked and run down that snowy hill."

No sooner were the words out of his mouth than these two kids were stripping down and charging toward the hill, jacked up on adrenaline. Mike turned to me and shrugged. "If they're going to be that dumb, they deserve the trauma." He kept his end of the bargain though and did give the two fans the passes for their trouble.

I'd spent my late teens and twenties living a pretty buttoned-up life. I went to college, I worked hard, I started a software company, I hung out with my family, and while most people my age were partying, I was meeting with lawyers and translating court documents. So it was during this time, in my early thirties, when I did my best to make up for lost time. By rock 'n' roll standards, my version of decadence was relatively tame. I drank almost daily, smoked a bunch of weed, and tried some of the drugs that were offered to me.

I was fortunate not to have the predilection for addiction that others had. I also may have thought about drugs differently than some of my peers. To me, these were opportunities to have an experience, to learn more about myself and the people I was with, to connect more deeply. For others, maybe less so.

The first time I tried mushrooms, I was with Daron, at a Nine Inch Nails/Marilyn Manson show. The Jim Rose Circus Sideshow—a sort of roving carnival of freaks—performed between sets and I have a searing memory of watching a guy onstage hanging stuff from his balls while I was tripping. I looked down at my hand and was convinced that it was covered in blood. Alarmed, I pointed it out to Daron.

"Don't worry, bro," he told me. "You're just tripping." He later admitted that he saw the blood all over my hand too but was trying to calm us both down.

I did mushrooms again after our final Ozzfest show in Los Angeles in 1998. After the tour ended, we had scheduled another show in Vegas with Primus. Walking in the hot desert, spaced out on mushrooms, after not having slept all night is something my constitution could've only handled in my twenties or early thirties. On another Ozzfest, I took mushrooms while driving across Kansas on our friends Clutch's tour bus. As the endless rows of wheat, soybeans, and rolling fields whipped by outside the window, I stared at green pastures filled with cows and was sure that I could feel my forehead growing in real time. Not sure if there was any wisdom that I was supposed to glean from that, but it made passing the time a lot more interesting.

———

Out on the road, the hardest thing to find is peace and quiet. There is always something happening, something that needs to be done, even when those somethings are really nothing. During short stretches back at home, you'd spend all your time dealing with all the stuff you'd neglected while you were out on tour—laundry, overdue bills, or maintenance on your car, your home, your relationships. As a creative person, though, peace and quiet isn't a luxury—it's a necessity. At least it is for me.

That's what I was searching for during one of these gaps in our relentless touring schedule when I borrowed my brother's orange VW camper van and retreated to the serene mountains near Ojai. It was around the middle of 1999, and I brought with me only a notebook, a pen, a book, and some water. After months upon months of being absolutely overwhelmed, I needed to strip everything away in order to clear my mind. I camped out by a wise old tree, fasted, and started to write.

By nightfall, the sound of the animals in the forest convinced me to get back in the camper van, pop the roof open, and lay down on the loft bed. From that vantage point, I could see the stars painting the night sky. Thoughts drifted in and out, like rivers through time. I tried to flow with them, not against them.

The following morning, I woke up and drove to the beach in Santa Barbara. I'd spent so much time the last few years being observed; now, I wanted to be the observer. I watched cars speed by, with their hubcaps turning and their headlights flashing. I climbed up on a nearby hill overlooking the ocean and laid down on a picnic table, my head hanging so I was watching the waves upside down. I breathed in deeply, and it was as if I could feel the ocean surging inside me. As it got dark, festive reveries of flashlight-toting beach-goers grew louder as they came in from the surf and gathered around bonfires on the sand, eating, drinking, talking. Words and phrases danced through my mind—"somewhere between the sacred silence and sleep," "the toxicity of our city"—and I scribbled them into my notebook, carefully tucking the early seeds of "Toxicity" into the crinkled, sea-stained pages.

On my way home the next day, I felt like the quiet, the fasting, the meditation, the writing had put me in deeper touch with myself, with the universe, and strangely enough, with my brother's aging VW van. It had a penchant for stalling, but as I drove home, it was like I could feel the VW letting me know when it needed to stop and rest, to avoid overheating. It occurred to me that I had nearly forgotten how to feel those same things in myself.

Prior to my retreat, our manager, Beno, had been feuding with Fred Durst, the Limp Bizkit frontman, over a band they'd both been trying to sign. Fred, who'd previously been supportive of System, dropped us from their tour in response. As I walked back in the door of my house, still buzzing from my transformative experience in the mountains and at the beach, I suddenly had a clear vision of System out on tour with Limp Bizkit. Two hours later, I got a call from Beno letting me know that he and Fred had sorted their issues out, and the tour was happening.

"I know," I said. "I already got that message."

I was tuned in.

CHAPTER 8

ncestral land has a unique pull on your blood. It seems like an almost mystical idea, that the physical topography of a place you've never been to, full of people you've never met, could exert such a strong magnetic force, but how else can I explain my determination to finally visit Armenia for the first time in 2000?

Up to this point, Armenia had already proven itself to be a powerful and defining part of my life, but in a sense, my entire experience with it was ephemeral. Of course, the stories of my grandparents surviving the Genocide were tangible and real, but those were *their* stories, not *mine*. My AYF activism was certainly my own, my agitation for Genocide recognition was genuine, but at the center of all this was a kind of hazy void. What was Armenia to me? An idea? A mythical realm? I often spoke of Armenia as my homeland, but what did that really mean when I had no lived experience of the place? It was as if I had an itch deep down in my soul to breathe its air and feel its soil underneath my feet.

I convinced an Armenian-American friend named Jack to come with me on this journey to scratch that itch. Jack is a funny, interesting character. He was a travel agent, albeit one who at that time had never really traveled anywhere in his life. He was not necessarily eager to make this pilgrimage, but I harangued him enough that he ultimately gave in.

There was something truly magical about those two weeks I spent in Armenia. It felt like the culmination of something that I couldn't quite put my finger on, maybe the final chapter in the first part of my life, or possibly the first chapter of whatever was to come next. Even though modern Armenia is hundreds of miles from the area where my relatives came from in what is sometimes called Western Armenia (situated in present-day central Turkey), my arrival in the capital, Yerevan, felt like a homecoming. To suddenly be around the language, the food, the culture, the history, the people—it was as if I could somehow see and feel with more depth. My being suddenly didn't require a detailed explanation to those around me. I felt better defined. Living outside my ancestral homeland for my whole life, I was constantly giving everyone I met a quick primer on Armenian history—Noah's ark, first Christian nation, Genocide, etc. In Armenia, I didn't have to—we didn't just all know it, we *shared* it.

I was arriving at an interesting moment in Armenia's history. It was nine years after the collapse of the Soviet Union, of which Armenia had always been a member more out of necessity than ideology or fraternity. Russia was the country's only reliable defense against Turkey after the Genocide and World War I. By 2000, Armenia was just starting to crawl out from under the yoke of Russia's influence and find its own voice.

The preceding decade and a half had been tumultuous. Back in 1988, a devastating earthquake centered around the city of Spitak laid waste to whole swaths of the country, killing between twenty-five thousand and fifty thousand people. The scale of the destruction was exacerbated by substandard building construction, which was itself a product of the widespread graft, bribery, and institutionalized theft that was endemic to the Soviet system at that point. To make matters worse, most of the hospitals in the region collapsed, killing a huge number of doctors and other medical personnel, which greatly hindered vital emergency services when they were needed most.

In isolation, the earthquake would've been enough to set the country's development back years and slow any push toward the kind of modernization that was commonplace in Western Europe. As it happened, though, the quake came just as a war with neighboring Azerbaijan over the region of Nagorno-Karabakh was beginning to simmer. The territory, also known as Artsakh, is surrounded on all sides by Azerbaijan but has historically and culturally been considered part of Armenia. This geographic anomaly is the fallout from Stalin's choice in 1921 to reverse a decision made by Soviet leaders to keep Nagorno-Karabakh within Armenia, instead making it part of Azerbaijan. But the geography didn't drastically change the demography. In 1923, the population was 94 percent Armenian, and even following decades of attempts to "Azerify" Artsakh by importing Azeris and pressuring Armenians to emigrate, it was still 76 percent Armenian in 1988.

After the Nagorno-Karabakh parliament voted to become part of Soviet Armenia that same year, Azeris responded with a pogrom against Armenians living in the city of Sumgait. Azeri enmity toward Armenians was so vehement that when the Spitak earthquake hit in December of 1988, there were reports of celebrations across the border in Azerbaijan. Sporadic ethnic clashes followed for the next few years, and once the dissolution of the Soviet Union became real in 1991, the newly independent nations descended into all-out war.

The First Nagorno-Karabakh War was a brutal conflict that killed nearly fifty thousand people and displaced more than one million. The Azeris blocked oil and gas deliveries to Armenia, plunging the country into a largely pre-modern existence. Families often only had an hour or two of electricity a day and had to rely on wood stoves for heat. When an uneasy ceasefire was finally declared in 1994, Armenia was in control of Nagorno-Karabakh, but much of the region lay in tatters.

I visited Artsakh during this life-changing pilgrimage in 2000, traveling in a van with a veteran who'd lost his leg in the war, and a kid named Mher who'd lost both his arms when he handled a downed electrical wire. The roads were pitted with holes and craters from bombs and other ordnance. Signs warned not to stray from the paved surface as the areas on both sides were heavily mined. At points, though, the way was simply impassable, and the van's driver had no choice but to delicately pick a path through the neighboring fields while we all held our collective breath. I only later discovered that Mher was also traveling with a nail bomb in his backpack.

As it happened, there was unexploded ordnance all over Artsakh and the bomb was just something Mher had picked up. Watching him, without arms, hopping down a long staircase on one foot, holding the unexploded nail bomb with his other foot was surreal to me but somehow fell within the range of normal for those who lived there. But seeing the aftermath of war in Artsakh, with its bombed-out homes and barns—it was like a flashback to my childhood in Beirut. Same feeling, different place.

It took ages before our van finally arrived in Stepanakert, the region's capital. The infrastructure there was still largely in ruins. We stayed in one of the city's only functioning hotels in a room with two cots. There were a handful of us, so I slept in a sleeping bag on the floor.

Artsakh itself was beautiful, its hillsides swathed in brilliant shades of emerald like the Irish countryside, topped with high mountain peaks and cut through with clear, freshwater streams. We took Mher home to his family, who honored us with a feast centered around a lamb they'd sacrificed for us, along with traditional Armenian dishes. Being vegetarian at the time, that grossed me out a bit, but I understood the value of what we'd received. We ate, drank, and sang late into the night, especially my friend Jack, who got so drunk he wanted to ride their horse but ended up riding the outhouse toilet instead.

System Of A Down was completely unknown in Armenia at the time, so I was able to travel the country like any other Armenian-American tourist. Traveling around during that first visit, I was struck by how old everything felt. To some extent, the destruction and enduring deprivations from the war enhanced this effect, but the footprints of ancient civilizations were all around regardless. I visited Garni, a pre-Christian temple, and passed through small villages that looked untouched by time. Europe felt young by comparison.

At one point, I visited Geghard, a monastery complex that was carved out of a mountainside in the Azat River Gorge in the fourth century. It was initially constructed on the site of a mountain spring, which still flows through a cave into a basin in a cathedral there. The day I visited, I was able to climb up to a church that was completely empty. I walked in and sat down, totally alone, humbled by this ancient structure chiseled from rock.

The last few years of my life had been so busy, so frantic, so noisy. My mind had often been a reflection of exactly that: busy, frantic, noisy. Sometimes what the mind and body need most is deprivation—fasting—the removal of all those stimuli. And that's what I found in this primeval house of worship, which felt like an inextricable part of the stone earth it was sculpted from. I closed my eyes and concentrated on the sound of my own breathing, in and out, in and out. The stillness was intoxicating. I stayed that way for a while—it may have been ten minutes, it may have been thirty—and when I opened my eyes, I glanced down at the rock formation on the floor. It looked exactly like Jesus. The moment was transcendent.

Armenia was the first country to adopt Christianity, but I've never considered myself very Christian, much to my mother's chagrin. Organized religion has never held much appeal for me. At that moment, seeing that image of Jesus, I didn't suddenly become a believer, but what I became was an *understander*. It made complete sense that Jesus's image would be here. This, after all, was one of his houses. And beyond that, it made sense that people who saw that image before me, people who were under siege by the Mongols, by the Persians, by the Turks, by the problems in their lives, would find shelter and comfort in it. There was clearly something special, something beautiful, and something holy about that place, and you didn't need to believe in the divinity of Jesus to feel that.

The whole trip changed me in profound ways. When I returned to the US two weeks later, I can still remember the unsettling feeling I had walking out of LAX. I'd been living in California since I was seven. I grew up there, my family and many of my friends lived there, my band was there, I knew the language and the culture. But there was no relief to be returning "home" after a long time away. In my mind, on arrival, the question circling my brain was "What the hell am I doing in this foreign land?"

———

In the fall of that same year, a resolution was introduced in the US House of Representatives to officially recognize the Armenian Genocide. Similar resolutions commemorating the Genocide had been introduced before but had never passed in both the Senate and the House. When the bill was in committee, the State Department and the secretary of defense warned that its adoption would anger the Turks, hurt US-Turkish relations, and potentially compromise American security in the region. When the committee voted to advance the bill to the House floor, Turkish officials threatened to torpedo negotiations with an American defense contractor over a $4.5 billion deal to buy attack helicopters. The Turkish parliament threatened to bar the US from using Incirlik Air Base in northern Turkey—a base, incidentally, set up on Armenian-owned lands that had been stripped from their rightful heirs during the Genocide. A few hours before the bill was set to be debated, Speaker of the House Dennis Hastert pulled it, supposedly at the recommendation of then president Bill Clinton.

To the Turks, Genocide denial was not just about polishing up an ugly incident from their nation's history. At the conclusion of World

War I, the Treaty of Sèvres aimed to divide up what was left of the Ottoman Empire into various spheres of influence, with significant chunks of real estate going to the English, the French, the Italians, and the Greeks. American president Woodrow Wilson aimed to give Armenians a piece of their historical homeland in the East. The land that is modern-day Turkey, including the Black Sea coast, was to be split into two nations: one for the Turks, one for the Armenians. The Turks, awash in a rising tide of aggrieved nationalism, felt insulted, and cited a right to self-determination for the people living on the land that was ceded for the new Republic of Armenia. A majority of the population, they argued, was Turkish. This was technically correct but only because the Turks had exterminated 1.5 million Armenians, ethnically cleansing this land—land my own relatives lived on—of its Armenian past. They believed in their right to codify their campaign of cultural erasure, enshrining it as international law.

The Turks subsequently fought what they called their War of Independence, eventually forcing the abandonment of the Treaty of Sèvres, the end of the Wilsonian vision for a Republic of Armenia, and the establishment of the Republic of Turkey. As such, the Genocide is not just an unfortunate episode in the history of modern Turkey; it is the very *foundation* of it. For the Turks, Genocide recognition has therefore become an existential threat to their nationalistic founding myths. In the end, the Entente powers who won World War I were more interested in cutting deals with the modern Turkish republic over oil concessions and control over the Middle East than dealing with recognition, restorations, or reparations stemming from the Genocide.

———

Having recently returned from Armenia, I watched the demise of the congressional resolution on Genocide recognition with great consternation and felt fired up with a sense of purpose. I wrote letters to both Speaker Hastert and President Clinton, criticizing their actions. It's always been my belief that in a democracy, when you want something from a government and you're not getting it, you have to take your cause directly to the people. With System Of A Down, we were regularly playing in front of thousands of people, and our crowds only seemed to be getting larger. I had promised my grandfather Stepan as the band started to get some success that I would use our growing platform to keep talking about the horrors that he and millions of others had lived through. I suggested to the band that we put on a benefit show to raise awareness of the Genocide and raise money for those fighting for its recognition.

It was an easy sell.

As Armenian-Americans, it wasn't really political for us—it was personal. We'd never intentionally set out for System to be an Armenian-American band, but as Daron once put it, maybe subconsciously we did. We shared heritage, experience, culture, and grief, and those things were always going to be an intimate part of System, even if we had never written songs with explicit lyrics about our Armenian roots. As much as we would grow apart over the years—creatively, politically, and personally—our shared Armenian identity always bound us together.

That November, we played a sold-out show in Hollywood at what was then the Palace—now, the Avalon—that we called "Souls: A Benefit for the Recognition of the Armenian Genocide." We invited the Armenian National Committee to set up a table there with information about the Genocide, we screened a short film explaining the history before we took the stage, and we gave out a program with a personal message explaining the atrocities and our connection to them, along with the infamous, ominous quote from Adolf Hitler, "Who, after all, speaks today of the annihilation of the Armenians?"

The show was incredibly emotional and raised around $20,000 for the Armenian National Committee. I think it also made System Of A Down something more than just four guys playing music. "Souls" felt like one of the pillars upon which System would stand: although we enjoyed playing music for its own sake and as a career, to me at least, there was something more important to be done with all we were achieving. We had a passionate, growing fan base, and we'd certainly never hid our Armenian heritage, but now those fans were recognizing that we weren't just another new band making weird, heavy music. We'd always spoken openly about the need for Genocide recognition but now, for the first time, I was sure that message was being received.

CHAPTER 9

Remember that parable about how you have your whole life to make your first album? There's a darker second half to it: generally, you only have about six months to make your second one. Oh, and it's supposed to be better than its predecessor. That was kind of the vibe as the band started meeting up in a rehearsal space in North Hollywood to start working on new music. Our debut had exceeded expectations, which wasn't hard because there weren't really many expectations at all. Now there were.

Truthfully, I wasn't all that stressed about it. I'd never even imagined what we'd already achieved with System, and if it never got better, if it all went away, I knew I'd be fine.

I think others in the band, particularly Daron, felt the pressure more acutely. He'd talk about calls he was getting from management about how important it was that we "nail" the songs for this second album. Daron already treated music like it was the sun his whole world orbited around. All this just served to amp up that feeling even more.

It was an incredibly productive and creative time for all of us. I'd always written lyrics since before I even knew they were lyrics, but at this point, I was starting to craft more music, too. I really wanted to collaborate with Daron and had this vision of the two of us sitting with guitars, trading parts back and forth together as we banged out songs. Unfortunately, he didn't really work like that. He liked to work on his music at home alone and then bring it into the rehearsal space in a much more arranged format.

His disinterest in close collaboration was a blessing in disguise for me. It forced me to become better as an instrumentalist and a songwriter because I couldn't lean on his expertise in either realm for my song ideas. I had to figure it out myself.

The fact that I started bringing my own music into the rehearsal space meant there was a lot more material for the band to work through—but it also changed the creative dynamic. On our debut album, the division of labor had been relatively predictable: Daron wrote the music, I wrote the lyrics. There were exceptions—Shavo came up with some of the riffs we used, I added bits of piano and samples, Daron wrote some lyrics—but for the most part, everyone knew their roles. Now, I'd thrown a wrench into the works. And I got the impression that Daron felt like my songwriting was infringing on his territory.

Still, when Daron and I were on the same page, the creative dynamic between us was incredible. One of the new songs, "Prison Song," exemplified that. The contrast between the monstrous opening riffs Daron had come up with and my whispery vocals makes both elements feel even more powerful. Our band had always embraced dissonance and juxtaposition in our music, and this particular song—with its definitive starting chords followed immediately by long, drawn-out, tension-building silences, a handful of alternating tempos, monstrous howls that descend into smooth, velvety murmurs toward the end of the track—represented our evolution and growing confidence in our own experimentation. Plus, as the first track on the album, it really ups the stakes and sets the tone for the music that follows.

I'd written what was essentially a treatise about the failures of the criminal justice system. Anyone who knows anything about songwriting would've told me that sentences like "All research and successful drug policy show that treatment should be increased and law enforcement should be decreased while abolishing mandatory minimum sentences," or "Drug money is used to rig elections and train brutal corporate-sponsored dictators around the world," are not lyrics that belong in a song. But I didn't care; I just jammed them straight in there, and the brutality of Daron's music somehow complemented that stuff perfectly. At intervals, he chimes in with a goofy sing-songy line, "I buy my crack, my smack, my bitch right here in Hollywood." His line is the antithesis of my lines—similar to his vocals on "Sugar"—but it helps balance all the weightiness of the song. The interplay between us reminded Rick of the way Chuck D and Flavor Flav played off each other in Public Enemy. The comic foil makes the seriousness more palatable.

That said, I often took pride in being my own Flavor Flav. The world of heavy music is generally so self-serious—grizzled-looking dudes snarling and bellowing through their songs, never betraying even a hint of a smile—that I delighted in bringing unbridled, Frank Zappa–esque silliness to our music. The original lyrics to "Bounce" were about pajamas—really just me playing with the word in lines about "the Dalai Lama's pajamas." The rest of the band rarely had any issues with my lyrics, but they hated these.

The criticism was essentially that we were a heavy band, and these lyrics were so *not* heavy. To me, that's what I liked about them. Metal was so overwhelmingly male, so overbearingly gruff. I wanted to be an antidote to that. I decided it wasn't a hill worth dying on though, so upon Shavo's recommendation, I rewrote them to be no less silly—"BOUNCE pogo, pogo, pogo"—but vaguely sexual in a double-entendre way that the rest of the band could get behind.

The arguments over another song, "Needles," got even more heated. It all turned on one word in the chorus, where in the original version, I repeatedly sang the line "Pull the tapeworm out of my ass!" The other guys were not okay with that. If I could sum up their argument, it went something like this: as System's lead singer, if I was singing about pulling a tapeworm out of *my* ass, it was implicitly referring to all *their* asses too. I'm still not sure I buy this line of thinking, but they didn't like the idea of anyone pulling *anything* out of their asses. It sounded kind of homoerotic. They were okay with weird lyrics, but when it crossed the line into making the band look somehow effeminate, it got dicey. Me, I loved playing around with that shit.

The fact that something this absurd became an actual raging argument within the band is an indication of the hothouse environment we were operating in at that time. We were *all* in *all the way*. Rick found the argument hilarious, and he may have been the one who suggested what became the elegant solution: changing "my ass" to "your ass." For whatever reason, Daron, Shavo, and John were perfectly fine with the suggestion of *someone* pulling a tapeworm out of their own ass so long as it was not one of our asses.

I can't even write that ridiculous sentence with a straight face.

———

Thinking back on it now, I'm not sure if the friction within the band at the time was hindering System's creative process or fueling it. The idea that friction makes sparks is not only a scientific fact—it tends to be an artistic one, too. But to take the metaphor to its natural conclusion, constant friction will wear down its components, in this case, the band members themselves. It may even cause them to snap.

Daron's unilateral vision for System's creative course ground against my own artistic ambitions. He and John also had issues. Shavo was kind of Switzerland within the band; he was passive, avoided confrontation (especially with Daron), and tried to get along with everyone.

Even though John had joined the band before our first album was even released, I thought Daron frequently treated him like he was just a replacement member, a second-class citizen. He's talked about firing John multiple times over the years, and pretty much every time, I sat down with Daron and told him, "It's not going to happen. If he goes, I go." I felt like System was the four of us, and if you took one out of this unique formula, anyone, it would be a different chemical compound altogether.

Part of the reason Daron and John would argue over everything was because their personalities are actually very similar: both born under the astrological sign of Cancer, creative but extreme, and sometimes hard-driving and aggressive. For Daron especially, the only way he could seem to find resolution to anything in his life was through conflict. He sort of lived that cliché, "The only way out is through."

The issues between Daron and John came to a head one day in that rehearsal space. It had been tense between them for days. We were in the middle of rehearsing one of the new songs, when Daron said something rude to John, and John snapped back at him. We stopped playing, and the two of them just started yelling at each other. There was a couch across from the platform where our gear was set up, so Shavo and I just sat down, figuring we'd let Daron and John shout at each other until they lost steam.

Loud arguments were not an unusual event at one of our practices. This time, though, the argument kept escalating and eventually got personal, and although my memory of it isn't flawless, John may have made some sort of remark about Daron's girlfriend. Then, Daron lost his shit and hurled his guitar at John. If I remember correctly, John either caught it or dodged it, but at that point, it was clear that this was about to turn into an all-out brawl.

John is a physically powerful dude and Daron is, well, not so much, so this was not going to be anyone's idea of a fair fight. As I saw them rushing together, I ran up off the couch to break it up. Instead, I mostly just got caught in the middle. John was swinging around me to hit Daron, who was sort of on the floor beneath me. Then Daron picked up my mic stand, which had a thick, metal base, and swung it. I ducked and it hit John square in the forehead, splitting open a gash. I think the sight of blood running down our drummer's face finally broke the fever in that rehearsal space.

There was a lot of blood coming from John's head, so we drove him to a nearby urgent-care center to get stitched up. That ride to me was more harrowing than the fight. Shavo and I were up front in the car while Daron and John were in the back. They'd quickly put their animosity behind them, and both seemed to agree that the fight and the bloodshed were actually one of the best things to happen to the band.

I can remember Daron turning to John and saying something like "This is good, man. This will make us a stronger band."

John immediately agreed. "You're right, dude."

I guess it was some sort of macho guy thing—bonding over blood—but to Shavo and I, they sounded like total psychopaths. Putting the group before the person is a commonality among communities and nations that's usually done for mutual protection and preservation when survival is only possible in larger numbers. The intention in this case, though, was clearly more caustic—to save the band while simultaneously saving face.

For me, I felt no differently than when I'd seen violence as a kid. It was just a stupid, uncreative way to solve problems. This is what happened when you ran out of ideas, arguments, or things to say. It was an undignified reversion to our basest animal instincts. The nineteenth-century French novelist Gustave Flaubert once wrote, "Be regular and orderly in your life so that you may be violent and original in your work." That was a lot closer to my way of thinking than bloodying my bandmates to settle petty disputes. Of course, Flaubert never opened for Slayer.

On the way home, I made it clear how I felt.

"Look, I'm glad you two are getting along again, but to be clear, I *don't* think this was a good thing. I don't want to be part of a band where this is how we work out our problems. This is fucked up! If anyone does this to anyone else in this band ever again, I don't care who it is and I don't care why it is, I'm leaving the band. No questions asked."

The stress and the drama in those sessions was hard to escape. We were spending so much time and energy on the music, and even though I was thrilled with what we were coming up with, the strain could be a lot to handle. Usually, whenever I got stressed out or overwhelmed, I'd take a hot shower to unwind some of that tension. I'd stand there, eyes closed, head bowed underneath the shower head, with the scalding hot water pounding on the back of my head and neck, as the steam rose up all around me. More often than not, that would be enough to turn off all the noise and center me. But things got so bad around this time that when I'd close my eyes in the shower, I'd immediately be gripped by an almost existential fear. I'd be consumed by this very specific nightmarish vision of a large man standing behind a towering panel of electronic instruments. My pulse would race, my breathing would get shallow, and I'd be close to passing out. It happened again and again.

It wasn't a huge stretch to see that vision as a distorted, fun-house mirror version of our recording process, or of my life, and to understand my reaction to it as a minor panic attack. Something like this had happened to me occasionally in the past, and in retrospect, it may well have been a case of the hot water in the shower lowering my blood pressure to a point where I was hallucinating and nearly losing consciousness. But it had never been this bad. I told Rick about what was happening, and he recommended that I go see a woman named Nancy de Herrera. Nancy had been an evangelist for transcendental meditation going back decades. In her younger years, she'd studied bacteriology at Stanford, then worked as something of an ambassador for the American fashion industry all over the world. She hung out with Jimmy Stewart, Esther Williams, and the shah of Iran. After the death of her second husband, a Formula 1 driver, a deep search for meaning had brought her to transcendental meditation. She visited India and Tibet dozens of times and became close with the Maharishi Mahesh Yogi. If you watch clips of the Beatles with the Maharishi in India in 1968, you can see Nancy, blonde and beatific, serving as a conduit between the Beatles and the guru.

Her proximity to the Maharishi put her in the orbit of a lot of interesting people. She rode camels on an expedition with Sir Edmund Hillary. She and the Dalai Lama chatted about yetis. In California, she'd become something of a TM teacher to the stars. Madonna, David Lynch, Lenny Kravitz, Rosie O'Donnell, and Sheryl Crow had all learned from her.

Of course, you'd know none of this by meeting her. She didn't talk much about herself and didn't come off as particularly showy. She was this sweet, older woman who looked very much like someone's grandmother. When I arrived at her house, a beautifully manicured manor in Bel Air off Coldwater Canyon Avenue, we sat down and talked over tea and cookies.

I'd had some experience with meditation before. I'd read Jon Kabat-Zinn's *Wherever You Go, There You Are* a year or two earlier and had tried meditating in dribs and drabs, but I'd never really committed myself to it before I started meeting with Nancy. The fact that she didn't have the outer trappings of being some guru—there were no flowing robes, no turban, no trail of obsequious minions walking behind her—appealed to me. It was as if her very being was a reminder that meditation didn't require superpowers. Anyone could do it.

Nancy gave me a mantra to focus on and taught me to repeat that mantra in my head, over and over, until it was all that remained. Everything else would begin to fall away. I'd just breathe in and out, in and out, and a calmness would descend. It was so simple yet unmistakably magical.

The goal was not so much to clear your mind as it was to slow it down. Nancy taught me that thoughts will always come when you meditate, and if you try to fight their arrival, they'll only return with more insistence. So, the key is to watch the thoughts come but gently tell them that it's not the right time to deal with them. Find a place in your mind where they can sit until later. She would even take phone calls during meditation sometimes. She'd tell me, "Don't be so hard on yourself. If you have to pick up a call, pick up a call." The goal was to make meditation a basic thing in your life, something accessible and easy to do every day, like walking.

Her home became such a tranquil place for me that I didn't even need to meditate there all the time to gain some benefits. I can remember turning up there once while she was out walking her dogs, and before she even got back, simply being there, alone and quiet, had blissed me out. Just that pause in my day, in my week, in my life, had been enough.

Our lives tend to be such a hectic race of "Go! Go! Go!" that often what we need most is just to "Stop!" People are addicted to smoking cigarettes in part, I believe, because of the power and necessity of that spiritual pause. When people smoke, they're getting in touch with their breathing. I'm not discounting the genuine addictiveness of nicotine, but in modern life, the physical act of smoking cigarettes is a ritual that often involves taking yourself out of a situation—work, dinner, whatever—standing outside and breathing in and out, over and over. That has value that stands apart from the sheer chemistry.

I found meditation incredibly emancipating, and the impacts for me were tangible. My meditation practice reminded me to listen more and react less. It also quickly brought on euphoric feelings of peace and made me think twice when I noticed judgmental thoughts creeping in. Essentially, the more I meditated, the easier it was for me to see the inherent good in people. Everyone is born pure, and it's the very act of living—fighting for our survival—that beats the purity and goodness out of us. We're all on the same journey together, different parts of a greater organism. So, if I'm out honking at some guy who just cut me off on the 405, that guy who just cut me off is also me. I've been there, I've done the same thing, so why heap my scorn on him? How is that serving either of us?

Meditation became a daily routine as important to me as eating and sleeping. It became so vital that I could really tell the difference if I hadn't had time to meditate. I wouldn't be as focused, as aware, as settled. It created this unique space for growth, change, and acceptance of whatever came my way. It gave me the tools to deal with the incredible metamorphosis that was going on in my life at the time. Every interaction was appreciated, every experience was accepted. I started to have more compassion toward others and their plight in what the author William Saroyan once termed this "human comedy." I began to understand myself better, and why I had been the way I'd been for my whole life. I also began to appreciate the struggles of my band members better and their needs to be seen or heard or accepted. Being truly aware means taking in the full experience of someone else, knowing their history, empathizing with their story, and understanding why they make the decisions they do.

Meditation also opened my mind to new philosophies. I'd long been interested in indigenous cultures, and the more I learned about them, the more the idea of living in harmony with nature made sense to me. It felt not only important, but practical. I could see changes in my songwriting almost immediately. For the song "Aerials," those lines, "Life is a waterfall, we're one in the river and one again after the fall / Swimming through the void we hear the word, we lose ourselves, but we find it all," are not something I would've conceived of before I'd started transcendental meditation.

My budding awareness from meditation enhanced and widened my activism, too. I became more sensitive to the inequities and injustices in our world, whether it was human rights abuses, invasions, wars, or environmental issues. It cleared the fog, in a way. I saw the injustice and was also able to understand the perpetrators of that injustice at the same time. From spiritual books, I segued into books about our combined indigenous past and its intuitive understanding of our journey on this planet. Stories about Native Americans, Aboriginal Australians, Māori, and indigenous communities from the Middle East shared similar customs, beliefs, and an underlying conviction about the importance of living within nature.

Inevitably, my outlook on life itself began to change as all of these new ideas took root. "Civilization is Over!" became my eco-political axiom. For ten thousand years starting with the agricultural revolution, humans evolved from hunter-gatherers to farmers, placing huge amounts of species into extinction over food competition. And yet, there's a glaring irony here: even though we grow more food than we need, we haven't been able to rid the world of hunger because the distribution of this food is based on privilege. The accelerated rate of destruction of natural resources on this planet coupled with the accelerated rate of overpopulation has been creating an inverse graph, making our current lifestyle increasingly unsustainable. Add to that the climate crisis and the human-footprint-based carbon warming and we have a real existential issue on our hands. So, the real question is what's next? Is there a way out? To me, our only path forward is to match the intuitive understanding from our indigenous past with our modern intellect, technology, and logic. It's the marriage of male and female energies. Without this cosmic marriage, we are doomed.

My spiritual awakening shifted the way I thought about our music, too. I'd recently learned about Buddhist sand mandalas, these intricate and beautiful pieces of art constructed by monks with colored sand. The most amazing part about them was that once they were finished, they'd quickly be destroyed or allowed to wash into the sea, vanishing without a trace. The destruction itself is in fact part of the artwork, a symbol that our time here on Earth is temporary, and its transience is what makes it so beautiful. It's the process of making the art, the process of living itself, from which meaning, truth, and beauty are derived, not the product of that process. The product—whether it was a sandcastle, a painting, or an album—only offers an illusion of permanence. These too will eventually decompose and disappear, albeit on a different timeline. The art is always in the doing, not the memorializing.

I had to become okay with that impermanence, that my songs, my art, would one day fade into the ether from which they came. Doing so allowed me to ease my grip on the music, to begin to unravel my ego from the work. As artists, our job isn't so much to create as it is to be open to the act of creation. The art is out there already; we just need to make sure we're tuned in so that we can receive it and then present it skillfully.

It's easy to get very New Age–y about all this, but meditation is a genuinely powerful tool. Our forebears understood this. A section of the Dead Sea Scrolls describes a nonreligious, nondenominational form of prayer—meditation, essentially—that was practiced thousands of years ago, which gave humans the power to materialize the reality they envisioned. This isn't magic exactly, but the more you learn about it, the more it can seem like it.

And it's not just the ancient sages who recognized this. It's doctors and scientists, too. In 1981, a physician from Harvard Medical School traveled to the Himalayas to study Buddhist monks who practiced a meditation technique called *g-tummo*. These monks had been living at high altitude, in small, unheated huts for more than a decade. The doctor attached thermometers to the monks' bodies and was able to document their ability to raise their body temperature by as much as seventeen degrees Fahrenheit after just a few minutes of using this meditation technique. Later studies documented similar feats, with monks able to dry wet sheets with only their body heat, raise the temperature of the room, or sit out in the mountains on subzero nights wearing nothing but a thin, cotton shawl. It's literally mind over matter.

To be clear, I don't heat my home with the power of meditation or go camping in the mountains without a warm coat and a cozy lodge at my disposal, but what meditation and my spiritual practice does for me is in many ways even more profound. I came to meditation looking for a way to relieve stress, to slow my mind from always running a hundred miles an hour, to help me learn to manage interpersonal relationships inside and outside the band. On a certain level, it helped to do all that for me quite quickly after adopting it.

Meditation is really the search for a feeling. If you've ever had a moment—maybe you've got headphones on, you're listening to music, you're staring out the window, or maybe your eyes are closed but you're not asleep—and for just that moment there is nothing *but* that moment. There are no bills you're worried about paying, there are no fraught conversations you're replaying in your mind, there are no concerns of what came before or what comes next; *that's* the feeling I'm aiming to conjure when I meditate. I've always thought of it as a portal to the most comfortable room in the house, the one I'm trying to get my being into. There are larger, more holistic goals, too, of course: to learn to exist in that moment all the time, to live a fully integrated life, to be a force for good in the lives of others, both those I know and those I don't. I recognize these are goals I'll never fully realize, but the very act of constantly striving and reaching for them is the whole point.

I've always felt that on the day of reckoning, if there is one, we will not be divided into believers and nonbelievers, but instead we'll be divided between those who truly feel at one with all beings and the universe, and those who don't. The greatest act of love is the opening of a door to a complete stranger. Acts of kindness are inspirational and often create a ripple multiplier effect that render a high quotient of positive productivity.

My meditation practice has evolved over time. Nancy first introduced me to TM, but since that time, I've learned more about it, adding and subtracting frequently to create a regular routine that works for me and changes as I change. Over the years, I've incorporated body meditation, Native American sun salutations, and even a vocal meditation for before I sing. I've created my own gratitude mantra—it's really almost a poem—that I recite whenever I meditate now.

I admit I've become a bit of a spiritual dabbler, as my practice borrows elements from Buddhism, Sufism, and various indigenous cultures. I've absorbed the writings of Vietnamese monk and peace activist Thích Nhất Hạnh; Indian musician, poet, and philosopher Inayat Khan; and Tom Brown Jr., a naturalist and survival instructor from New Jersey. For me, the point is not to become someone's acolyte, but rather to recognize that wisdom can come from many disparate sources. When you study meditation, you're not only studying how to meditate more effectively, you're studying how to *live* more effectively.

That said, spirituality does not exist in a vacuum. I can read books about it, I can talk to others who have wisdom and understanding, but real growth cannot be only theoretical. It's lived experience that becomes your spiritual North Star. In other words, you often need to do things wrong to learn how to do them right.

———

Sometime in 2001, my bandmates and I were working at Cello Studios in Hollywood in Room B. It's a really great-sounding space with high ceilings and isolation booths that line the live room, and it's where we recorded much of the material that ended up on that second album. We had a song we were calling "Suicide" back then; actually, if you listen to the track now, you can even hear me mumbling "we're rolling 'Suicide'" right before the first guitar notes sweep in. Anyways, the earlier version of the song had all these really cool pieces to it—staccato verses, winding melodies, tribal drumbeats, and a memorable, moody chorus about "self-righteous suicide" that Daron had written about drugs, I think. The song whipsawed back and forth between different tempos and had this great middle eight section that needed lyrics, but I couldn't come up with any. Whatever I wrote didn't seem to fit what was already around it.

Rick saw me frustrated, struggling to craft lyrics, and suggested we meditate together. So, we did, right there in the little mixing room at Cello. It was as if my mind was running at warp speed, then I just closed my eyes, and slowed it all down. Afterward, we went back to his house on Miller Drive. I still hadn't written any lyrics for that middle eight section, so we went into his library. He asked me to trust the universe and pull a book off the shelf, open it to any page, and stick my finger onto a sentence or word randomly. When I did, I saw the line: "Father, why have you forsaken me?"

I felt goosebumps on the back of my neck. I can't remember what the book was called, but it was a quote from Jesus.

"That's it," I breathed. "That's the line."

I wrote a little bit more to flesh it out, and the line completely transformed the whole song. It gave depth to the darkness of the chorus Daron had written and made the whole song sound like an angry lamentation toward an indifferent god. It was somehow the exact words that song needed, and there they were just sitting in this book on Rick's shelf. There might have been a time when I would've resisted such a mystical artistic course, but not anymore. The song wasn't mine to write or Daron's to write. It was just ours to discover and then present to the world.

We wrote and recorded almost forty songs during those sessions. I suggested that since we had so much music, we should put out a double album. It was quickly pointed out to me that this might be a little presumptuous for a band whose debut had exactly zero radio hits. I mean, not that many people even knew who we were. Daron and I had both brought so much music to these sessions that a lot of the songs were inevitably not going to make the final cut. However, when we finally picked the fifteen tracks that would appear on *Toxicity*, only one of them, "Shimmy," was among the ones I'd written the music for.

To be fair, the songs we picked were the ones that danced best together, that felt like a cohesive album. Thinking back to those sand mandalas and the idea that the art was about the process of creation and not the product of it, I was content. The fact that the final song on the album, "Arto," was a largely instrumental, tribal-sounding adaptation of an Armenian prayer-hymn called "Der Voghormia" (or "Father Have Mercy," in English), which I played alone with a musician-friend named Arto Tunçboyacıyan, seemed to support that very idea.

Besides, it was hardly as if I was unrepresented on the album. I'd written a majority of the lyrics, including those for the title track, which were based on the writing I'd done while on that little personal retreat in the mountains in Ojai and at the beach in Santa Barbara. I'd been able to write about the prison-industrial complex, overpopulation, food insecurity, the protests at the Democratic National Convention, the failures of our education system, and my own spiritual rebirth, and then finesse all that into an album that was going to be released by one of the largest media and technology conglomerates in the world. That felt like a subversive triumph.

Everyone seemed to agree that the first single should be the song that we were calling "Suicide." A lot of stories came out subsequently claiming that Sony forced us to change the song's title, but I don't remember it like that. I mean, you don't have to be a multibillion-dollar international corporation beholden to share-holders to come to the conclusion that "Suicide" is a pretty bleak title for a song, particularly one that isn't even about killing yourself. Changing it to "Chop Suey!" on the other hand, was a kind of meta inside-joke about the title itself. Both the song and the title had been cut up, diced, mixed around, so the new title seemed to make sense—it was the chopped version of "Suey" or "Suicide." I liked it.

The record label had supported us after we'd released our first album, when it wasn't at all clear that there was going to be a big financial upside for them. Sony and Columbia trusted Rick, so he had a lot of rope to do what he wanted. When we played *Toxicity* for them, though, the label reps seemed legitimately excited and told us they could hear "big songs."

About a year earlier, before we'd started working on the album, Rick had had a conversation with Kevin Weatherly, the program director at KROQ, about trying to get us into regular rotation on the station. At the time, Kevin was a powerful gatekeeper. If KROQ added your song, most of the rock stations in the country would soon follow. MTV took their cues from him, too.

Kevin told Rick that he really liked us, loved the energy we played with on our first album, and thought we were intensely creative—but our music was just too out there for commercial radio. "Their songs are just so wacky," he explained. "I don't think we could ever play System Of A Down on KROQ. Ever."

I've always liked Kevin and hadn't taken his assessment personally. It was just business and I understood it. What he was saying was objectively true: System Of A Down was hardly an obvious commercial prospect. Our music was often dissonant and challenging.

On one level, our songs were generally constructed like standard pop songs, with only occasional variations on the classic verse-chorus-verse-chorus-bridge-chorus-outro structure that everyone from the Beatles to the Cure to Green Day to Miley Cyrus have employed for decades. Within that structure though, there was an anything-goes aesthetic—well, *almost* anything goes—that could make things sound, in Kevin's words, "kind of wacky."

But at that moment, the rock mainstream was changing faster than even Kevin realized. The grunge that had dominated in the early nineties had given way by the middle of the decade to more middle-of-the-road fare like the Wallflowers, Hootie & the Blowfish, and Matchbox Twenty. By now, though, many of the bands we'd been performing alongside and hanging out with for the previous few years—Korn, Deftones, Limp Bizkit, Incubus, Slipknot, Linkin Park, A Perfect Circle, Godsmack, Papa Roach—had hits on the radio and/or were selling millions of records. This was the vanguard of a heavy music renaissance that people were calling "nu metal." While I didn't necessarily feel a musical affinity with all those artists, undoubtedly their successes softened the ground for us. By dint of sheer luck and good timing, the landscape of popular music was shifting definitively in our direction.

A year out from Kevin's declaration that KROQ would never play System Of A Down, we were about to become the most played artist on his station.

CHAPTER 10

My first thought was "That's a *lot* of people."

It was Monday, September 3, 2001. We were standing in a mostly empty bar in Hollywood, across the street from a parking lot, adjacent to the famous Roosevelt Hotel, where a makeshift stage had been constructed for us. *Toxicity* was set to come out the following day, and we'd agreed to do a free concert, sponsored by KROQ, who'd been playing our first single, "Chop Suey!," in heavy rotation since we'd released it a few weeks earlier.

The bar was essentially serving as a green room for the gig, and once we got there, we could see the fans packed into the parking lot and spilling out onto the street. We'd originally figured that we might get about three or four thousand of them at this show, but there were easily more than twice that many, probably at least ten thousand people milling around, waiting for us to play. Apparently, a large cohort had been camping out since the night before.

We'd envisioned this show as both a way to thank our core fans in our hometown, and a nice little promotional event for *Toxicity*'s release. Our debut album had done well, and we'd gradually been building a fan base out on the road, town by town, fan by fan. Looking out at the throngs of people before us, it was clear that our days of slow, steady growth were over. With "Chop Suey!" all over the radio and the video on MTV, something had popped.

We'd outgrown our own gig.

The fire marshal agreed. As more and more fans arrived and pushed forward, trying to get closer to the stage, they'd dismantled some of the barricades that had been set up for security purposes. With the barricades gone and the show overcrowded, the event now violated safety codes. The fire marshal declared that it was too dangerous, and the concert would have to be canceled.

To me, calling off the show and disappointing ten thousand diehard fans sounded more dangerous than playing, and we said as much to the LAPD officer who seemed to be in charge of the situation. Some of these kids had been here since yesterday, and if the show was just summarily canceled, they were going to be *very* angry. I'd seen what hordes of sweaty, angry metalheads looked like when we'd toured with Slayer. You don't want to get between them and the thing they want.

We suggested to the officer that maybe we could play a couple of songs, then apologize to the audience that we couldn't do more but promise we'd be back to play another free concert at a larger venue soon. That seemed to me like a safe, fair compromise.

The cops didn't agree.

"What if we just got up there, and didn't even play?" I tried again. "What if we just explained the situation and promised to play another free show at a later date?"

The answer was unequivocal: No. Way. In fact, I was told that if we so much as went onstage, we'd all be arrested.

At this point, I huddled with my bandmates to consider our options. There were no good ones, so I proposed a fairly radical one: Let's call the LAPD's bluff. Let's just go up there and play anyway. Were they really going to arrest us in front of ten thousand rabid fans? People would go fucking apeshit. And even if they did arrest us, what better way could there be to introduce System Of A Down to people?

The band's lawyer was nearby at the bar and overheard my proposal. He called me over to a window that looked out on the parking lot where the fans were gathered and opened it.

"You see everyone over there?" he said, pointing out of the window. "They're all going to sue you. If you guys get up onstage, regardless of whether you get arrested or not, if shit gets out of hand, if people get hurt, everyone here is going to sue you. And you'll be screwed because you'll have violated the fire marshal's orders."

It was a sobering moment. Just the mention of a lawsuit stirred enough bad memories for me to drop the idea entirely.

We left the bar and went back to a nearby hotel room that we were using as a home base that day. In the meantime, we figured that someone—the promoter, the fire marshal, the police—would get onstage and explain that the show was off but would be rescheduled.

But that didn't happen.

No one got up and announced *anything*.

Instead, the crew at the location simply began disassembling the stage. When they pulled the "System Of A Down" banner off the brick wall behind the drum riser, the crowd figured out what was going on. Then all hell broke loose. Fans rushed the stage. They destroyed our gear, toppled amplifiers, fought with our road crew, threw rocks and bottles at the cops, broke windows, and knocked over the portable shit cans.

The LAPD responded with the kind of restraint the LAPD had long been known for at the time: they showed up in riot gear and on horseback, shot tear gas and water cannons at the fans, and then beat the shit out of as many of them as they could seem to get their hands on. The riot raged through the streets of Hollywood for six hours before everyone was dispersed. In the end, six people were arrested, many more were injured, and the damage ran into the hundreds of thousands of dollars. We were scheduled to do an in-store signing at Tower Records in West Hollywood the next day to celebrate the album's official release. It was canceled out of concern that there could be more trouble. The promotional rollout for our album was not exactly going according to plan.

The thing about that riot that so many people seemed to miss at the time was how unnecessary it was. The moment was clearly a powder keg, but it took really detached and irresponsible decisions by the LAPD to light the match that set it off. In a city like Los Angeles, where everyone is always in their cars, where people don't often walk next to each other in the street, the police have less rapport with citizens. Everything they did that day—from not letting us even announce the cancellation to showing up dressed and ready for war—was done from a position of fear and posturing. And fear is contagious. Nothing seems to precipitate a riot faster than cops showing up in riot gear. It gins up everyone in an already charged atmosphere and becomes a self-fulfilling prophecy. And that's before you even get into how police budgets work: it's use it or lose it. If cops don't deploy their riot gear or any of their other high-tech military toys, money for it is often stripped out of their budget the following year. That creates a perverse incentive for further militarization and mass conflagrations.

Every news channel seemed to pick up the story about the riot. As terrible as it is to say, I can look back now and say that it almost certainly ended up as a better promotional event than if we'd actually played the gig, though I imagine that the people who got their teeth kicked in by the police or ended up in jail might not see it that way.

It certainly set a chaotic tone, which would only intensify in the weeks to come.

———

A little less than a week later, I was sitting behind a long table, alongside my bandmates, at the Virgin Megastore in Manhattan, signing autographs for a line of fans. We'd flown to New York to do a bunch of promotional events and interviews and play a show at Irving Plaza. This signing was one of the last things on our schedule before we'd fly back to Los Angeles the next day.

Typically, at signings, fans often hand me gifts, letters, or little trinkets that they want me to have. I don't usually have time to read the letters or notes right there and then, so I put them aside for later.

We flew back to LA the following day, and that night, I started reading through a pile of the notes I'd been handed. I came upon one that really struck me. The guy who wrote it was unemployed and clearly depressed. He asked if we could hire him as a roadie and described a series of tragedies that had recently befallen him. He seemed to be in desperate straits. I was worried that he might be suicidal. A few years earlier, my friend from high school, Paul, who'd inspired the lyrics for the song "Soil," had taken his own life. I was left asking myself those terrible questions that people often ask in that situation: *What more could I have done? Did I fail him? Could I have made a difference?* Even though this person who'd written the letter was a stranger, he was also a fan, which maybe put me in a unique position to actually have a positive impact on him.

So, I did something I'd never done before and have never done since: I called him.

Needless to say, he was surprised to hear from me. When he got over the initial shock, we actually had a really good conversation. I was trying to get him to see that things weren't as hopeless and grim as he thought they were, and by the end of the call, I felt like he was coming around. I went to sleep that night feeling pretty good. That was September 10.

Early the next morning, I was startled awake by the sound of my phone ringing. It was my girlfriend at the time.

"Just turn on the television," she said. "I'll talk to you later."

It was the kind of phone call that I imagine millions of people got that morning. On TV, one of the Twin Towers at the World Trade Center was in flames. The newscasters were struggling to explain what was happening.

As I was digesting the situation, the phone rang again. I figured it would be my girlfriend, calling back. Instead, it was the fan I'd spoken to the night before.

"What the FUCK!!" he yelled. "Oh my god!! What's going ON!?!" He was completely unhinged. I tried to calm him down, telling him that everything was going to be alright. At the time, I really wasn't so sure it was going to be, but this guy needed a steady hand, so I was doing my best to provide it for him. We were still on the phone when the second plane hit the towers. At that point, he was just screaming into the receiver. When I finally settled him down enough to get off the phone, I sat watching the news coverage, stunned.

Everything felt like it was spiraling out of control.

Sometime during that day, I got a call from Beno letting me know that our record, *Toxicity*, which had come out a week earlier, was now the number-one album in the country. I don't really remember taking the call. I don't remember what was said. It's hard for me to imagine a career triumph feeling more cosmically insignificant.

I was numb.

The next few weeks were probably the most stressful of my entire life. I spent the day or so after 9/11 writing "Understanding Oil," the essay I described at the beginning of this book, which turned a critical eye to US foreign policy, the injustice it caused, and the anger it fomented toward the United States. The essay made me—and by extension, the band—a media piñata, as everyone rushed to prove their patriotism by condemning anyone who dared criticize the US. There were death threats, calls to boycott our shows or for our label to drop us, and I had to go on Howard Stern's show to try to quell the furor.

The day I posted the essay on the band's website, Clear Channel—which controlled the largest block of radio stations in the country—put out a memo telling their programmers not to play 165 songs that they deemed "lyrically questionable," including "Chop Suey!"

The two events were unrelated but indicative of a troubling truth: free speech is always the first casualty of war.

I understand that Clear Channel is a private company, and that most of those who took aim at me and System over "Understanding Oil" were not bound by the free speech protections guaranteed by the First Amendment the way government entities would be. But what was happening was more insidious and more troubling. A national tragedy had invited massive self-censorship. My friend Maria Armoudian wrote a great book called *Kill the Messenger* about the media's role in major wars and genocide throughout modern history. In places like Nazi Germany, Northern Ireland, Rwanda, and the former Yugoslavia, the media stoked anger and resentment toward minority groups, marginalized criticism of the government, and ultimately shaped the way conflicts were perceived.

In the days and weeks after 9/11, we saw this happening in the US as well. Newscasters everywhere solemnly intoned how this day would forever change America, and they were right—just not necessarily in the ways that they thought. Private media companies policed the bounds of acceptable expression and became uncritical, full-throated supporters of the government's actions. There is nothing like war to unify a nation in deep sociological turmoil or juice the profits of the media conglomerates pushing it. Investigative reporting was largely shoved to the margins as major newspapers and TV networks lined up like lap dogs to regurgitate every word coming out of the Oval Office, the Pentagon, and the State Department as if it was the gospel truth. A toxic brew of fear and patriotism was emanating from nearly every household. An attack on our country became a test of our democracy, our freedom of speech, and our right to express ourselves without censorship or threats. It was a test that we failed *miserably.*

With more than two decades of hindsight, we can begin to take the full measure of the consequences: two catastrophic, mismanaged, deadly wars; state-sponsored torture at Abu Ghraib, Guantanamo Bay, and elsewhere; the rise of ISIS; trillions of dollars in debt for US taxpayers; multiple refugee crises; the ostracism and scapegoating of Arab-Americans; a suicide epidemic among military veterans; unspeakable suffering for the people of Iraq and Afghanistan; and the withering of America's moral standing around the globe. In light of all this, Howard Stern giving me a hard time or radio stations not playing "Chop Suey!" are certainly very small potatoes, but they're all part of the same problem.

Even if you try to view Clear Channel's decision to ban certain songs as nothing more than a clumsy attempt to shield already distraught listeners from reminders of a horrible national trauma, it's impossible to justify some of the songs included on their list. John Lennon's "Imagine" and Louis Armstrong's "What a Wonderful World" merely dare to envision a brighter future than our miserable present. Cat Stevens's "Peace Train," Edwin Starr's "War," and Black Sabbath's "War Pigs" suggest there are ways to respond to a foreign policy challenge that don't involve guns, bombs, and bloodshed. And it's difficult to see the inclusion of the entire Rage Against the Machine catalog on this list as anything but political. Some voices were just not welcome to the public debate.

In the case of "Chop Suey!," the chorus—"I don't think you trust in my self-righteous suicide / I cry when angels deserve to die"—certainly did have some eerie resonance with the horrible events of that Tuesday morning. It would be easy to pass off the parallels as nothing more than coincidence, and I suppose in a literal way, that's true. But I believe that when artists are operating at their highest level, they can tap into a collective unconscious. We aren't writing songs so much as we are receiving them. We aren't making art; we are transmitting it from an ethereal plane into something you can look at, listen to, or touch.

I can say this with a certain amount of creative detachment because in this particular case, it was Daron who wrote those lines in "Chop Suey!" I sincerely believe he was channeling something he wouldn't have been able to explain. We all were.

Several months before 9/11, another friend of mine, Boots Riley—a rapper, songwriter, filmmaker, activist, and lead vocalist of a group called the Coup—designed the cover art for their album *Party Music*. The photo that was set to appear on the cover featured an explosion at the World Trade Center, as Boots and his bandmate were pushing a detonator in front of it. They intended the cover art as a harsh critique of capitalism, but if you Google the photo now, it's uncanny how much the explosion on the Twin Towers looks like a photo from the morning of 9/11. Coincidence? Sure. But it's hard not to look at that picture and feel like there was something in the ether that Boots was tapping into.

Unsurprisingly, the Coup's album, which had originally been set to come out in mid-September, was delayed, and their record label, a division of Warner Bros., insisted that the cover be changed. Boots fought that change for many of the same reasons I articulated in "Understanding Oil." As he put it back then, "There's been a whitewash in the media over the past couple days over what the US's role

My classic wheels in Beirut
in our backyard.

Good to be young.

Early days in
the US.

My friend Suren and I at ninth-grade graduation.

Drunk on the floor playing air guitar with a broom.

With my brother Sevag decked out for a wedding or something.

With my friend Kev in Mexico.

Playing my Roland D-50.
    I loved that synth.

Playing "Question!"
(Greg Watermann)

SOAD Rockin'.
(Greg Watermann)

Working on *Elect the Dead* with Dan Monti. *(Greg Watermann)*

Elect the Dead photo shoot. *(Greg Watermann)*

We all wore these on tour with the F.C.C.
(Greg Watermann)

Serj Tankian and the F.C.C.
(Greg Watermann)

Axis of Justice Radio Network. *(George Tonikian)*

Dad and I preparing for a show. *(George Tonikian)*

"Souls" show with special guitar. *(Greg Watermann)*

Singing with the orchestra. *(Greg Watermann)*

in the world is, and the fact that they kill hundreds of thousands of people per year to protect profit. . . . What's happening right now in the media is so dangerous to the political state of people that if I kept that cover, it would give me at least a platform to expose the realities of what's going on." Warner held firm though, and eventually they changed the cover over his protestations.

Boots was one of very few artists who stood up back then and spoke unpopular truths at a difficult time. It was a lonely crew of us that included Rage Against the Machine, Tool, Madonna, and the trio then known as the Dixie Chicks.

Much of the criticism directed at me and at System was also spiked with anti-immigrant rhetoric. We were portrayed as "the other," not *real* Americans, even though we'd all grown up here. I was sometimes told that I should "Go back home!" Whenever I heard that, I would think, "Great. Where is that?" And also, "Unless you're Native American, you can *fuck off*!"

I don't think I'd ever felt more like a man without a country than in the days, weeks, and months after 9/11.

———

In an irony so delicious that you couldn't make it up, we were slated to go out on a co-headlining tour with Slipknot on September 14 that, weeks before, had been titled "The Pledge of Allegiance Tour." I have no idea where that name came from but perhaps from that same collective unconscious that seemed to be serving as an all-purpose wellspring of creative inspiration. The tour was delayed a week because the country was still largely shuttered, and even then, we were one of the first bands out on a major tour after the terror attacks.

It was an odd time to be out on the road. September 11th had been a genuine national trauma, and no one seemed to know what was going to happen next. Security procedures were ramped up, often rather haphazardly, pretty much everywhere. The media was constantly guessing where the next attack might be and when, and there were many warnings about the potential for a mass casualty event at big public gatherings. So, playing an arena tour amid all that was about as nerve-wracking as you can imagine.

On one level, I was concerned that some terrorist would try to blow up one of these venues we were playing. On another level, I was concerned that someone who was angry at me for being so outspoken would take a shot at me or my bandmates while we were onstage. I was looking over both shoulders at all times. I already found touring to be a trying ordeal, so adding in life-threatening risk wasn't making it more pleasant. Every night, I felt like I was in a constant state of alert, wondering, "Are we safe? Are the fans safe?"

I remember waking up on the tour bus the morning of our show at the Continental Airlines Arena, in East Rutherford, New Jersey, just a few miles from New York City, and strolling into the arena on one of the loading bays. There was no security anywhere. If someone wanted to plant a bomb or do something else awful, there was no one there to even try to stop them. I mean, this was *one month* after 9/11! I freaked the fuck out, called our management, and told them to tell the promoter that we weren't going onstage until they swept the whole place with explosive-sniffing dogs. They did, in fact, bring in dogs, and the show went off without a hitch, but that jittery vibe pervaded the whole tour.

In spite of this, we still found moments of lightness, fortunately. One of the other bands on that tour was Rammstein, this German metal band with a wicked sense of humor and a taste for over-the-top stage antics. We ended up hiring one of their friends to work security for us, an ex-wrestler known as Herman the German. Herman was a sweet guy with an almost impenetrably thick German accent. One day, Daron couldn't find the black leather pants that he liked to wear onstage, so Herman was running around the backstage area in a frenzy, going room to room, yelling "Whegh argh Daron's lazer pants?!" Watching this large German man scurrying around shouting about "lazer pants" sent the rest of us into fits of unstoppable laughter. The mere mention of the phrase "lazer pants" became a surefire way to lighten the mood throughout the rest of the tour.

———

Despite the supernatural levels of stress, at least from a business perspective, things had never been better for System Of A Down. Radio play and MTV had introduced us to legions of new fans. Our audiences, which had been overwhelmingly male, were suddenly dotted with more and more women. We also began to get people coming out to shows who only knew our "hits"—initially "Chop Suey!" but later, "Toxicity," and "Aerials," too—which was a strange phenomenon.

Perhaps there was no greater symbol of our transformation from scrappy underdog outsiders to celebrated industry insiders than when "Chop Suey!" was nominated for a Grammy for Best Metal Performance, and we were invited to perform at the ceremony. When I got the call from Beno about all this, my reaction was immediate.

"Nah, fuck that," I told him. "We shouldn't play there."

It wasn't so much a considered opinion as it was a gut feeling. The Grammys at the time felt cheesy, and to show up to perform in the hopes of being rewarded with a little gold statue felt unbecoming for our band. The whole idea of treating art like it was a competitive sport, with winners and losers, was just so counter to my ethos. You really can't rank art. One song or one album is not objectively better than another. Different people respond to different music differently. That's the whole point. Grading art is like grading emotions.

Daron agreed with me, so we turned down the invite, and—*surprise, surprise*—did not win the Grammy. I felt good about our decision; it seemed like the punk-rock thing to do. When I look back on it now, though, I must admit that I don't feel nearly as militant about it. If the me of today was doling out advice to the me of back then, I'd just say to go play the damn show. I still think it's stupid to be declaring one song or one album to be the "best" anything, but it's just not that big of a deal. We're still part of the industry, so not showing up at some awards show doesn't really change that. Besides, it's a chance for an interesting experience, and life is too short to walk away from those.

———

Success only magnified the growing dysfunction within the band. Inevitably, more fame and more money inflated all our egos, mine included, and put more yes-men in our orbit to tend to those egos.

Between the backlash to my 9/11 essay, our lyrics, and our various avenues of activism, it was perhaps unsurprising that the media began to portray System much like they did Rage Against the Machine: as a political entity. The rest of the band resisted being viewed in this light, and I understood their frustration. Politics were certainly a big part of System's music, but they weren't the whole enchilada. Daron, in particular, bristled at all the focus on our political messaging because it drew attention away from the music itself. All this served to further alienate him from me at a time when there was already growing discord between us.

In spite of all the public criticism I was getting over "Understanding Oil" or my general willingness to take politically unpopular public stands, very few people actually confronted me personally about any of this. These days, if you're in the crosshairs of any public debate, you are undoubtedly getting lit up on social media—but that just didn't exist back then. I'd talk to fans after shows, and political controversy would almost never come up. No one in any of the bands we were on the road with in the months after 9/11 seemed to have any problem with my outspoken opinions either.

In early 2002, System did a short tour of Australia and New Zealand for the first time ever, as part of a traveling festival called Big Day Out, along with Garbage, New Order, the Prodigy, Silverchair, and the White Stripes. We arrived in New Zealand first, and after the epic flight across the Pacific from California, I was in a weird state of being half-asleep and half-awake as I checked into the Metropolis Hotel in downtown Auckland. They put me in a room on a high floor, with big floor-to-ceiling windows that looked out onto the harbor.

A friend who worked at Interscope Records had given me an album by this great band Dredg, and I put it on the stereo. I remember standing in that room, with the windows flung open to reveal the lush blue of the water and verdant green hills in the distance. I stood there, breathing in deeply, watching the white, cottony dandelions dance in the air outside my windows as the music filled up that room. In that moment, I could sense the tension that had been coiling within me for weeks, months, and years gently unwinding. The weight of the world was lifting off my shoulders. I felt physically different.

I'd never been to this strange island nation on the other side of the world before, but there I was, looking out that hotel window, my first day there, wondering to myself, "Could this be the place? Could this be 'home'?"

It was an odd, largely unfamiliar sensation.

I finally felt like I was somewhere I belonged.

CHAPTER 11

S itting in the Birmingham City Jail in 1963, Martin Luther King Jr. wrote an open letter in the margins of a newspaper a visitor had brought him. Following his arrest for marching against racial segregation in the city, several white local clergy members had condemned him in the very issue of the newspaper he was holding. They'd criticized him as an outsider coming to their city to march in their streets in violation of local laws against public demonstrations. In response, King wrote that "injustice anywhere is a threat to justice everywhere. We are caught in an inescapable network of mutuality, tied in a single garment of destiny. Whatever affects one directly affects all indirectly."

As a teenager, activism to me was always personal. When I'd march in protests or pass out flyers, the cause was always more or less the same: Armenia. We might've been trying to draw attention to the Armenian Genocide or to raise money for the victims of the Spitak earthquake, but I always felt like it was a personal quest. After all, I was advocating for *my* downtrodden people, on behalf of *my* ancestors, telling what was essentially *our* story.

The older I got, the more I began to understand exactly what Dr. King meant in those lines he'd written sitting in jail in Alabama. One injustice isn't cordoned off from the rest of the world. It breeds like a cancer. The Armenian Genocide begat the Holocaust. Corporate greed begets climate change which begets poverty which begets crime which, in turn, begets mass incarceration. Of course, these relationships are not linear. Illegal wars and the climate disaster spawn refugee crises which in turn lead to nativist, anti-immigrant policies which empower authoritarian rulers who are prone to launch more illegal wars which will create more refugees and so on and so forth. Each injustice is both the cause and effect of countless more injustices. This is part of the "inescapable network of mutuality" that Dr. King was writing about. If we're willing to stand on the sidelines because one injustice doesn't directly impact us, just wait—it will soon enough.

We live in an interconnected world. I don't mean this simply referring to the age of mass media and the internet. Those things have only magnified an interconnectivity that has always existed, a physical, political, and spiritual interconnectivity. In such a world, injustice for one is inevitably injustice for all.

For me, activism and fighting injustice are ultimately part of a spiritual journey. Making the world a better place and making yourself a better person are two sides of the same coin. It has to be this way because standing up to injustice isn't easy or comfortable. Remember, Dr. King wrote those words about injustice *from a jail cell*. He could see the promised land but was assassinated before he could reach it. He understood deeply that spiritual, personal suffering could not be overcome without addressing worldly suffering.

Love was the antidote to it all. Love is the raison d'être of social justice and activism.

Of course, these simple, elegant ideas start to get challenged when put into practice in the real world.

———

The first time I met Tom Morello we barely spoke. We were at a New Year's Eve party in 2001 at his house with around three hundred other people spread out across his backyard. I was a big fan of Rage Against the Machine, and Tom and I had plenty of friends in common—he'd actually come with Rick Rubin to the Viper Room the very first time Rick saw us play—but I didn't want to impose myself on him at his party. Tom reached out a few months after that party with an idea he wanted to talk to me about. Tom had been to Ozzfest and other heavy music festivals and was disturbed by what he'd occasionally experienced: young fans sporting tattoos and t-shirts with racist and fascist slogans. He wanted to see someone or something pushing back against this far-right messaging. He imagined a sort of traveling "freedom school" offering a counter-narrative and promoting progressive causes. Tom initially figured Rage could champion this initiative at their shows. There was just one problem: before he could get this idea off the ground, Rage broke up.

When Tom and I began talking, he and Rage's rhythm section had just started rehearsing with Soundgarden frontman Chris Cornell. They were calling their new band Citizen Kane then—they'd eventually rename it Audioslave—and there was talk of them possibly playing Ozzfest the following summer. But the band wasn't ready. His vision needed another public-facing advocate that was already out there. As it turned out, System was playing Ozzfest that summer, and he was hoping I could help get this "freedom school" and these progressive causes in front of those fans. The more we talked, the more we realized how aligned our larger visions were. Then the wheels started turning: *Why limit this sort of activism to Ozzfest? Weren't there a lot of places where we could use our platform for the greater good?* These conversations led to us founding a nonprofit, Axis of Justice, in 2002.

The organization was set up to connect musicians and fans with grassroots political organizations to fight for social justice. Under the banner of Axis of Justice, we invited nonprofits like Amnesty International, Anti-Racist Action, Greenpeace, RAINN, and Food Not Bombs to set up booths at Ozzfest and other concerts. Some people scoffed at the idea that a bunch of metalheads were going to give a shit about economic justice, ecological disaster, or the plight of domestic abuse survivors, but the Ozzfest crowds were receptive.

We weren't just talking the talk, either; we also got involved with direct actions. In Santa Monica, the city council had passed a law making it illegal to distribute food to the homeless. We brought a group there to give out box lunches to homeless people, in defiance of the law, and invited the press out to chronicle it. Later on, when the grocery workers union went on strike in Los Angeles, we organized a benefit concert for them.

We also did a series of Axis of Justice concerts. Tom was incredibly good at wrangling other artists into playing with us, so these were some amazing shows. Chris Cornell, Maynard James Keenan from Tool, Eddie Vedder, Flea, Boots Riley, Pete Yorn, Michael Franti, Dave Grohl, and Wayne Kramer from MC5 all came out to play with us. We used the shows to raise money and awareness for the organizations we partnered with. In 2004, we even played a show to protest the Republican National Convention in New York.

Those shows were charged with so much positive energy. Once, we were backstage with Boots during a gig at the Troubadour when he noticed a guy in the audience wearing a Confederate flag belt buckle. Boots pointed it out to me, and then said, "I'm going to go talk to him." In my head, I thought, "I'm not sure that's such a great idea, Boots," but I watched from a distance and was kind of amazed. The conversation never got heated. Boots and this fan spoke calmly for a few minutes, shook hands, and then Boots walked backstage again.

"He wasn't racist," Boots clarified. "He just thought it looked cool. It was a fashion thing. So I explained to him why it wasn't cool at all and we talked it through. He gets it now." I hadn't seen many artists handle confrontation with such compassion and grace before. I was genuinely impressed.

Mixing music and politics can often feel like walking on a tight-rope. For years, I'd been disparaged for my activism. "Shut up and sing" was the unimaginative rejoinder frequently lobbed in my direction, as it is at any performer who dares give voice to an unpopular opinion. Because my formative experiences as a music fan came at those AYF shows—events that were inherently and inescapably political—I've never really understood those who insisted that music and activism should somehow be kept separate from each other, as if one might infect the other.

This sort of criticism was often disingenuous, anyway. People generally have no problem combining music with politics—as long as they agree with the politics. "Shut up and sing" is really a comment that comes from someone struggling to reconcile the fact that artists they admire have political beliefs that don't align with their own. Rather than examine the validity of those beliefs, they try to shut down the conversation before it starts.

What perhaps frightens those people the most is that when done right, music and activism can work together incredibly effectively. Music has a unique ability to deliver hard truths, heal divisions, and rally people to a cause. I'll never forget the first time I heard Peter Gabriel's song, "Biko," about the South African anti-apartheid activist Stephen Biko. At the time the song came out in 1980, there wasn't worldwide outrage over South Africa's racist apartheid system. There weren't widespread protests against the government. The struggles of South Africa's black majority weren't being chronicled every night on the news. So, for a teenager in Southern California, this is how you heard about injustice happening halfway across the world—in a Peter Gabriel song.

The South African government recognized the danger the song posed to them, and immediately banned Gabriel's album within their borders. *Shut up and sing.* But outside the country, the song—which told the story of Biko's abuse and death at the hands of South African police—spread the word: first to other musicians and music fans, then more widely.

Of course, there had been thousands of activists working to undermine apartheid long before Gabriel came along with "Biko," but he amplified their message exponentially. In doing so, he helped kick-start a movement that encouraged divestments from South Africa and cultural boycotts. He helped put South Africa on the news every night, further ramping up the pressure on the government there. "Biko" didn't end apartheid, but it was a pebble in a pond whose ripples had an enormous impact.

I've never felt like the cultural megaphone I had because of System's success meant I had any sort of responsibility to be an activist or to speak truth to power. Those things are just part and parcel of who I am as a human being. I'd be fighting for what I believe in *regardless* of what I was doing for a living. That said, when you're standing onstage, holding a microphone in front of an audience, you command tremendous power. The question is: What are you going to *do* with that power?

There is a famous photo of Bob Marley onstage in Kingston, Jamaica, in 1978, with the political leaders from the country's two major parties on both sides of him, as all three clasp their hands above Marley's head. At the time, Jamaica was embroiled in an undeclared civil war. The supporters of the two opposing political parties were literally murdering each other in the streets. The idea of these two politicians shaking hands—or their supporters dancing side-by-side in the audience—was outlandish. This concert was intended as a truce, a way to build some momentum for peace in the country, or at the very least, to press pause on all the killing.

It was Marley's first show back in Jamaica in two years, when he'd played a massive concert just two days after being shot by would-be assassins. He was an artist, not a politician, but he knew that as the most popular and unifying figure in the country, if he stood onstage, with tens of thousands of adoring fans in front of him, and invited the two warring politicians to shake hands, they couldn't very well refuse. He knew the power he wielded and was prepared to use it.

Bono and the Edge replicated this type of political performance when the plans for a unity government in Northern Ireland were in jeopardy.

In the summer of 2008, I performed solo with my backing band, the F.C.C., at the Reading Festival in England. At these massive festivals, people in the crowd often hold up huge flags on poles. These flags are primarily functional, a way to find your friends in a crowd of one hundred thousand. People tend to use flags they feel somehow represent them personally—rainbow Pride flags, or "Don't Tread on Me" flags, or flags supporting one sports team or another. At Reading that year, I remember standing onstage, looking out and seeing an Israeli flag on one side of the crowd and a Lebanese flag on the other. The two neighboring countries had been fighting a low-grade war for decades, fueled by bloody cross-border skirmishes and actions by, among others, Hezbollah and the Israel Defense Forces. Between songs, I asked if we could get those two flags to come together, side-by-side. Slowly, I could see the flags begin to inch closer to each other as the people hoisting them made their way through the crowd toward the center. When they finally met in the middle and the two flag-bearers embraced, the entire audience erupted in cheers.

I'm not naïve. Getting those two flags and their bearers together did not bring peace to the Middle East any more than Bob Marley's gesture stopped all the bloodshed on the streets of Kingston. But images matter. Symbolism is powerful, and it's imperative to try to make positive change where possible. If we can't even envision the peaceful world we hope to live in, we have no chance of achieving it. If we fail at making small gestures, we won't have the courage to try big ones. And if you're not using your microphone, your stage, and all the clout that comes with it to try to make some sort of real impact in this world, then what the fuck are you doing and who are you?

I know for a fact that I've lost fans over my politics and my activism—probably thousands of them. I'm okay with that. Being an artist should never be a popularity contest. I've always felt like my job was to tell the truth. When I slammed on the brakes of my Jeep on that winding road through Laurel Canyon years before, I didn't yell "I want to sell millions of CDs!" or "I want to play in front of thousands of fans!"

No.

What I wanted then, what I'd wanted ever since I first started tinkering away on that Casio, was to make music. I wanted to be an artist. I wanted to express myself, to show people what the world looked like through my eyes. I still do, whether that's ten people or ten million.

———

System had recorded close to forty songs during the time we put *Toxicity* together. The album ended up with fifteen tracks, which meant there was a lot of great material that got left off it. Sometime in 2002, we became aware of a bootleg that was circulating that had been titled *Toxicity II*. It featured recordings of thirteen more songs from those sessions that had been leaked online.

This was an era of music leaks. File-sharing services like Napster and LimeWire had made searching for and trading large files on the internet relatively simple and had upended the entire music industry. The most disturbing thing about the *Toxicity II* leak was that the music itself was unfinished. I wanted people to hear those songs, sure, but not the raw, uncompleted versions. We needed to put our finishing touches on them and mix and master the tracks for release.

I suggested to the rest of the band that we do exactly that. Daron wasn't initially into the idea, and Shavo and John were pretty lukewarm, too. There was fear that it would be perceived as a "B record" right after *Toxicity*, which it wasn't. I made the case that since these songs were already circulating, shouldn't we make sure we have the best recordings of them out there?

Plus, a lot of the tracks we were talking about were ones for which I'd written the music, and I wasn't sure how much that might have been factoring into Daron's reluctance. It seemed to me like he wanted to be the one masterminding the band's music. This album might undercut that idea. The argument went round and round for a while. It was solved by what often solves arguments: money.

By offering Sony this extra record that they weren't expecting, we were able to renegotiate our contract with the label in a way that was much more favorable to us. When the rest of the guys in the band realized the dollar figures involved, their feelings about releasing another album from those *Toxicity* sessions changed quickly.

Toxicity had been selling very well up to this point, and we were already playing bigger shows, but this renegotiation was the first major financial windfall for the band. It was the kind of payday that could change your lifestyle, but I did my best to ensure that it didn't change mine. I bought a house and started a savings account, but beyond that, I didn't really go in for the typical rock-star excess. I'd already ridden the rollercoaster of American capitalism with my parents once and wanted to do my best to avoid its nausea-inducing peaks and valleys for a second time.

When it came to the new album, Daron had the amazing idea to design the cover art to look like a pirated CD-R, which I thought was brilliant. And in keeping with the theme, we decided to title it *Steal This Album!*—a nod to Abbie Hoffman's counterculture classic, *Steal This Book*.

By this time, the band had been on tour for the better part of five years with only a short break, which we'd mostly spent writing and recording. I was worn out from the road, and I think the rest of the guys were ready for a break, too. Still, we wanted to do something to promote the new record, so we all met in Beno's office one afternoon to talk about it.

As we sat down, the first order of business was picking a single to push to radio. "I-E-A-I-A-I-O" was being touted as a good possibility. I love that song. It opens with tripwire tongue-twisting lyrics that all start with "P," has a chorus that sounds like a European soccer anthem, a middle eight that interpolates the theme from the 1980s TV show *Knight Rider*, and a few lyrics inspired by a chance meeting John had with *Knight Rider* star David Hasselhoff at a convenience store when he was kid. I mean, what's not to like?

But I had other thoughts about promoting *Steal This Album!*, so I raised my hand and made a bold suggestion. Knowing Daron's somewhat contrarian attitude, I prefaced my words with "You're probably not gonna like this idea," but then said, "Let's not release *any* singles from the new album. Instead, let's make a video for the song 'Boom!' Let's fill it with images from anti-war protests from around the world, and let's have Michael Moore direct it." I envisioned it as a strong statement against the brewing invasion of Iraq.

When I stopped talking, the room got very quiet for what felt like a long while. Remember, this was the late fall of 2002. Our singles from *Toxicity* were still in heavy rotation on radio stations and MTV. Meanwhile, the US had already invaded Afghanistan, and George W. Bush was in the process of manufacturing justifications and a so-called "coalition of the willing" to launch a war in Iraq. I felt like if we were going to take up any more of people's bandwidth, we better have something worth saying. Michael Moore, who had recently directed a Rage Against the Machine video on Wall Street that forced the New York Stock Exchange to shut down, would be the perfect person to help make sure we did it right.

Daron finally spoke up to break the silence.

"We're overplayed on the radio," he said. "We don't want to be one of those bands people get burned out on. I like that idea."

Daron and I have had our personal and creative differences over the years, but I'll always love him for having my back that day. The record label, on the other hand, was predictably unenthusiastic about the idea of spending hundreds of thousands of dollars on a video to protest a military action that roughly 70 percent of Americans supported at that point—all while not even having a single on the radio to help sell more records. A couple of days after that meeting, I got a call from Beno informing me that Sony had rejected the idea. I didn't get angry. I didn't curse anyone out. But in a matter-of-fact voice, I told our manager to inform the label that I was out of the band.

This was no rock-star diva move. "If we can't make a creative decision on something as important as a war and have the support of a company that we've made millions of dollars for, then I don't see any point in being a part of this," I explained. It was a stark threat, but it wasn't a bluff. I was ready to walk over this. Beno relayed my ultimatum, and Sony backed down. In the end, we made the video exactly as we wanted to.

The fact that the whole band backed me on this was incredibly meaningful. Although Daron and I haven't always seen eye-to-eye creatively, we both understand what this band means to each other and to our fans. He and I have always been very careful about weighing opportunities that could potentially sacrifice our standing with our fans and in our own minds. Many of our peers have raked in millions in random corporate sponsorships for tours or other events. We saw how that kind of stuff could discredit the art and didn't engage in it. To this day, we're still *very* careful about sync offers—allowing our music to be used for TV shows, films, video games, and that sort of thing—and other commercial opportunities. I can confidently say that we've turned down millions in film sync business alone. That incident with the "Boom!" video was one of those times I felt like we stood up for what we believed and didn't blink.

"Boom!" is one of my favorite System Of A Down songs and *Steal This Album!* may be my favorite of our records. The verses to the song are almost completely spoken-word and feel much more urgent because of it. The words themselves vacillate between poetry and political manifesto, drawing a direct connection between various rancid *isms*: consumerism, globalism, nationalism, and, of course, militarism. The angry, staccato choruses drive it all home. In some ways, the roots of that song go all the way back to my family's apartment in Beirut, where Sevag and I crouched down, listening to the bombs drop, and feeling the walls shake. Once you've been on the receiving end of that, it never leaves you.

"Boom!" is explicitly anti-war, and it was part of a handful of anti-war songs that ended up on that album, including "A.D.D.," which stands for "American Dream Denial," and "Bubbles." When the album came out in late 2002, war was in the air. In fact, we filmed that "Boom!" video at simultaneous worldwide protests the month before the US invaded Iraq. But interestingly enough, all those anti-war songs were written and initially recorded *before* the September 11th attacks. I guess war was already in the air even then. It goes back to that collective unconscious that I mentioned before. Sometimes, as artists, we can be tuned in to frequencies we wouldn't be able to pick up otherwise.

To be anti-war in the years immediately after 9/11 was not necessarily easy. But time tends to be the great revealer when it comes to geopolitics. Eventually, a majority of the American public realized that the Bush administration's reaction to 9/11 was a complete disaster. They'd been blatantly lying about weapons of mass destruction in Iraq and created a decades-long generational war in Afghanistan that the US has only recently extricated itself from at an astronomical cost in blood and treasure.

The fact that a majority of the population came around to the idea that the wars in Iraq and Afghanistan were a mistake is cold comfort to those who argued against them at the time. Frankly, when I survey the damage done, the barbaric crimes committed, and the silencing of public opinion that came in the wake of 9/11, I would rather have been wrong about all of it.

In the spring of 2004, we were getting ready to play a second "Souls" benefit show that we'd scheduled at the Greek Theatre in Los Angeles for Genocide Remembrance Day, April 24, when I got a call from Beno. After years of working at a frantic pace, System had been on a relative hiatus for much of the past eighteen months. The "Souls" benefit would be only our second show of the year. When I got on the phone, Beno told me that Daron didn't want to play.

"Why?" I asked.

"I'm not sure," Beno replied. "Can you talk to him?"

"Of course."

It all seemed very strange. If there's one thing Daron always wanted to do, it was to play. Music is his life. For him to write off performing—and at a show to raise money and awareness for the Armenian Genocide, no less—was hard to wrap my head around.

When the three of us got on a call, Daron confirmed that he didn't want to do the show. His explanation was a little convoluted. He felt like the band had made our opposition to the war in Iraq very clear. I'd been extremely outspoken about the lies the US government told to get us into the war and the atrocities committed by the American military once we were there. He believed there was some sort of hypocrisy in criticizing the US on one hand, then asking them to recognize the Genocide on the other.

"Daron, let me simplify this," I said. "What we're talking about is injustice. That injustice could be the invasion of Iraq or the Genocide of the Armenians. They're *both* injustices. That's what we're against. There's nothing hypocritical about it. We're on the right side of this."

The line went quiet for a few seconds. Finally, Daron spoke.

"Okay," he agreed, at last. "That makes sense. We can do the show. I'll talk to you later." And then he hung up.

I still don't totally understand what that phone call was really about. Daron is a smart guy, but I think emotions were clouding out logic. His family's roots are in Iraq—they're Iraqi-Armenians—so he had complicated feelings about the war there. On one hand, I think he liked the idea of the Baathists being forced out of power; on the other, he may have realized that things were likely to get worse without them, as they eventually did. Beyond that, I think the fact that System had become so associated with activism made him uncomfortable. Not because he necessarily didn't agree with the politics—I think he did—but although he liked the anti-establishment punk-rock ethos of the band, I think he had a harder time articulating himself when it came to politics. He'd rather talk about music. The more the focus turned to politics, the more I became the band's de facto spokesperson. It created the perception that System was *my* band. And to be fair, it was not my band, it was *ours*. Daron and I had started it together and we'd always been a team, its twin artistic engines.

The "Souls" show ended up being pretty amazing. The Greek Theatre, built into a hillside in Griffith Park, is a beautiful location with impeccable acoustics. Saul Williams, a poet I'd become close with, performed, as did a great band called Bad Acid Trip, who were friends of mine and who I'd recently signed to my own record label. Along with all the messaging about the Genocide, Axis of Justice also set up tables and passed out information. To me, it felt like exactly what a System Of A Down show should be.

If I'm being honest, though, my most enduring memory around that gig happened the night before. We sound checked at the Greek, and then I went to a friend's birthday party. I was there hanging out with some friends when I noticed someone I'd never seen before, a young woman with short, cropped blonde hair. I felt immediately drawn to her. I needed some sort of pretext to go over and meet her. I knew the brother of the guy she was talking to, so I walked up and asked him for a cigarette. When I did, he introduced me to her. She told me her name was Angela.

"What do you do?" she asked me.

Most of the people at the party were Armenians and knew exactly what I did. I initially assumed Angela wasn't Armenian—at the time, you didn't find many Armenians with blonde hair and long legs—but she was. She just had no idea who I was.

"I do music," I told her.

"Oh, is that right?" she said. "I sing a little too."

"I'd like to hear you sing sometime," I smiled.

We talked for a while about music and about Armenia. She had grown up there, but I think she was impressed that I actually knew quite a lot about the country despite having only visited once. She was young, just twenty at the time, but she talked with such wisdom and clarity. It was clear that she'd lived through a lot. At a certain point, I guessed her zodiac sign—which, yes, I know, is a pretty cheesy thing to do—but we were both Leos, and as I told her, I could see that fire in her eyes.

I loved the fact that Angela had never heard of me or the band. From the moment we met, I never had to wonder whether she was interested in me as a person or me as a public figure. We were just two people making a real connection.

When Angela left the party that night, though, I didn't get her phone number. I'd been in a long-distance relationship with a woman in Australia for a long time, and although that had come apart at the seams by then, I was really in no place to be jumping into another relationship. But I was enchanted with Angela nonetheless and knew in my gut that one way or another, I was going to see her again.

CHAPTER 12

Shortly after the first System Of A Down album was released, the four of us were in a limo together, headed somewhere I can't recall, to go do something I have no memory of. I feel a little bad that so many of my days during those hectic early years with the band are nothing but an incoherent blur, but most of the nice perks and day-to-day particulars that came with being in a successful band were never that important to me. Regardless, I remember looking around at Daron, Shavo, and John on that ride, and thinking to myself, "This band isn't going to last that long."

It was kind of a crazy thing to think because, really, at that point, the band had just started. As we were sitting in that limo, nobody was arguing, nobody had a serious drug problem—things were actually pretty good. Yes, Daron was complaining about something—maybe the limo itself—but surely some idle griping didn't spell doom for the whole project, right? Or maybe it did. Negativity has a way of seeping into the cracks in any foundation. I'd already spent enough time with those guys to know that what we had was combustible, and when you take something that's combustible, you seal it up for years in a tight place, and then you shake it a bit, it's going to explode.

System spent our first five years largely sealed up together in tour buses, recording studios, and rehearsal spaces. Maybe it didn't even matter who the personalities involved were. Arguably, if you put *any* four people in that environment for five years, there's going to be some volatility. Everyone always says a band is like a marriage, and I think there's some truth to that. But most bands don't start with thoughtful vows in front of friends and family, and sincere reflection on the commitment you're about to make. Bands start on whims and chance. Someone knows someone who plays bass. You need a drummer for a gig next Friday. Suddenly you find yourself married to people you never planned on spending the rest of your life with.

When we took some time away from each other, starting in early 2003, it felt—for me—like a welcome and much-needed bit of relief. Music had started to feel more like a job than a passion. It wasn't that I needed time away from music. I just needed time away from the people I'd been making it with nonstop for ten years. I still wanted to make music; I just wanted to make it differently.

During that time, I reconnected with a fellow musician named Arto Tunçboyacıyan, who we'd worked with on two of the tracks for *Toxicity*. I'd first met Arto a few years earlier at the Armenian Music Awards, where I'd seen him perform, tapping on and blowing into a half-filled Coke bottle, using it as both a percussion and a wind instrument at the same time. He was a tornado of creative energy. We wanted to make an album together, so we started meeting up at a studio in Burbank and then finished up at a home studio in the Valley.

I brought some song ideas, but mostly, we were just improvising, creating on the fly. Many days, we'd show up in the morning with nothing and have a couple of new songs recorded by the end of the day. It was so different from my experience with System, where we'd spend months writing and rehearsing material before we even stepped foot into a recording studio. I'd gotten used to thinking of the studio not as a place where ideas are born but where they're repeated, again and again and again and again, until they're perfected. The process of making a System album would take six to nine months. With Arto, we spent a week and a half in the studio and came out with an album. We called it *Serart*.

What we came up with bore little resemblance to what I did with System. The songs on *Serart* are a free-flowing, experimental mix of poetry, jazz, electronic music, and a globe-trotting potpourri of different strains of world music.

In April of 2001, I'd done a deal with Sony to have my own imprint label, Serjical Strike; I wanted to use it to bring bands to people's attention that normally would not be seen and to put out my own records as well. *Serart* was the first release on the label. It felt like the perfect mission statement for the kind of unfettered, genre-surpassing creativity I was hoping to foster. I signed a couple of bands I really liked, a gothy punk band called Kittens for Christian, and that band Bad Acid Trip, who'd played the second "Souls" show and would eventually make this amazing thrash-metal-meets-the-circus kind of album that Daron produced. But nobody embodied the label's commitment to unfettered creativity more than the enigmatic guitarist Brian Carroll, a.k.a. Buckethead. I'd met him through Bill Laswell, an avant-garde bassist and producer, back when Buckethead was playing guitar for Guns N' Roses. We'd send each other music or books we liked, we'd hang out sometimes, we'd talk about music. One day, Bucket called me and told me he needed money and wanted to make an album for my label.

"Look, if you need money, I can just give you some money," I told him. "We don't have to make a record."

"No, no, no," he said. "Let me make a record for you."

I'd recently built an eight-hundred-square-foot studio right next to my house, so we started bringing different artists to that studio to work with Bucket. Saul Williams did a track with him. The guys from Bad Acid Trip collaborated on a song. Shana Halligan, a singer who was also a neighbor and friend of mine, sang on a track. My friend Azam Ali, an incredible world music singer, contributed. I wrote a couple of songs with Bucket, played and sang on them, and co-produced the whole album. Through Bucket, I also met a guy named Dan Monti, who became a great friend and longtime collaborator.

Working with Buckethead was, to put it simply, *quite* an experience. It's not like when he takes the KFC bucket off his head and puts away his mask that he's just a regular guy. A regular guy he is most definitely *not*. Sometimes, he'd call me at four in the morning and leave a fifteen-minute guitar solo on my voicemail. He had ambitions to open an amusement park for chickens. He is eccentric and acutely sensitive but such a singular creative spirit. He's a sweetheart of a human being—caring, compassionate, funny. We made a completely bonkers music video up in Big Bear for one of the songs on the album, "We Are One," in which Bucket plays a taxidermist who picks up a bunch of roadkill and then Frankensteins their parts together into some sort of monstrous super-animal.

A couple of years after we made that album, he called and asked me to play a show with him at his old high school. I think Bucket's dad was a coach at this school, and if I remember correctly—and I may not—the event was a "Battle of the Bands." Bucket had pulled in a few ringers for our band including me and Primus's drummer Bryan "Brain" Mantia. We set up in the school gym and just jammed out, with me making up the vocals as I went along, pure stream of consciousness. The kids at this school went nuts.

After doing things in such a regimented way for years with System, this looser approach to everything was incredibly refreshing. I recorded a little with Saul Williams and played a handful of shows with him, Money Mark (a key collaborator of the Beastie Boys), and Zack de la Rocha from Rage. We didn't really have any songs; we'd just go onstage with a few ideas and develop them up there. I'd play an electric sitar through a bass amp, Zack was playing drums, Mark was on keyboards, and Saul would get up in front of the microphone with a newspaper and freestyle poetry inspired by the news. Of course, the output was hit and miss, but when it came together, when it worked, to be there for that spark of creation was electrifying. These sorts of projects were, in a way, a manifestation of my spiritual journey, an artistic exhortation to live in the moment.

My label, Serjical Strike, was always conceived as an outlet for working with artists I love. I didn't have any real commercial ambitions for it. That notwithstanding, I narrowly missed out on signing the British band Muse in 2002 and early 2003, just before they became huge stars in America. "Narrowly missed out" is a diplomatic way of putting it. I was kind of screwed over.

I'd seen Muse play at European festivals where System was performing. At the time, the band already had a big following in Europe but hadn't broken in the US. In fact, their American record label, Maverick—a Warner Bros. subsidiary run by our old buddy Guy Oseary—didn't even release their second album, *Origin of Symmetry*, in the States. Their music is this infectious blend of progressive rock and European pop with deep-seated classical influences, but I guess the label thought American audiences wouldn't get it. I spoke to their manager about trying to negotiate an exit from their Maverick deal so I could sign them, and he seemed amenable to it. The guys in the band were genuinely good dudes. They came to my house, we jammed together in my studio, they even played with my dog.

Maverick wanted half a million dollars to let Muse out of their contract, so I went to Sony and pitched them, essentially telling them, "Front this money. This band will be worth it and then some." Sony hemmed and hawed. At the time, Muse was working on another album, and Sony wanted to wait to hear it before they'd commit to ponying up the half million dollars to pry Muse away from Maverick.

Around this time, I was spending a lot of time in Australia and New Zealand. This is before I met Angela, and I was still trying to salvage my relationship with my ex-girlfriend, who I'd met on my first trip down to Sydney. Everyone knows that long-distance relationships are tough to maintain, but I'd really fallen for this Australian woman and wanted to try to make it work. I left to go down there for a few months and told my lawyer to let me know when the advance copy of Muse's album arrived, so I could pitch the band again to Sony. It would seem my lawyer failed to do that.

In the meantime, a VP at Sony tried to go behind my back and sign Muse out from under me. By the time I heard anything about any of this several months later, the whole ship had sailed. Warner Bros. heard the new Muse album, *Absolution*, moved them off Maverick, and was making arrangements to release the album through a different subsidiary. To date, it has sold more than 3.5 million copies worldwide. The band's follow-up, *Black Holes and Revelations*, has sold more than five million.

Now, to be fair, from a business standpoint, I did so many things wrong here. First, I should've gone directly to Guy about releasing Muse from his label. We were old friends, and we might have been able to work out something far less onerous than the $500,000 Maverick was asking for. Second, when Sony balked at paying that money, I should've found it somewhere else or put it up myself. Third, as annoyed as I was at my lawyer for not letting me know that the album had been delivered, I should've been calling in to check on it. I was way too Zen about the whole deal. My spiritual practice seemed to be teaching me to believe that if it's meant to be, it will be. I wasn't going to force anything. But that's not really the way the music business works.

All that said, ultimately, I came away from this pretty annoyed with Sony. For a record company that I'd made a hell of a lot of money for to not only be unwilling to invest in my vision but to actively undermine it was galling. The fact that their machinations ended up scuttling what would've been an extremely lucrative deal for both my company and theirs is even more so.

When it came time to start working on new material for another System Of A Down album in late 2003, my head and my heart weren't fully in it. At the time we started writing, my relationship with my ex-girlfriend had completely cratered, and I was grieving that loss. I had been so deeply in love with her and thought this relationship was going to be for keeps. When it turned out that it wasn't, I sank into a deep depression. I lost a lot of weight and didn't really want to leave the house much. In some ways, though, I welcomed the idea of going into a rehearsal space with Daron, Shavo, and John because it gave me something to do other than sit around stewing about the demise of this relationship.

The practice space didn't turn out to be the haven I'd hoped it would be. Having worked with other artists in the interim, I'd seen other ways of making music than the way we'd done it in System. I was writing songs and I was desperate to collaborate, to be creative, but everything within the band felt rigid and inflexible. No one wanted to change anything or even experiment with it.

As we started working out of our North Hollywood practice space, most of the songs we spent time on were ones Daron had written. The music I brought in was shuffled to the side. If I mentioned that I had a song I wanted us to take a crack at, Daron would never outright refuse, but it was always "Let's work on that one next week," or "How about we finish up this batch of songs first?" We rarely ever seemed to get to my songs.

I found this all extremely frustrating and discouraging, but I really wasn't in the emotional headspace to put up a fight about it.

Instead, I thought about the things I'd learned through meditation. I didn't want to get so tied up in what's *mine* and what's *not mine*, so I took a deep breath—literally and figuratively—and just let it go. This might've alleviated the tension in the moment, but it didn't make me any happier or more content in the long run.

After a few weeks, at a band meeting with Rick and Beno, I told everyone that after we finished this album cycle—recording, promoting, and touring—I was going to take some extended time away from the band. I wanted to work on my own music. I wanted the machine to stop so I could focus on being an artist again rather than a musician married to a fixed schedule on the road, in service of commercial ends. I wasn't quitting the band forever, I assured them, but it was going to be an indefinite hiatus.

In the moment, everyone seemed to understand. They knew I'd really been struggling since the breakup with my ex and hadn't been happy working on the new music. I don't think anyone was surprised by my announcement, but I'm sure they all assumed that once I had some time and breathing room, I'd change my mind. Maybe, deep down, I thought the same thing.

In the short term, I hoped that by making it clear how unhappy I was in the band, Daron might be more willing to cede some creative control, to allow a more egalitarian ethos to take hold. I thought he might reflect on what was making me so miserable and try to alleviate it. In fact, the opposite was true. It seemed to me that Daron felt the band falling apart, so he gripped the reins even more tightly to bring it under control. As I sensed that happening, I totally disengaged. I was physically present at those sessions, but not spiritually.

It would be easy to blame Daron for all this, but honestly, he was just being the person he had always been. For me to expect something else was naïve. If I wanted to make a change in the way the band operated, *I* had to be the engine of that change. *I* had to be proactive.

Unfortunately, though I couldn't see it then, my spiritual practice was actually making me more passive. I wanted to avoid stress, to not be in constant conflict with Daron or anyone else, to not hold on so tightly to things like status and ownership. I was also insecure about some of the songs I had written. I felt like if I could let that stuff go, if I could embody the Buddhist ideal that material possessions weigh us down and that attachment to worldly things is the root of our suffering, then I'd be more at peace. None of those principles are necessarily wrong, but my interpretation of them back then was severely flawed. I simply figured that avoiding confrontation and conflict was more evolved than engaging in it. While it did mean that I wasn't spending all the time in our practice space or in the studio clashing with my bandmates, I was pushing my problems to the side more than I was actually dealing with them.

Those recording sessions were both interesting and strange. We were working with Rick again, this time at his manor on Laurel Canyon Boulevard. It was across the street from Harry Houdini's old house, and the rumor was that there was an underground tunnel connecting it to the Houdini mansion. If his place on Miller Drive was a bit spooky, this place felt downright haunted. At night, it groaned and creaked. Doors would slam shut randomly. You'd hear sounds from rooms that no one was in. Other bands who'd worked with Rick there like the Red Hot Chili Peppers and Slipknot had reported similarly bizarre experiences.

Daron was also singing lead on a lot more songs than he had in the past. That didn't really bother me because I felt like if he'd written the lyrics and the song suited his voice, he should sing it. I wanted the band to be a living, breathing organism that would evolve and change as we all evolved and changed as artists. Just because I'd been the lead singer in the past didn't mean I had to be in the future. Just because fans were used to a certain version of System Of A Down didn't mean that we had to keep being that. There were times when I thought Daron's voice didn't work that well with the music, sure, but I didn't want to step on his toes. I thought that if I gave him the room to grow as an artist, he would eventually do the same for me. But it didn't work out that way.

Despite all the issues, the sessions were incredibly productive, at least in terms of the sheer quantity of music we churned out. We once again recorded a plethora of songs, and some of them were great. "Holy Mountains" is a powerful anthem about the Genocide, and a sort of companion piece to "P.L.U.C.K." from our first album. "Lost in Hollywood" and "Soldier Side" are two of the best songs Daron's ever written. The former is a simple story song about being chewed up and spit out by the entertainment industry, but it's executed so beautifully. As for "Soldier Side," it's an incredibly emotional anti-war song written from the standpoint of soldiers and their parents. To this day, I have a hard time singing those harmonies with Daron without getting choked up.

"B.Y.O.B." is another anti-war song. I wrote the verses, which are angry, political, free associative poetry, and then Daron wrote the lyrics for the chorus, which are lighthearted jaunts about partying. How many songs can you think of that have references to Fort

Knox, oil, fascism, and government corruption, all centered around a chorus about "dancin' in the desert / blowing up the sunshine"? On one level, I suppose you could see that dichotomy as indicative of the ways in which Daron and I weren't on the same page at those sessions. In fact, though, his lighthearted chorus was exactly what that song needed. Much like our earlier collaborations, these parts really work off each other—one deadly serious, the other completely unserious—and the contrast makes the song sharper and more surprising. It was what we'd always done best.

One of the few songs of mine we recorded during those sessions was called "Question!" I'd written the song on an acoustic guitar in my living room. At the time, I lived in a beautifully serene two-story, nestled among trees in a cozy little community not far from Malibu. The verses were in a strange time signature, one that immediately put me into a kind of trance while playing and singing them. The pre-chorus switched to a straightforward 4/4 time, opening room for a huge, anthemic chorus where I sing, "Do we, do we know when we fly? / When we, when we go, do we die?" It felt like there was a real profundity and depth to the song. It was serious.

I brought "Question!" in relatively early in the process, and I think the song caught Daron off-guard. He had a habit of bringing his B-level material into our sessions first, before building up to his stronger songs. I'm not sure why, maybe he wanted to lower expectations so he could exceed them later. At any rate, I think "Question!" forced him to up his game right away.

Early in System's existence, Daron told me that he didn't think it would be fair to divide our publishing royalties into four equal shares since he and I were doing the vast majority of the songwriting. That seemed reasonable back then, and it was in my financial best interest to agree with him anyway. Instead, I devised a formula for figuring out the publishing shares on each song, which, according to my business manager, was a nice, scientific way of breaking it down. If you contributed the music to a verse, chorus, or bridge, you got a certain percentage. Ditto for the lyrics. It was all worked out on a spreadsheet. Although all big band decisions were decided by a vote of all four members, in the case of the publishing splits, since Daron and I were the primary writers, normally the two of us would simply hash it out and decide what was equitable. On "Question!" in particular, I'd written both the music and the lyrics, and Daron had just contributed a little guitar tagline, which—if I'm being charitable—was worth about 5 to 10 percent of the publishing. But when it came time to divvy it up, he received 20 percent. It seemed far-reaching, especially since I was only getting 5 to 10 percent on most songs on that album. It's not as if Daron forced this on me, but again, I got Zen about it and decided this was not a fight worth fighting. I let him have it. This was a pattern that repeated itself on several of the songs from these sessions. Whatever the creative conflict was, my answer was almost always passivity.

At the end of the recording, we once again had multiple albums worth of material. When it came time to figure out which songs would make the final cut, I leaned on the lesson we'd learned the last go-round. I suggested that we divide the songs into two albums and release both. Part of me knew this was my last hurrah with the band—at least for a while—so it seemed to make sense to get the most mileage we could from it. I had no intention to tour behind two separate albums, but I figured if they were released closely enough together, we'd just do one big run of shows to support them both.

Initially, this suggestion was not much more popular than my suggestion to release *Steal This Album!* had been, but once everyone—the band, the management, the label—realized that it might be a long time before they got anything else out of System, they came around. We put out *Mezmerize* in May 2005, and its companion, *Hypnotize*, dropped six months later.

Looking back, that release scheme looks like a marketing masterstroke. We became one of very few artists to ever hit #1 on the Billboard charts with two different albums in the same year. It was a huge commercial triumph for the band, albeit one that I had a hard time getting very excited about. In many ways, despite having some great music on them, those albums felt like a personal nadir for me. When I listen to them, even now, I'm reminded of all the heartache I had when we began making them, all the concessions I made along the way, and the spiritual confusion that let it all happen.

CHAPTER 13

Tour documentaries are a dime a dozen. It's a proven formula: send an ambitious, young filmmaker out on the road with a band, gather some flattering performance footage, clips of screaming fans, and bits of the band clowning around backstage or on the tour bus, then edit it all together and you've got yourself a perfectly serviceable promotional item to stoke interest in the band's upcoming album. There's nothing at all wrong with these films, but I wouldn't be that excited to make one. Fortunately, when Carla Garapedian came to me in 2004, wanting to make a documentary with System Of A Down, this sort of self-serving fluff was not what she had in mind.

Carla was a former BBC journalist who'd already made films about homeless orphans in North Korea and the plight of women in Taliban-dominated Afghanistan. Now, she wanted to make a film about the Armenian Genocide.

As we began to talk, it occurred to me that we had a chance to do something really subversive. Under the guise of a typical hagiographic documentary, we could slip in a hard-hitting film about

Genocide denial and its effects. I convinced the rest of the guys to let Carla and her small crew trail us around off and on for the next six months or so—on tour, at home, wherever. She filmed me with my grandfather Stepan, who was then living in a nursing home, and used older home footage of him talking about his personal experiences living through the Genocide. She also filmed our third "Souls" show at the Universal Amphitheatre in Los Angeles and interviewed fans outside the show.

When we were on tour in Chicago, we realized that we were only a few miles from Speaker of the House Dennis Hastert's local office. Hastert had made himself a chief impediment to official recognition of the Genocide by the US government. In 2000, he'd withdrawn a resolution from the House floor that would've formally recognized the Genocide, even though the International Relations Committee had forwarded it out of committee for a vote by the full House. He insisted that it was an appeal from President Clinton, claiming the bill would damage US-Turkey relations, that caused him to withdraw it before a final vote. In later years, it was reported that FBI wiretaps had revealed Turkish covert relations with Hastert. He denied the allegations that unnamed Turkish agents had paid him $500,000 to pull the resolution from the House floor, threatening to expose evidence of the child molestation he eventually went to jail for if he didn't. Though Hastert never faced charges related to the bribery or blackmail, the fact that he became a lobbyist for the Turkish government following his time in Congress didn't exactly quiet those concerns.

In the fall of 2005, when we were in Chicago, the International Relations Committee had once again forwarded a bill on Genocide recognition, and Hastert was once again the man holding the power to kill it or put it to a full vote. In twenty-four hours, we arranged a rally outside his office. John and I both went to help lead the protest, give interviews to the media, and deliver to Hastert a petition and a letter I'd written about my grandfather's experience during the Genocide. He either wasn't there or wouldn't see us, so I left the material with his staff.

That night, we had a show at what was then called the Rosemont Horizon, an arena near the Chicago airport. My security guy told me that he'd gotten a message from friends of his at the FBI letting him know that Turkish intelligence was tracking me and my movements. There were vague threats. Apparently, the noise I'd been making about Genocide recognition and the news coverage of the ad hoc protest at Hastert's office had gotten their attention, and not in a good way.

Logically speaking, I knew that it was incredibly unlikely that the Turks were going to hire an assassin to take out the lead singer of a popular rock band on American soil. Logic, though, has a way of being unsettled by fear. Your mind keeps drawing the worst possible conclusions. The Turks viewed Genocide recognition as an existential threat to their state, and as one of the most visible proponents of this recognition campaign, what *wouldn't* they do to shut me up? I can remember feeling very jittery up onstage that night—and for most of the rest of that tour. I'm sure if you were to watch video of those shows, you'd notice that I'm moving a lot more than usual, darting around in sudden, unpredictable directions. As ridiculous as it sounds, somewhere in my brain, my thought was *"If some sharpshooter wants to take a crack at me, I'm not going to make myself an easy target."*

Still, I wasn't going to let the threats change my course. A few months after visiting Hastert's office in Illinois, I went to Washington, DC, to meet with members of Congress about the resolution, which was still languishing in limbo. The meetings were arranged by the Armenian National Committee of America. I was under no illusions; I knew that I was getting access to the halls of power in return for lending whatever celebrity I had to the cause. Some of the younger members of Congress were actually System Of A Down fans and wanted to meet me. Other older ones wanted a photo for their kids or grandkids. It's kind of a sketchy trade-off, but I wasn't about to waste the opportunity to buttonhole people who were in a position to help.

A few of the House members I met, Democrats like Adam Schiff and Frank Pallone, were already big supporters of the Armenian community and Genocide recognition. Although I certainly identify to the left on the political spectrum, the recognition campaign doesn't necessarily align with one political party or another, and I was willing to cross the aisle to win support. Devin Nunes was then a Republican congressman representing a district in central California with a big Armenian population. He didn't seem particularly engaged with the issue but knew it was important to the people who vote for him, so he was all for the resolution.

Nunes introduced me to another Republican congressman and told me that this particular congressman was a huge music fan. I can't recall this guy's name, but he was an interesting study in contrasts. Unlike a lot of the other congressmen I met, this guy was whip-smart and politically astute. But his conservative political views didn't seem to match up *at all* with his musical taste. He had a poster of John Lennon on his office wall and told me he was a big fan of the radical left-wing proto-punk band MC5. I knew MC5 founder Wayne Kramer through his work with Axis of Justice and arranged for Wayne to send him some cool merch.

On the issue of Genocide recognition, this congressman knew the issue inside and out. "I will lay out for you exactly why the United States doesn't recognize the Genocide," he told me. "We sell Apache helicopters to Turkey, a NATO member. Turkey allows us to use the Incirlik and Izmir air bases which are absolutely vital to support our forces in Iraq. I know it's wrong, but that's why the government won't allow this resolution to pass. It's just geopolitical priorities."

I appreciated that this guy was being honest about why so many congressmen wouldn't support the resolution, though I found his coldhearted assessment bracing. No one was making qualitative arguments about whether or not the Genocide was a historical fact. Everyone acknowledged that it was. It was just political cynicism that was standing in the way of saying it outright.

At one point, I sat beside Eric Cantor, who was then part of the Republican majority's House leadership, along with a table full of his constituents, all of whom were speaking passionately about the importance of formal recognition. He nodded in agreement and muttered things like "Yes, it should be recognized," but remained noncommittal in terms of any real action. Finally, I looked over at him and said sharply, "So, are you going to pressure the speaker to bring this to a full vote?" He looked annoyed and gave me another non-answer.

Ultimately, the resolution had more than enough support to win passage, it just came down to whether Hastert would schedule a vote on it. He still wouldn't meet with me, but by chance, I saw him in the Capitol rotunda talking to some sort of youth group in matching shirts. I couldn't pass up the opportunity to corner him but did it very politely. With Carla's documentary crew in tow, I introduced myself and asked if he'd had a chance to read the letter I'd delivered to his office. He claimed not to have seen it yet. I explained to him that everyone I'd met with that day in Congress agreed the Genocide was a historical fact and that the fate of this bill, which was so important to our community, was entirely in his hands. He smiled, shook my hand, and promised, "I'll take a look at your letter." Then, he walked away.

Brushing so closely to the country's levers of power brings with it an undeniable charge, a little endorphin rush. But once that passed, it was hard not to come away from that day on Capitol Hill feeling incredibly discouraged about how our democracy works. Here was a truth no one was disputing, a bill most everyone agreed with on its merits, but it could still be scuttled because one guy, who may or may not have been bribed and blackmailed by Turkey, had the power to do so. Is that really the way a democratic republic is meant to function?

———

Within the music industry, there were definite mechanisms that created a sort of political favoritism as well. Certain causes and ideas got noticed and supported; others did not. In 2006, I fell into a situation that allowed me to see these gears turning up close, and it was not pretty. I was in New York to meet with Craig Kallman, the CEO of Atlantic Records, at the label's offices. I went there with this amazing progressive rock band called Fair to Midland, who I'd signed to Serjical Strike. They had a little buzz behind them, and we were looking for a major label to partner with to release their album. It was down to Atlantic or Universal, and both companies were anxious to make a deal.

I like Craig a lot, and the meeting went well. When it was over, we walked out of the conference room, and he pulled me aside.

"Hey, do you want to meet the old man?" he asked.

"What old man?"

"Ahmet," he clarified. "His office is right next door."

Ahmet Ertegun was a music industry legend. As a Turkish immigrant, he'd founded Atlantic back in the 1940s, then helped launch the careers of icons like John Coltrane, Ray Charles, Aretha Franklin, the Bee Gees, and Led Zeppelin, among many others. By this time, he was in his early eighties and had more of a ceremonial position at Atlantic, but I imagine his stature was helpful for closing deals. Regardless, I had a lot of reverence for his legacy and was excited to meet him.

I was ushered into his office, a plush cavern of dark woods and leather furniture that looked like something out of the 1970s. Ahmet was sitting behind a big brown desk and introduced himself. We made some small talk, and I told him what an honor it was to talk to him. It was all very cordial and inconsequential until I mentioned that I was Armenian. He stiffened a little and something in the air changed.

"The first person I hired at the company was Armenian," he told me, a little defensively.

"That's great," I said.

I brought up my friend Arto, and wondered if Ahmet might know Arto's brother, Onno Tunç, who was a very famous songwriter in Turkey. He did, but the conversation continued to feel stilted. After a few more minutes of chitchat about musicians and Armenia, I thanked him for his time, and left.

Later that day, I was flying back to LA, and something about that short meeting continued to gnaw at me. I opened my laptop and plugged Ahmet's name into Google alongside the word "Genocide." It was then that I finally understood why he'd gotten so uncomfortable when he found out I was Armenian. Ahmet had a history of funding organizations and university chairs that trafficked in Genocide denial. His family had a deep history in this area. Ahmet's father had been a close advisor to Kemal Atatürk, the founder of the modern Turkish republic. Later, as the Turkish ambassador to the US, his father had fiercely fought against the making of a film adaptation of *The Forty Days of Musa Dagh*, a popular novel set during the Armenian Genocide. As recently as 1998, Ahmet had acknowledged that Armenian deaths had taken place in 1915, but he maintained that they were not part of an extermination campaign, claiming that there were "different interpretations of what happened."

Learning all this created a conundrum for me. How could I potentially work with a company whose founder and figurehead was a Genocide denier? But was it right to tell the guys in Fair to Midland—who were not Armenian—that they couldn't make a deal with Atlantic because of a ninety-year-old grievance? What was my duty to them as a business partner, if you will, versus my duty to the Armenian cause? For the moment, I kept it all to myself and marinated on it.

Craig called me a few weeks later to take my temperature on the deal. I told him the band hadn't made a decision yet, which was true. I'd always respected Craig, so I decided to level with him.

"There is a thing I want to mention to you," I said at last. "It's about the old man."

"What about the old man?"

I told him about my meeting with Ahmet and then my later discovery of his history of denying the Armenian Genocide. Craig was shocked and knew nothing about it.

"Let me look into this and get back to you," he reassured me.

A few days later, I was out walking my dogs in the rain when my cell phone rang. It was Ahmet. He was anxious to talk and try to smooth things over. When I pointed out his blatant support for so-called scholars that denied the Genocide at chairs he had endowed at various universities or think tanks he'd sponsored who recommended the US government not recognize the Genocide, he said those scholars are no longer there. He also said that he believed that the Genocide occurred, and that Turkey should recognize it properly but, if I'm being honest, I was skeptical of the ardor of his belief. After all, he was close with top officials in the Turkish government, including Recep Tayyip Erdoğan, who was then the prime minister and later became the country's autocratic president.

"You have to understand, this isn't just activism for me," I explained. "This is personal. My grandparents lived through the Genocide. I have spent most of my life advocating for this cause. If I go into business with you, that's going to make me look like a hypocrite."

"No," he said. "It's not like that. We can work this out."

I suggested a solution. "How about if you write a letter on Atlantic Records letterhead that says, 'I, Ahmet Ertegun, recognize the Armenian Genocide,' sign it, and send it to me? I will never publicize the letter unless my back is against the wall with my own people. I'll keep it quiet."

"I can't do that," he told me.

"Why not? You *just* said that you recognized the Genocide. Why can't you put it on paper?"

"Because if anyone discovers that letter, they will burn my house down in Turkey," he said. "I would be in serious danger."

I thought about it. Putting this old man in peril didn't seem like a good solution to this quandary. "Look, I don't want anything bad to happen to you," I said at last. "Don't worry about it."

"Give me a little time and let me see if there's something else that I can do," he told me. We left it at that.

A week later, Craig called me and was blunt. "If you're waiting for the old man to do something, he's not going to," he said. I could tell he was upset about the whole situation but there was nothing he could do. The guys in Fair to Midland eventually decided to do a deal with Universal instead of Atlantic, anyway. I didn't nudge them in any way or let them know anything about this whole subplot until after they'd made up their minds. Their decision had nothing to do with it. Nonetheless, on some level, it still felt like karmic justice.

There has to be a cost for Genocide denial. And even if the only real cost I personally exacted was making Ahmet uncomfortable and forcing him to answer for his support of Genocide denial, that was not nothing. This was one of the most powerful and beloved figures in music industry history. To know that he was not able to live his whole life without paying a price for serious ethical failings makes it easier for me to believe there's spiritual balance in the world. As Martin Luther King Jr. once put it, "The arc of the moral universe is long, but it bends toward justice." In a small way, I could feel that bend.

Not too long after all this went down, Ahmet died after tripping backstage at a Rolling Stones show. Shortly after his death, Harut Sassounian, an Armenian journalist, published a story in which he wrote that Ahmet had reached out to him a few years earlier to disavow his previous Genocide denial. Ahmet told Sassounian the same thing he'd told me—that he couldn't go public with this because it would make him a target for Turkish extremists—so Sassounian had waited until his death to reveal it. I'm not sure if it makes me happy to know that Ahmet was apparently genuine in what he'd told me that day on the phone and wasn't just trying to close a deal, or if it makes me sad that he felt like it wasn't safe for him to speak the truth. Maybe a little of both.

———

Around this same time, Carla was shopping for a distributor for the documentary she had made with us, which was titled *Screamers*. The film had turned out to be an amazing piece of stealth political activism. Yes, it has many of the things you'd find in a normal tour documentary—System rocking out onstage, declarations of love from fans, behind-the-scenes footage from the tour bus—but it's all wrapped around brutal images of genocides through the past century, and interviews with diplomats, journalists, experts, and survivors explaining how denial of the Armenian Genocide opened the door to all the rest.

Because System was such a big part of the documentary, Carla was talking to a lot of record companies about distributing the film. I was helping out wherever I could. Carla told me that Lyor Cohen, who was then the CEO of the Warner Music Group, had vetoed his company distributing the film out of loyalty to Ahmet, whom he considered a great friend and mentor.

This really upset me. Ahmet's father had successfully quashed one film about the Genocide decades earlier, and now here was his son doing the same thing again *from beyond the fucking grave*. What was even more upsetting was that Ahmet had insisted—at least to me and Harut Sassounian—that he believed that Turkey *should* recognize the Genocide. So how was Lyor honoring his friend's legacy by standing in the way of a film advocating for that?

This was a pivotal time in my career, as I was getting ready to sign a solo deal with Warner Bros. Records, a division of the Warner Music Group that Lyor headed. In light of all this, I made sure to insert a clause into my contract with Warners to prevent them from impeding my political activism. Tom Whalley, who was the president of Warner Bros. Records, was also involuntarily put in the middle of this *Screamers* issue, as was the aforementioned Craig Kallman. And though I loved Warner, I made it clear to Tom in the same way I had to Craig that this was a very real issue that caused me serious discomfort: Genocide denial cannot simply be shrugged off.

When I got on the phone with Lyor, I explained all this, recounting both my family's history and my conversation with Ahmet. As an Israeli Jew, I told him, surely he could understand the importance of acknowledging genocide. Lyor took it all in, and to his credit, he did understand.

"I made that decision, and I'm sorry," he acknowledged. "I'm happy to purchase the film."

"Look, I'm not actually on the phone trying to sell you the film, as it looks like Sony is gonna pick it up," I said. "I just want to let you know why this was an issue for me."

Carla ended up going with Columbia, a division of Sony, to distribute *Screamers*. It was always her film, not mine. But the band's success had put me in a position where I had some leverage with decision-makers, so if I wasn't going to use that leverage to question the decisions they were making, what was it all for?

About six months after *Screamers* was released, I was in New Zealand, on the treadmill one afternoon in an empty gym, half-watching CNN as I jogged, when I suddenly recognized a face on the screen. It was Hrant Dink, a Turkish-Armenian journalist and activist who had been prominently featured in *Screamers*. Hrant lived and worked in Turkey, where he eloquently and courageously advocated not only for Genocide recognition by the Turkish government but also for reconciliation between Turks and Armenians, who had lived side by side for hundreds of years. He'd just been assassinated in front of his newspaper's offices in Istanbul.

I stepped off the treadmill in complete shock. I'd met Hrant at the *Screamers* premiere and we'd really connected. He'd been arrested multiple times for speaking out about the Genocide, and had faced threats before, but he was soft-spoken and gracious, less a bomb-throwing revolutionary than a diplomatic man of principle. I considered him a friend. And now, he was dead.

The killer was a seventeen-year-old Turkish nationalist who, after shooting Hrant three times at point-blank range, smiled for photos with Turkish police officers who were supposed to be arresting him. As I stood there in that empty gym, looking at the TV and then staring out the large glass window with tears running down my face, I felt scared and angry, almost like I needed to take cover. I thought back to the threats I'd personally received when I was out on tour. Maybe I wasn't being alarmist after all. It felt like they were coming for all of us. I mean, *what won't they do to shut us up?*

———

While I was excited to have Carla along documenting parts of our tour, being back out on the road after a couple of years of only sporadic shows quickly reminded me why I didn't like the touring life. We did almost one hundred shows in 2005, with long treks through Europe, North America, and Australia and New Zealand—and it was exhausting.

For one stretch of our US tour, I'm pretty sure our bus driver was on crack. He'd regularly wake us up yelling to himself while he was driving, shouting things like "I'm gonna get you! I'm coming for you!" At one point, the bus slid into a ditch on a snowy road. At another, it broke down completely, and he just went outside and started kicking it.

Trucker crack is apparently a hell of a drug.

As challenging as it could be, touring life was never all bad. John and I would always go out to restaurants together on the road. Shavo would join us sometimes, though ordering food with Shavo required a level of patience only practiced in high-level yoga. Onstage, Daron would always crack us all up with funny voices and other antics. When he first sang a romantic version of our song "Cigaro," he tweaked the lyrics and sang, "My cock is much bigger than yours / Can't you see that I love my cock? / Can't you see how stupid this song is?" When Shavo and I heard that onstage, we were both practically on the floor, laughing. At our best moments, System gigs would be half performance, half inside-jokes.

Some of the shows on those tours were genuinely great, but no matter how good they could be, for me, the highs of being onstage and performing didn't seem to balance out all the lows it took to get there. At a big festival in Spain, high winds blew the roof off the outdoor stage and forced the promoters to postpone our set. They wanted to cancel but apparently some of the thirty thousand people in attendance had already started setting shit on fire and destroying stuff at the news of the mere delay in the show. The promoters were afraid of what they might do if the concert was canceled outright, so we waited backstage for hours, hoping the wind would subside enough that we could play. It never really did, but after the backstage area ran out of food and water, we finally took the stage around 3:45 a.m. The wind was still whipping around, and I was getting mouthfuls of sand and debris as I tried to sing. It felt practically apocalyptic. When we finally finished our set around 5 a.m., the Prodigy, who'd had a massive hit several years earlier with the frenetic and (hopefully) tongue-in-cheek electronic music blitzkrieg "Smack My Bitch Up," still had to play after us! I remember walking off the stage and seeing poor Keith Flint, the group's normally manic, orange-haired frontman, walking toward the stage with a dead-eyed look on his face.

I nodded and just shrugged, "Sorry, bro." He shook his head and kept walking.

In some ways, although nights like that weren't particularly enjoyable while they were happening, they did at least serve to break up the monotonous blur of touring. The rest of the guys seemed to cope better with life on the road than I did. I think Daron, Shavo, and John had all dreamed of living this life. They'd grown up desperate to be rock stars, and now they were doing it. I never was interested in that part of it. I wanted to be an artist. I'm not saying that the rest of the guys didn't care about music or art—they did—but they understood everything that came with being successful and were fully onboard for it. For me, System was becoming a day job so that I could continue to be an artist.

When the tour finally ended in October, I was relieved. By then, I'd started dating Angela, who I'd met the night before our "Souls" show in 2004. I'd finally gotten her number from a mutual friend and called her, and everything in that relationship was still bright, sparkling, and new. The two of us had even planned to take a trip to Armenia, so I could meet her father and grandparents. They were from Vanadzor, a city about two hours north of the capital, nestled in the mountains. Angela's father was a giant man with a portly laugh who was a connoisseur of all good things in the area. Her grandfather was the real family patron, an engineer by trade who had run the largest construction company in Armenia for years. Her paternal grandmother was an English teacher, which explained why Ange's English was fluent from day one despite her not having lived in the US for very long.

Unlike during my first trip to Armenia five years earlier, now, people on the street often recognized me. I had really long, curly hair then, which was unusual for men in the country at the time. When I was recognized, I'd get approached by well-wishers and autograph-seekers, and when I wasn't, I'd get approached by people who were laughing at my long hair and making fun of me. Either way, I thought, it was good to see people smile in a country that had dealt with so much hardship over the last decade.

While we were in Armenia, I met with Vartan Oskanian, who was the foreign minister at the time. A friend of mine worked for him and had arranged the meeting. It was enlightening. We spoke a lot about Armenia's challenges at that moment in time. There was an influx of money, people, and energy in the capital, Yerevan, but that same vibrancy wasn't being felt in the countryside. Villages and towns were experiencing serious depopulation due to lack of investment in infrastructure and employment.

The early years of Armenian independence after the collapse of the Soviet Union had been difficult. The 1988 Spitak earthquake, the First Nagorno-Karabakh War, and the complete devaluation of the ruble had plunged newly independent Armenia into the cold of winter. The infrastructure erected by more recent Soviet regimes crumbled quickly because of the hierarchical corruption embedded in the late-era Soviet system. Contractors took payoffs to look the other way when the well-connected stole cement and other building materials. Doctors had often obtained their medical licenses with well-placed bribes, and as a result, the whole health care system was in shambles. You never knew if the doctor you were going to had actually gone to medical school or just paid for a certificate to hang on his wall. Ditto for educators, engineers, and those in many other sectors of professional society. All post-Soviet states were mired in this same cacophony of corruption. Modernization was slow in many regions of Armenia. Ange told me about how growing up, she'd go to school in the winter in full snow gear because the only heat came from wood-burning stoves, for which students would have to chop wood. Electricity was intermittent at best, and she was often reading by candlelight in the evenings.

I'd long felt a deep, spiritual connection to Armenia and its history through my family, but this trip felt like the beginning of building a relationship with the country as a contemporary entity. The longer I was there, the less I felt like a tourist, and the more I felt a part of it.

———

A few months earlier, back during the North American leg of the *Mezmerize* tour, we played two shows back-to-back in Quebec City. I managed to find enough time during those two days to go on a short hike. While on the hike, I got an email from our management that mentioned the possibility of the band playing some shows in 2006. Eager to stay focused on the nature around me, I responded with something along the lines of "Sounds good. We'll talk about it later." I'd already told Beno and the whole band that after the current touring wrapped up, I'd be taking time away from the band, so I'm not sure why I wasn't more declarative about it in response to this particular message. Frankly, I just didn't think that much about it. I figured that management was presenting options for us to consider for the following year, and I didn't much want to think about it right then while I was hiking.

When I was finally back home in Los Angeles, after the Armenia trip, the issue was raised again, and this time, I was more definitive.

240

I *needed* time away and had no interest in touring next year. The rest of the band didn't take this very well. Touring for us was undoubtedly lucrative, but my time and peace of mind were worth more to me than any paycheck.

It's not like Daron, Shavo, and John didn't have a reasonable argument. We hadn't done a tour to support the release of *Hypnotize*, so wouldn't it make sense, business-wise, to do a run of Ozzfest dates, at least? The thing is, I wasn't arguing about whether or not it made business sense. I, personally, was *so over it*. I was completely burned out on the band and on touring. I'd only survived the eighty-plus shows we did that year because I knew that there was a light at the end of the tunnel. I'd already told the band about my plans for a hiatus when we'd first started working on *Mezmerize* and *Hypnotize* two years earlier, so it's not as if I was dropping this on them out of left field.

This argument was simmering within the band as we rehearsed for a couple of one-off shows we'd agreed to do at the end of 2005: one for MTV in New York, and the other, KROQ's Acoustic Christmas concert in LA. On a break from what were definitely tense rehearsal sessions, Daron was riding in the passenger seat of my car as I drove, when he revealed that Shavo was thinking about suing me if I didn't agree to do Ozzfest the next summer.

I was so stunned that I almost had to pull the car over.

As Daron explained it, Shavo's view was that when I responded to management's initial inquiry about next year's shows, "Sounds good. Let's talk about it later," that was a binding contract. Daron didn't come out and *say* that he was going to join this lawsuit, but he also didn't say he *wasn't* going to, instead muttering something along the lines of "We'll do what we've got to do." (John, for his part, made it clear he'd never sue me.)

I felt completely violated. For whatever creative friction and personality conflicts existed within the band, I still considered all the guys to be more than just my friends, something closer to family. We'd been through so much together and created something incredibly special, which had transformed all our lives. This felt like the sacred trust we'd built was being destroyed in the worst way. They all knew how scarred I'd been by the lawsuit that financially wrecked my family. To now be potentially facing the same thing from people I'd thought of as brothers was like being stabbed in the back. It was traumatic. I honestly would rather Shavo have punched me in the face. And to think it was done for a paycheck was even worse.

In retrospect, I probably shouldn't have ever taken the lawsuit that seriously, but having seen what kind of damage can be done by one, I hired lawyers to help evaluate whether this threat was real. I spent several thousand dollars on legal fees and was advised to find an amicable solution. In the end, I signed an agreement promising to do the Ozzfest dates in return for collective liability dissolution, a.k.a. nobody suing me. It was both ridiculous and tragic. It felt like something in the band broke that day, perhaps irretrievably.

Meanwhile, we still had to play that KROQ Acoustic Christmas show. It was probably the least enjoyable gig of my life. I broke down crying before we even went on, and then trashed my keyboard onstage out of sheer rage. My passion had become my career and now I felt like my career was choking the life out of me.

By the time we went out on Ozzfest the following summer, I was more in control of my emotions but no happier to be there. I tried to put on good shows each night—after all, why should fans who shelled out their hard-earned money get shafted just because we couldn't get along?—but spent a lot of my downtime on my own bus, writing and recording material for *Elect the Dead*, my first solo album.

In many ways, the shows themselves were fine. The crowds were great, the band was as popular as it had ever been, and we'd been playing together for so long that we were a well-oiled machine. But emotionally, I was totally checked out. A lot of people got in my ear then or shortly thereafter and asked me why I'd leave a band at the absolute height of its popularity. While it may not have been the shrewdest business decision, that was never my motivation for playing in this band. I could see that my path was diverging from the band's, and I simply had to follow it wherever it was going to take me. The decision was financially suspect but spiritually sound. In many ways, it was no different than ditching Ultimate Solutions when it was highly profitable but otherwise not very enriching for me.

We played our last show of that Ozzfest tour at an amphitheater in West Palm Beach, and I tried to appreciate the moment for what it was, knowing that it represented the end of an era for me. The closing of a door. I hadn't said I was quitting the band forever, but when we said our goodbyes after the show, I knew things would never be the same for the band ever again.

And they weren't.

CHAPTER 14

When I started playing my Casio keyboard in college to take my mind off the mess my world had become, I couldn't have imagined a series of events that would follow which would have led to me one day sitting in my home studio, playing my music for an Oscar-winning director. But there I was, in late 2005, hanging out with William Friedkin, who'd directed *The French Connection* and *The Exorcist*, among many other films, letting him listen to clips of unreleased music I'd recorded.

There was a lot of it. I'd been writing music pretty much every day for a number of years. I was building this vast library of songs and musical pieces, but with System Of A Down, we were only going to put out fifteen or twenty songs, tops, every few years. Much of this music would've never fit into System anyway—it was closer in spirit to goth, jazz, or classical music—and even the stuff that could've fit hardly ever did. I was experimenting with samples, prepared piano, ethnic instruments, strings, and programming beats. System songs almost always started with guitars, but so much of the music I was making was more piano-based. I had tracks upon tracks of music that I'd never done anything with. I wanted a way to get some of it out into the world and had long been interested in composing music for films. A friend, Jay Faires, who ran the music division at Lionsgate, suggested that I meet with Friedkin. He was directing a psychological thriller for them called *Bug*. They already had someone who'd composed the score, but they were looking for some additional music.

Bill—as Friedkin insisted I call him—was actually a big fan of System. He was enthusiastic about what he heard in the studio that day, and for the movie, I ended up doing what were essentially a few character themes—music that would set the vibe when a certain character came on screen. It was my first foray into making music for films and TV, and I was hooked. Friedkin was great to work with and a very generous guy. When System won a Grammy in 2006, he sent me a beautiful bouquet of flowers.

There is something about the process of scoring that really appeals to me. A lot of the work is really in the conversations you have with the director before you even play a note. What's the tone they're aiming for? What sort of emotional palette do they envision? Which instruments do they hear? Once you figure out the vibe, the actual music falls into place pretty easily. It's a different sort of creative puzzle to solve than writing songs for a band. I guess some artists might find all the parameters limiting, but I find them liberating.

The world of film music is almost completely separate from the one I'd been working in with System. The fact that I'd fronted a multi-platinum rock band for a decade carried very little cachet with music supervisors and directors. No one really cared that I'd commanded the attention of fifty thousand people at the Reading Festival or that I'd had hits on MTV. Maybe it would get me a meeting with a music supervisor, but it wouldn't get me work. I had to prove my worth all over again—and I loved that. It was a new challenge.

Not too long after working on *Bug*, I was in one of those meetings at my studio with a major music supervisor named G. Marq Roswell, playing him music, talking about my enthusiasm for scoring, when he interrupted me.

"Wait, I'm a little confused," he confessed.

"Why are you confused?"

"Well, if you're interested in this kind of work, why did you say no to *The Passion of the Christ*?" The controversial Mel Gibson–directed film had come out two years earlier and was nominated for an Oscar for Best Original Score. I think Marq could tell by the look on my face that now *I* was the one who was confused. "I was helping put that together and wanted you to do some music for it," he continued. "The answer I got back was that you weren't interested."

"Huh?" I stammered. "I said what?"

"I was told that you passed on it," he said.

"This is the first I've heard of it," I told him. "Who did you talk to?"

"Your agent," he replied.

After Marq left, I tried to trace what had happened. I called my film agent at CAA, and he knew nothing about it. Then I tried my booking agent at William Morris, a guy named Don Muller.

"Don, I was just meeting with Marq Roswell about some film music," I said. "Did you tell him I couldn't do *Passion of the Christ*?"

The phone line got quiet.

"Yeah," he admitted, barely above a whisper.

"*Why?*" I asked. "Why on earth would you tell him that?"

Again, silence. Then he just spoke a single word: "Beno."

I hung up with Don and called my manager, David "Beno" Benveniste. I recounted the saga to him and then simply asked, "What happened?"

"I don't remember," he said.

"You don't remember?"

"I don't remember any conversations about that," he said, pointing out that it was a few years ago. He has lots of conversations about the band, and people ask us to do things all the time, but this one didn't ring a bell. To this day, he insists that he has no memory of ever being asked about me contributing music for *The Passion of the Christ* or of turning it down.

I want to give Beno the benefit of the doubt. He's a good manager who did a lot of things right to help a not obviously commercial band achieve great commercial success. But it seemed to me that there were some conflicts of interest with him managing me as a solo artist. In the case of this *Passion of the Christ* opportunity, if I had worked on it back around 2003 or 2004, that might've further distanced me from System at a time when I was already floating out of the band's orbit. With System being the big cash cow, my thought at the time was that Beno had a vested financial interest in maintaining the status quo. I'm not saying he did that, or that his dropping the ball on this opportunity was somehow intentional, but it was hard to avoid wondering about it.

That, in itself, was a problem.

With this in mind, I decided I needed a new team to work with. I already had a new record label, Warner Bros., and now, I got a new management team—Coldplay's manager Dave Holmes, along with my friend George Tonikian to handle the day-to-day stuff—and a new lawyer, too. It felt like the clean slate I needed in order to start marching forward confidently as a solo artist.

———

If the latter days of System felt increasingly like a creative prison for me, making *Elect the Dead* was like finally being set free. I had all these songs—ones I'd originally written with the hopes the band would record them, ones I'd written on my tour bus during that final Ozzfest run, ones I was continuing to write each day—and now the only arbiter of whether they were worth recording was me.

In 2006, I started working in my home studio, building tracks in exactly the opposite way we used to do it in the band. This wasn't out of some stubborn determination to turn my artistic life on its head; it was out of pure necessity. I didn't have a band yet, so the usual method of laying down the drum tracks and then building the song around them wasn't going to work. Instead, I started with the acoustic guitar or piano and worked from there. I don't think I wrote a single song on electric guitar, which served to make the songs more melodic and harmonic. Once I had the acoustic guitar or piano down, I'd lay down rough vocals, so I'd know my melodies. Then I'd program drums to discover my rhythm. Usually, it was only at that point that I'd start to add electric guitar, bass, keys, strings, and anything else. With a song like "Praise the Lord and Pass the Ammunition," I used loops and samples to build the structural skeleton, and then added various instruments. My motto throughout was: "No limits. No rules."

Working mostly alone suited me. I had such a clear vision of what I wanted to accomplish that hiring other people would've likely just gotten in the way. Eventually, I did bring in Dan Monti, who I'd met on those Buckethead sessions, to play additional guitar and bass and help with the engineering. I asked Bryan "Brain" Mantia to play most of the live drums, except on a couple of hard-hitting punk-rock tracks for which I enlisted John. To his credit, despite what was happening with System, John was an enthusiastic participant and even tried to refuse payment for his work on the sessions.

As versions of the songs started to come together, I invited a few other friends in to give me feedback. My friend Jay brought his eleven-year-old nephew along to listen. Just observing this kid gave me the most honest, unfiltered sense of which songs were working best. Whereas adults will couch their reactions with diplomacy, kids don't have that sort of discretion. The songs he liked, he'd start banging his head to and jumping around. The ones that didn't move him, literally didn't move him.

The album is a pretty good indication of where my head was at back then. The first single, "Empty Walls," is about the lack of empathy people seem to have for victims of humanitarian catastrophes. "The Unthinking Majority" is a loud, angry thrash-metal song that takes aim at dictators.

I'd been reading a lot about indigenous cultures, and the way they saw themselves as existing in harmony with nature rather than trying to triumph over it. That was heavily impacting my own spiritual outlook and finding its way into songs like "Honking Antelope," "Feed Us," and "Sky Is Over" that were concerned with the environment and overpopulation. I wrote "Saving Us" on acoustic

guitar while sitting with Ange, and it's basically about the tumultuous first few years of our relationship. "Money" exorcises some of my
issues with System, and despite lyrics like "Self-absorbed delusion /
Inclusion of dysfunction," and "The causes of my servitude can be
traced to the tyranny of a down," no one—including Daron, Shavo,
and John—ever seemed to pick up on it, or if they did, they never
mentioned it.

"Baby" literally came to me in a dream. I can recall watching
a hand play the chords on acoustic guitar—I think it was actually
Daron's hand—and a voice singing the words. I woke up and immediately picked up my cell phone and recorded it. That's the only time
that's ever happened to me, but it felt like proof of that idea that we
don't really create music, we just receive it from the ether of humanity's shared history.

One of my favorite songs on the album is "Beethoven's Cunt." It's
an interesting progressive rock tune but part of the reason I love it so
much is that I was able to smuggle the word "cunt" into its title. It's a
harsh word and a real taboo in the US, but I always hated the idea of
certain words being somehow out of bounds. By 2007, I was spending a lot of time in New Zealand. After falling in love with the place
on my first visit, I was trying to establish residency, which required
spending at least three months there, uninterrupted, for a couple
of years. In Australia and New Zealand, the word "cunt" carries a
much different connotation than it does in the US, and, in fact, is
more often positive. A "top cunt" is a good friend, a "sick cunt" is an
icon, and to call a group of people "cunts" is a term of affection.

When it came time to put together a touring band, I called
them the F.C.C. The name was, of course, a play on the Federal

Communications Commission, which regulates the public airwaves in the US, but the acronym of our F.C.C. actually stands for the Flying Cunts of Chaos. In 2011, we were performing on *The Tonight Show with Jay Leno* on a night when one of his other guests was Robin Williams. I met Robin backstage; he was pretty subdued—particularly in comparison to his frenetic stage presence—until I told him the name of my band. Once I did, it was as if I freed the genie out of the bottle. He went running down the hallway of the studio, shouting, "Jay! Jay! The Flying Cunts of Chaos are here!" I considered that as much of a ringing endorsement for the name as there could possibly be.

Elect the Dead is a rock album, and of all the music I've made as a solo artist, it's likely the closest to what we did in System, which I suppose makes sense, since I was only a year or so removed from being in the band when I made it. The album did well. It sold over a million copies, "Empty Walls" was played a lot on the radio, and when we went on tour—first playing theaters, and then opening for Foo Fighters on an arena tour—the response was amazing.

Touring as a solo artist was different than touring with the band. It was my name on the marquee, so whatever pressure existed was squarely on me, but I got to make all the decisions, too. It was wonderful. Oddly enough, life on tour also felt more social as a solo artist than it had in recent years with System. We were all on one bus—as opposed to multiple buses or flying between dates with System—and that sense that we were out there together working hard to try to win people over fostered a camaraderie I hadn't felt in years.

None of this changed the fact that I couldn't sleep on a tour bus or that every day on tour felt like a barely altered version of the day before it, but it did make it all more bearable and occasionally quite enjoyable. Still, when I was offered the support slot on a Metallica tour in 2008, I turned it down even though it was a great opportunity. I was completely fried from touring and ready to be done with it.

The success of *Elect the Dead* also hit me differently than any of our highs in System. Although I'd long maintained that I didn't really care that much about selling CDs or concert tickets or getting my songs on the radio, that is quite obviously an easier stance to take when you have, in fact, already sold lots of CDs and concert tickets and had your songs on the radio. After all the years of having Daron and the guys treat my musical songwriting dismissively in System, I think it helped to have some outside validation. It filled me with confidence not only in my musical abilities but also in my own power of artistic discernment.

I had something to prove—not to anyone else, but to myself: I could do it without the band. And by "it," I don't simply mean commercial success. I mean making a good album, putting together a band that gets along, mounting a tour I actually enjoyed, and coming away from all that more energized to make music than I'd been when I started. The experience changed the way I thought about System, but it also changed the way I thought about the kind of music I wanted to make going forward. The reaction to music, or any kind of art, might be interesting, it might make you feel good, but it should never be the only reason you make it.

A year or so after we finished the *Elect the Dead* tour, I was offered a chance to perform the album live with the Auckland Philharmonia

Orchestra in New Zealand. I'd written some rudimentary string and brass sections for System songs in the past, but I'd never taken on a project like this. I was immediately fired up at the challenge. I wrote some basic parts, and then was introduced to an amazing Greek-Kiwi composer named John Psathas who helped me flesh out the arrangements. I would take the stems of the songs from *Elect the Dead* and then strip them down to just acoustic guitar and vocals, or piano and vocals. Then, I'd add strings and brass lines. Basically, I was losing the band, and building an orchestra. But I didn't have the experience at that point to go much beyond rudimentary orchestration so that's where Psathas came in to build the arrangements into something bigger and fuller. I wanted to record the show with an eye on maybe releasing it, but it was going to be a costly endeavor, something on the order of $60,000. I pitched Warners on it but was fully prepared to pay for it out of my own pocket if they balked. They didn't.

The day of the show was a little nerve-wracking. There was an issue with the sound truck, and although the show itself went great, the recording quality was subpar. I sent the tracks to a bunch of world-class mixers to try to fix it, and although they improved the audio a bit, it was still not great. Finally, I sent it to Tom Holkenborg, the Dutch DJ/producer/composer who records under the name Junkie XL. He stripped the whole thing apart then put it back together and magically fixed the problem. I am forever in his debt for that. It's his mix you hear on the *Elect the Dead Symphony* album and the DVD that came out in 2009.

Having sung in front of smaller bands for so many years, the feeling of being onstage surrounded by the power and grace of an entire symphony orchestra is invigorating. I was anxious to repeat it, and in 2010, and again, later in 2013, I organized short tours, mostly through Europe and Russia, playing with a local orchestra in each country. I could really see the musical and temperamental differences between countries manifest themselves. We'd typically show up in town a couple of days before the performance and would only have a few rehearsals with the orchestra. The ensembles in Eastern Europe—places like Germany, Austria, Poland, and Russia—were on-point and disciplined. You gave them charts; they could play them flawlessly. In Saint Petersburg, the orchestra was tight, talented, and meticulous. When the conductor put down his baton, everyone followed his lead and stopped playing on a dime. That was a great performance. In Italy, they had great, emotive soloists, but as a group, they couldn't always hold it together.

The worst show of that run was in Atlanta. The venue was beautiful, a tiered outdoor amphitheater built into a hill, and the orchestra itself was reasonably capable, although the players themselves were mostly on the older side and didn't have much of a feel for the songs. It didn't help that we'd flown in directly from Rome and had no chance to rehearse.

Even with all those things working against us, the show might've been salvageable if not for the one element you can never totally control: the audience. The venue was filled with people who were diehard fans of both System and my solo album, but I'm pretty sure none of them had ever been in the presence of a violin or a cello. So, while a coterie of aging, formally clad classical musicians were struggling to follow along with the arrangements, long-haired yahoos in black concert t-shirts pressed themselves forward toward the front row, double-fisting beers, pounding on the stage, and shouting for us to play "Sugar" and "Chop Suey!" It was like one group came thinking they'd be playing Wagner to retirees, and the other came expecting the mosh pit at Ozzfest. After the show, my piano player came off, shaking his head in disbelief, muttering "They're just uncivilized!"

Nonetheless, I was hooked on the thrill of playing with orchestras. I always knew my second solo album was going to be more of an artistic leap—in fact, I'd structured my deal with Warner Bros. in a way to accommodate for that—but now I knew exactly what I wanted to do. When I started writing songs for what would become *Imperfect Harmonies*, my overarching idea was that I wanted to write for the orchestra like it was an electric guitar. The goal was to create a sound I'd never really heard before, an orchestral-electro-rock fusion. It was a big endeavor.

I played the songs for an A&R rep at Warners, and he suggested that I meet with David Foster, who was then an in-house producer at the label. Foster is an accomplished songwriter, producer, and musician, and is kind of *the* guy when it comes to orchestral pop. He's been around forever, has worked with everyone—Barbra Streisand, Josh Groban, Celine Dion, Dionne Warwick, Andrea Bocelli, Michael Jackson, Paul McCartney, Aretha Franklin—and has more than a dozen Grammys. The thought was that maybe Foster could produce the album or at least work on it in some capacity.

David rolled up to my house one day in a big, black Mercedes AMG, and got out of the car, wearing this giant, red Ferrari t-shirt. We sat down on my couch, and I made him some coffee. We started chatting and he was clearly an incredibly nice guy. I asked him what it had been like to work with Bocelli.

"You like Bocelli?" he asked me.

"I love his arias," I said. "I'm not really into his gooey pop shit." As that second sentence was literally coming out of my mouth, I was looking into David's eyes and realized, *Oh, right, this guy I'm sitting on the couch with wrote those pop songs.* To his credit, David didn't even flinch, and just kept the conversation moving, totally unfazed.

We listened to my songs, and he had some nice feedback. He was constantly surprised by the odd chords I used, which I told him was largely a function of the fact that I had no formal musical education and didn't know the way I was supposed to do it.

When we finished listening, he turned to me and said, "You're really talented and I'd like to work with you but I'm pretty busy for a while." He paused and seemed to be doing some calculations in his head. "Why don't you call me in 2014 and maybe we can work together then?" At the time, it was 2010. Maybe that was his way of getting back at me for the Bocelli crack, maybe that was his way of blowing me off, or maybe he just really was that busy. I thanked him for his time, and he left.

I ended up producing the album myself. When I turned the record in to the label, I was immediately told, "You realize there's no single here, right?" And I did realize that. They warned me that the album wouldn't be on the radio, and definitely wouldn't sell like *Elect the Dead* did. I was okay with all of that. It was the music that had come to me at that time, so regardless of commercial factors, it was the music I was excited about releasing then.

Much as everyone predicted, the album didn't sell like *Elect the Dead*, and it didn't really get any radio play. I did a European tour supporting the album, but the North American dates ended up getting cut. Despite all that, I was just as happy with *Imperfect Harmonies* as I'd been with *Elect the Dead*. In fact, I might've been even happier. I'd just wanted to make the thing I wanted to make exactly how I wanted to make it and let the chips fall where they may. I wanted to make art without worrying about commerce. Now, I finally felt like I had.

—————

The European tour for *Imperfect Harmonies* wasn't entirely European. We played one show in Yerevan, too. It was the first time I'd ever played in Armenia, so it was a big deal, both for me and, thankfully, for a lot of Armenians. The show was broadcast live on Armenian national television.

I'd been trying to figure out a way to play in Armenia for years, but the infrastructure for concerts and touring there was simply nonexistent. It was only slightly more existent when I arrived in 2010. We played in this theater where there was this gigantic sculpture of Lenin's head—like, twenty feet high—which had been taken off a statue and was sitting there in the back of this theater. It was totally surreal.

The F.C.C. all wore what was essentially a uniform onstage: sharp black outfits with matching top hats. Just before the band was about to walk onstage, the venue's security stopped them because they didn't have the correct passes. Our drummer, Troy Ziegler, who is a 6'3" Black guy—and who I'm willing to bet was, at that very moment, probably the only 6'3" Black guy dressed in a uniform and wearing a top hat in all of Armenia—politely tried to explain to the security that they were the band, hence the outfits. But this security guard—actually an army soldier as there were no private security firms in Armenia at the time—just wasn't having it. The incredulous look on Troy's face was priceless.

Finally, we got onstage, but we weren't quite out of the woods yet. One of the guys on the crew was an alcoholic, and he did not have his shit together that night, not only with regards to his drinking but just his general abilities to do his job. The first ten minutes of that show, I had the mic in my hand, and I was singing into it, but no sound was coming out of the speakers. Whenever I'd look back at him to try to get his attention, he was ducked down behind the console, either hiding or maybe taking swigs off his canteen.

Luckily, the sound was eventually sorted out, and the rest of the show went off without any issues. Midway through, we played a mournful ballad from *Imperfect Harmonies* called "Yes, It's Genocide." The lyrics are entirely in Armenian, and while I don't think you need to speak the language to understand what the song is saying, it occurred to me that that audience was probably the only audience I'd ever played to that had ever fully grasped what it meant.

For an encore that night, I came out and performed an Armenian folk song called "Bari Arakeel" on acoustic guitar. It was a song that I used to sing with my father back in Beirut when I was a kid, and it got as big a reaction as anything I played that night. As the audience sang along, I realized that there was something in that theater, in that country, that I couldn't replicate anywhere else in the world. I was being fully seen for who I was, for who my ancestors were, for where I came from, for what I cared about. It was a feeling that was certainly worth enduring alcoholic crew members and overeager security guards to experience, and one that, as soon as the show ended and we flew on to the next destination, I was immediately eager to feel again.

CHAPTER 15

When you've had a certain amount of success fronting a popular rock band, you get offered lots of opportunities to do things that are probably a bad idea—act in a movie, be on a reality TV show, run for political office. When I got a call from the playwright Steven Sater around 2008, I assumed this was going to be one of those ideas. He'd just won two Tony Awards for *Spring Awakening* and was now looking to make a modern musical adaptation of Aeschylus's ancient tragedy *Prometheus Bound.* All that sounded fascinating but not exactly my cup of tea.

When we first met up at a vegetarian restaurant in Santa Monica, Steven—a slight, curly-haired figure with piercing green eyes—told me he was a fan, and then laid out his vision for what he was hoping to do: a rock musical of the mythical tale of Prometheus as the original prisoner of conscience. In the Greek myth, Prometheus steals fire from the gods to give it to mankind. Zeus punishes him by chaining him to a rock where an eagle eats his liver every day, only for it to be regenerated each night so the torture can begin anew. In Sater's reading of it, Prometheus was the ultimate humanist; the fire he stole represented technology, art, and civilization itself. Zeus's brutal reaction made him a stand-in for any ruthless dictator or unrestrained tyrant. I told him right away that his idea was intriguing, but there was one looming issue.

"The thing is," I said, "I don't really like musicals. In fact, I kind of hate them. I know that's what you do, but there's something about most musicals that feels really false and cheesy to me."

He wasn't flummoxed. "Well, what do you find cheesy?"

We talked a bit about different musicals, and it came down to the fact that the music itself rarely felt authentic. It always felt a little too bright, a little too, well, theatrical.

"Well, that's *your* problem," he told me. "*You're* going to be the one composing all the music. I'm just writing the words. If you don't want the music to be cheesy, don't make it cheesy. You can do whatever you want."

Whatever I want? Could I really say no to that? I was also worried that I didn't really know shit about musical theater. It wasn't my field of expertise. But should I walk away from an opportunity that married so many things I cared about—art, music, human rights—just because I might fail at it? I began thinking about all the music I'd been writing recently and immediately saw that this could be another way to get it out in the world. If it turned out to be nothing more than that, hell, that was enough.

"Okay," I agreed. "I'll do it."

In the end, it was so much more than that. I look at the work I did on *Prometheus Bound* as one of the most satisfying musical adventures of my life. Across nearly four years, I worked with musicians, actors, choreographers, directors, arrangers, and crew, and learned so much.

As a composer, I had six musicians, a conductor/musical director, and eight or so actor/singers all with their own unique talents and ranges. I had to adapt my compositions to their strengths, and work with them on the fly to adjust the music based on the changes in the script and the instructions of our director, Diane Paulus. Through an amazing vocalist named AnnMarie Milazzo, who typically worked on musicals, I learned how to apply my harmonic knowledge to something more than a two- or three-part harmony, establishing unique rhythms inspired by many different musical genres.

The challenges were unlike any I'd faced before. I remember being in rehearsals at the Oberon Theater in Boston, and the scene we were working on needed to be extended, so our director Diane just turned to me and said, "We need more music. Can you add something here and end with that same little piece we had before?"

It took me a second to realize that she meant she needed me to write more music on the spot. Like, *right now.* They were going to run the scene again in two minutes. In less time than it normally takes for a band to tune up their instruments, I had to compose new music and teach it to the musicians, despite the fact I don't read music and certainly can't notate it. Fortunately, the musicians were total pros and could decipher what I was trying to tell them. Once they did, the scene worked better, the director was happy, and we moved on. Shit like that happened all the time. It made me work faster on my feet and trust my intuition.

The tone of the entire production was so different from what I was used to. Instead of all the macho rock 'n' roll posturing, the theater world is essentially dominated by a more LGBTQ+ vibe and more feminine energy. It was such an interesting change. When the show opened, we partnered with Amnesty International and emphasized the political aspects of the story. We drew attention to the cases of eight specific prisoners of conscience—several, including Dhondup Wangchen, a Tibetan filmmaker; Nasrin Sotoudeh, an Iranian human rights lawyer; and Đoàn Văn Diên, a Vietnamese labor leader, are still in prison today—and created ways for the audience members to highlight their cases during the actual show, folding them into the performance. It was a wildly innovative way to marry art and activism.

The company's actors—which included Uzo Aduba and Lea DeLaria, who'd both later star in *Orange Is the New Black*—were incredible, and the whole production was breathtaking. It was performed not just in the round, but with the actors and the band mixed among the audience members, many of whom were standing like they would in the pit in front of the stage at a concert. Diane's vision was very punk rock: she wanted to break down the barriers between the audience and the performers, and have the show engulf them. If you bought a ticket, you were literally in it. The show was happening all around you.

Unfortunately, *Prometheus Bound* never got to go to Broadway, but the process itself was genuinely inspiring. I'm not sure I've ever worked so hard to make so little money in my life, but it was worth every ounce of sweat. It was as if the goal wasn't just to tell a story, or even to simply have that story resonate out into the world, but to remake people's entire conception of this kind of storytelling and what it could achieve. That striving, that risk-taking, was what I wanted to focus on in my own art.

—

One Sunday afternoon, sometime in 2008, I was sitting at the kitchen table at my parents' house, finishing up lunch. When I'm in LA, I try to eat lunch with my parents every Sunday. My mom will often make cheese *boreg* with tabbouleh or some other Mediterranean dish, or we'll order kebab with hummus and salad, and talk about our week. After we'd cleared the plates, my mom was buzzing around the kitchen when she offered a casual suggestion, seemingly out of nowhere.

"You should make an album with your father," she mused.

My mother raised this idea without much forethought, in the same way she might tell me to go to the drugstore with him or show him how to use his phone. But as soon as she said it, I couldn't believe I hadn't already proposed it. I thought about my father as a teenager on that bus on the way to take a class from a master oud teacher, getting off to reroute his life into another direction. Then I thought about the way my journey had followed the opposite path, skidding my Jeep on a winding road, abandoning a plan for law school to pursue music. My dad had given up on his own musical ambitions to take care of his mother, then my mother, and then later, me and my brother. When I decided to focus my life on music, he'd encouraged me even though the family was in difficult financial straits. He even offered to get another job, so I wouldn't have to make the sacrifices he'd made. Now that I was in a position to do what I wanted musically, helping my dad rekindle his own dream felt like the karmic payback he deserved.

We made an album of Armenian folk songs called *Inchbes Moranank*—which means "How can we forget?" in Armenian—that we released on Serjical Strike in late 2009. The album included a recording of "Bari Arakeel," which he and I sing together on the record, much as we had when I was a kid. I approached some Armenian songwriters to compose new material, including an homage to my friend Hrant Dink, the Turkish-Armenian journalist and activist who'd been assassinated by a Turkish extremist with complicity from the state. To hear my father sing that song and add to the canon of Armenian revolutionary music that first got me excited about music and activism—it was as if everything was coming full circle.

The best part of all was that this album gave my father a platform to perform again. He began playing mostly at Armenian functions and festivals, but when we went back to Beirut in 2011, he was one of the support acts for my concert at that outdoor amphitheater, Zouk Mikael. He'd never performed at a major show like that, and I can remember how nervous he was before he went on. But for him to be able to go back to the country where he'd lived for so many years, the country where he'd had to abandon his musical aspirations, and to be able to play at that beautiful venue in front of all those people, was, I hope, a full-circle moment for him, too.

This period of my creative life really liberated me artistically. It felt so good to be completely free to pursue whatever projects fired me up. I made a jazz album with a bunch of friends called *Jazz-Iz Christ*. Some of that material originated in *Prometheus Bound*, and I even got Stewart Copeland from the Police to play on one song. I also composed a four-part symphony, *ORCA*, which grew out of some of my orchestral experiments for *Imperfect Harmonies*. In parts, it's very traditional classical music; in others, it's more contemporary, reminiscent of something you might hear from modern composers like Philip Glass or Ennio Morricone. I staged a live performance of it in Linz, Austria, with members of the famous Bruckner Orkestra, which we recorded and released on Serjical Strike.

Needless to say, none of these projects became giant global hits, and many die-hard System Of A Down fans likely don't know they even exist. They were the kinds of ideas most managers and major-label A&R reps would've thrown themselves in front of trains to keep me from spending time on—ambitious, time-consuming ventures that presented me with golden opportunities to alienate my audience while almost guaranteeing very little money in return for my troubles. That I did them anyway makes all the difference. The process of making each helped to unhitch me from the corrosive belief that art is somehow legitimized by the size of the audience it garners.

I have a hard time understanding why more artists don't venture further out of their creative comfort zones. I guess it's a fear of seeing the fan base they've built turn their back on them, but shouldn't that previous success encourage them to keep pushing, keep exploring? Do they really want to keep doing the same thing over and over? Is that really even art?

A good chef can make a great pizza *and* cordon bleu. One will have a plethora of diners, the other an interested few, but both are quality dishes by the same chef. Real art is about saying "yes" to the opportunities that scare you and the challenges that look too daunting to take on. Art exists for its own sake, much like the universe itself.

———

The importance of having the guts to say "yes" to the things that turn you on is matched only by the impact of learning how to say "no" to the things that don't. Most artists aren't good at saying "no." A lot of this comes from the artist's own vulnerabilities and not wanting to hear "no" as an answer. They don't like to deliver bad news themselves, and the apparatus that the entertainment industry builds around them makes it so they never have to. When you're a successful artist, you are surrounded by people whose job it is to flatter you and treat you like a delicate genius. These "yes-men" see it as their mission to make sure you never have to endure an uncomfortable conversation or an awkward moment.

As such, artists are assiduously insulated from being the engines of other people's disappointment. They are encouraged, or maybe even taught, to ignore a problem and assured that doing so will eventually make it go away. I can recall dozens of times when one artist or another flaked on returning my texts, emails, and calls. Just because you're a rock star or you're on tour, you don't get a hall pass from me: I am too and manage to respond, *always*. Artists shouldn't be given immunity from basic etiquette. It only encourages the egotistical monstrosity sometimes brewing within.

When it comes to any sort of project, idea, or proposal, a quick and decisive "no" is almost always preferable to an insincere or wishy-washy "yes." Of course, while I find non-answers aggravating, I fully understand the impulse. Telling someone you disagree or don't like something they've done is hard. But it's as important as just about anything you'll ever do, both as an artist and as a person.

It all comes back to an idea that could be called compassionate confrontation, something that I struggled with for a long time. As I've mentioned before, when I first started meditating, I mistook passivity for nonaggression. Whenever I was faced with problems within System Of A Down, my way of handling the problem was to retreat. Letting it go seemed better than mixing it up over the things that were making me unhappy. For a long time, I blamed Daron and the other guys for all this, but it wasn't that simple. It took getting out of the band, making music, and succeeding on my own to understand that I needed to own my part in this unhappiness. I needed to gain confidence in myself as a musician, as a songwriter, and as a person before I could see that clearly.

All those things I thought I was taking the high road on and "letting go" were things I cared about, things that ultimately mattered to me more than I was willing to admit. My mindset back then was: *Do you want to control the creative process? Okay, fine by me. You want to take credit for all these songs? Cool. I don't need credit.* But every time that happened, I was stockpiling negativity. My passivity only led to anger and resentment. What I thought was spiritual evolution was really just a lingering inclination to avoid confrontation. In a strange way, I had an easier time confronting strangers—politicians, journalists, CEOs, whoever—about political conflicts than I did confronting friends about personal issues. I think I had a clarity around my political opinions that I was slower to come to in my creative life.

I needed to learn how to advocate for myself without doing it at the expense of others. I wish instead of swallowing all that negativity, I could've just pulled Daron aside and said, "I love you, brother, but this is not right. I care about you, but I don't like the way we're operating." I walked away from the band rather than trying to deal with the problems I had in it head-on. My artistic vulnerability played me. That's on me.

All this was on my mind when the band reunited at Shavo's house in 2010. It was just the four of us hanging around the living room, talking, catching up. It had been more than four years since we'd performed together, and although we'd been in touch periodically, this was the first time we were talking seriously about playing together again. There was an offer to tour the following year, and I was considering it.

As much as I was fed up with everything when we parted in 2006, as angry as I was over the threat of a lawsuit, the way it all ended felt unsettled, unfinished. With everything I'd done on my own in the interim, my perspective on the band and my place in it felt radically altered. Judging by the conversation and jokes at that meeting, I have to admit that I wasn't really sure theirs had. Still, it felt like performing together again would be a chance to heal and to see if my new confidence and assertiveness could change the fundamental experience of playing in System for me. At the very least, I'd come away with no regrets or what-ifs as I moved forward with or without the band.

Getting onstage again together was like riding a bicycle, albeit a seventeen-crew-member arena-pumping bicycle. It was easy. I felt almost lazy. If someone slept too late, we'd skip soundcheck. No one seemed particularly concerned with things going exactly right every night. I kept myself pretty cocooned out on the road. I wasn't mixing too much with other bands, or even that much with my own. The general attitude within System wasn't aimed toward achieving any real goals, just having a good time. And a good time it was.

Because we didn't have any new music to promote, we didn't really have to do any press, which gave us a lot more free time. At the beginning of the tour, Daron and Shavo didn't really want to soundcheck, which may have made my monitor tech's job mission impossible and made my hearing onstage way less than optimal, but that was one more thing we didn't have to schedule. We could really just hang out all day, play at night, and then repeat. I still didn't love the touring life, but it was less stressful for me than it had ever been before. There was no greater goal than just being there to play, and that was fine by me.

At the time, I was juggling a bevy of different projects: *Prometheus Bound, Jazz-Iz Christ*, the *ORCA* symphony, working on songs for my next solo album, *Harakiri*, as well as occasional solo shows with an orchestra or with the F.C.C. Knowing what a busy year 2011 was going to be, I'd also attached a GoPro to myself with the idea of gathering footage for a documentary project, which would eventually transform into a biographical film called *Truth to Power.*

Just typing all that makes that time sound *more* stressful, not less, but I think the change in my perspective made all the difference. It was as if System Of A Down had gone from being *the* thing I do, to just being *a* thing I do. All my eggs were no longer in that one basket. If the reunion was a disaster, I knew I had a dozen other things on my plate anyway. When things felt like they were going wrong in the band, instead of just letting it go out of fear of upsetting anyone else, I confronted it, hopefully with compassion.

Almost immediately after we'd decided to tour, talk turned to making new music. It didn't feel like the band's creative dynamic had changed enough for it to be an appreciably different experience than the last time we'd recorded together. So every time they talked about going into the studio, I'd balk. In this way, I suppose the System reunion represented a culmination of both a courage to say "yes" to challenging enterprises and the value of saying "no" with empathy. I managed to decline their entreaties to record new material without ditching the band as a performing entity or severing my relationships with Daron, Shavo, and John. That seemed like progress.

I'd be remiss not to add that our hiatus had significantly increased consumer demand for System Of A Down. We were getting paid around seven times more for our shows than we had when we'd stopped in 2006. And keep in mind, it's not like when we quit, we were falling off commercially. We'd just had two number-one albums in six months. But absence does indeed make the heart grow fonder. Or at least it does for concertgoers. In retrospect, my walking away from the band five years earlier looked like a canny business move, albeit an unintentional one. It was almost as if the concert industry was paying us for all the shows we hadn't played in the previous five years. To put it in perspective, I was making more in three and a half minutes onstage with System than I had for three and a half years' worth of work on *Prometheus Bound*. That doesn't make the former more valuable artistically than the latter—in fact, it's quite likely the opposite.

———

A friend once told me that getting married is only for people who want to have kids. Obviously, that's not a very romantic view of the institution of marriage, but I wasn't sure that necessarily made it wrong.

For a long time, I didn't know if I wanted to have kids. The prospect of adding to an increasingly overpopulated planet felt irresponsible. Plus, I was an artist. I know it's a cliché, but I had all these songs, all these albums, all these projects, which I nurtured and treated as if they were my children. I wasn't sure I had enough room in my life for a child. Wouldn't I have to choose between my artistic and biological offspring? Would that mean giving less of myself to my art? Or, even worse, less of myself to my child? I wasn't completely against the idea of having kids, but I was skeptical.

Angela, on the other hand, was all in. She's always wanted kids. And after eight years together, our relationship had evolved deeply. She convinced me that I could be a good father and a good artist at the same time. I'd achieved so many of my professional and creative ambitions; lurching into the unexpected and the unpredictable felt like the exact sort of undertaking I needed the guts to say "yes" to. Before I did that, though, we decided to say "yes" to each other.

The first time I asked Ange out on an actual date had been back in 2004. That day, my dog Bowie had caught a hummingbird in her mouth. After I pried the poor bird from her jaws, I was overcome by the frail, desperate beauty of this creature my dog had just attacked. I felt responsible for its fate. I called around to a bunch of veterinary clinics before I finally found one, way out in Santa Monica, that would have a look at a hummingbird. When I got there, I handed this mangled little bird to the vet, then handed over my credit card. The vet didn't mince words: the bird was definitely a goner. That was a blow, but I felt some peace with the idea that Bowie was only doing what her nature commanded her to do, and I had done what mine commanded me to do too by trying to care for the bird. That had to be enough.

After this whole ordeal, I went to my favorite Indian restaurant in Santa Monica, sat down by myself, and had dinner. As I was eating, I was still thinking about the hummingbird, thinking about how fragile everything in life is, thinking about trying to make the most of the moments we have. Then I thought of Angela. She was the person I wanted to share all that with right then. So, I called her. The rest is history, *our* history.

That's perhaps a long way of explaining the venue for our wedding eight years later: the Hummingbird Nest Ranch in Simi Valley. Neither of us wanted to say our vows in a church, so we got married out in nature. The ranch spread across 123 acres, and the property had lush gardens, green fields, olive trees, a pool, a ranch house, and a Spanish-style mansion. We invited our closest friends and family, all those we were comfortable being emotionally naked around. We were married in green gardens covered by a canopy of trees gently dancing in the wind. The setting was beautiful, and the party was the best I've ever been to in my life. And I've been to some good parties.

———

Two years later, our son Rumi was born. His birth itself left me in utter disbelief and awe, watching a being—not just the flesh and blood, but the spirit—enter this world from the womb. It was such a surreal experience, and made me feel, as it likely makes all men feel, kind of powerless in this most auspicious of moments.

There is so much about being a parent that people can tell you or that you can read about, but most of it means nothing until you actually become one. There is a depth of love and fear and responsibility that's nearly impossible to explain to someone who doesn't have kids and unnecessary to explain to someone who does, so I won't try either way.

What I will say is that having a child made me think differently about all my creative endeavors. It became clear that all those albums and projects I'd described as "children" just a few paragraphs ago were not that. It doesn't mean that art and music became less important, but being a parent put their significance into a new perspective.

In a way, I was right to worry that parenthood would change me as an artist because it did. I don't just mean that I write songs about or am inspired by Ange and Rumi, though I do and I am. Being a father means I can no longer make music whenever the inspiration hits, because the inspiration might hit right when I need to make Rumi lunch or take him to the doctor or listen to Metallica with him for the first time. My artistic life had to start fitting into certain hours of the day. It's Ange who sometimes gives me a hard time about this. She tells me that I treat music like any other day job, and at times, she's right. If you want to be around for the important people in your life, that doesn't happen by magic. You must manage your time accordingly.

But the changes are also much more profound than that. Becoming a parent forever altered the way I see the world and my relationship to it. It made the idea of our connectedness to the Earth and our responsibility as stewards of it more tangible. I could see, in very real terms, how my spirit would one day carry on without me, the same way my parents' will and their parents' have. How could all that *not* change my art?

Fatherhood also made me a more cautious activist. My views, my advocacy, my politics—none of that has changed. If anything, my positions have been further solidified. I don't think I necessarily do anything too differently, or say no to political action I would've previously said yes to, or hold my tongue instead of speaking out. But I have become more thoughtful and deliberate. I look back at some of the things I did, pre-Rumi, and shake my head. If I'd been a parent, would I have jumped right back on tour after all the 9/11 craziness without more painstaking security arrangements in place? Maybe not.

Mostly, I just don't want my statements to ignite some sort of madness against me or my family. So, I try to be a little bit more careful when I speak about or do things that have the potential to be incendiary. It's a delicate balance. I also want Rumi to grow up seeing me stand up for what I believe in. If I don't teach him the power of "yes" and "no," of embracing challenges boldly and confronting wrongs with compassion, I can't expect him to have the confidence to one day do the same for himself.

CHAPTER 16

I was wearing jeans and a t-shirt, standing in an office at the TUMO Center in Yerevan, getting ready to play a show with the Armenian Opera Orchestra in the large public park next door. The TUMO Center is the brainchild of Armenian-American engineer and entrepreneur Sam Simonian and his wife Sylva, who built it as a technology hub to run afterschool programs for teenagers. The seventy-five-thousand-square-foot facility is a marvel and looks more like the Google headquarters than it does many other buildings in Yerevan, which are, for the most part, dominated by a mix of drab Soviet architecture and traditional Armenian red tuff, a kind of stone construction that's been used there since ancient times.

Sam himself is a genuine visionary who's as responsible as any other single person for the flowering of Armenia's tech sector over the past decade. There are now additional TUMO centers throughout Armenia and across Europe. I eventually helped him add a music program to the center's offerings, but back in 2011, Sam was just getting started, and he'd asked me to play this grand opening party.

Before any concert, there's a sense of excitement and uncertainty as you iron out last-minute issues and manage pre-show jitters. The scale and location of this show had amplified that, as had the announcement that the country's president, Serzh Sargsyan, would be in attendance. During rehearsals, I'd watched the bassists in the orchestra march outside the building to fistfight with some locals over an issue I thankfully remained oblivious to. Tempers flared, a few punches may have been thrown, the problem was apparently sorted, and they all were bundled back inside to resume the main activity that occupied most of the orchestra members' time when not performing: chain-smoking cigarettes.

I'd arrived two days earlier and had gotten to know and like quite a few of the musicians. For most of them, music was a side hustle, as they didn't get paid enough to be full-time musicians. They were architects and bricklayers and software engineers and whatnot. They were top-notch players, but their instruments were old and often in poor condition. It's not clear many of them had ever played to an audience as large as the one we were expecting.

More than eleven thousand people had crammed into the park for a concert we'd initially assumed would draw less than half that. The fact that it was a free show probably helped to attract more people. I was sitting upstairs in the TUMO Center offices, when Sam walked in and told me that the president wanted to meet me.

Serzh Sargsyan had become president of Armenia three years earlier in a much-disputed election. The opposition candidates had claimed the voting was marred by fraud, and their supporters filled the streets of the capitol following the announcement of the results. After nine days of peaceful protest, on March 1, the police initiated a heavy-handed crackdown. The resulting violence left at least ten people dead, many more injured, and an opposition candidate under house arrest. It was a national trauma. The government declared a state of emergency that allowed them to restrict press freedom and block access to certain websites. A law was later passed banning public rallies.

It wasn't an auspicious beginning to Sargsyan's term in office. Three years later, his government had eased many of those restrictions, and he was perceived to have done well handling the fallout of the First Nagorno-Karabakh War. That said, he'd not shown himself to be a clean break from the corrupt oligarchs who'd largely controlled Armenia in the years since the Soviet Union's demise. New protests against his government had begun earlier in 2011, with demonstrators demanding the release of prisoners jailed during the 2008 protests, accountability for those who'd killed protestors, and a host of other democratic and economic reforms.

Let's just say this was not a guy I was anxious to cozy up to.

Still, you've got to pick your battles. Snubbing the president backstage was not going to help anyone and certainly wasn't going to make this show for the opening of an important center for kids go any more smoothly. So, despite my hesitations, I agreed to meet him.

We sat together for several minutes, and Sargsyan was extremely polite, even charming. As much as it wouldn't behoove me to snub him, he had every reason to be nice to me, too. After all, I was a well-known, influential member of the Armenian diaspora about to get onstage in front of eleven thousand of his constituents, many of whom may have been protesting in the streets against him just a few months earlier. Having me on his side would only help burnish his public image.

The conversation was mostly small talk. I apologized for being dressed so informally while he was in a suit, but he waved it off.

"I wish I could be dressed like you right now," he smiled.

I asked him what he'd been doing that day so far, which is something I often ask when I'm talking to people who have some sort of lofty status. It seems to put them at ease. He told me that he'd just gotten back from a meeting in Kazakhstan regarding some sort of economic cooperation agreement.

"How have the rehearsals been going?" he asked in return.

"Well, the musicians are great, but their instruments are twenty or thirty years old," I said. "A lot of the drumheads are worn thin, and the strings on some of the violins and cellos need to be replaced."

At this, he bolted upright a little, and called to an aide who was standing nearby.

"I thought we just paid to upgrade the national orchestra's equipment," he remarked to the aide.

I interrupted. "That was the *national* orchestra," I corrected him. "This is the *opera* orchestra."

"Well, I'll take care of it," he said, reassuring me.

I knew he was just saying that to impress me, but it spoke to everything wrong about the oligarchic system. It's all about putting people and institutions in the leader's personal debt. It's paternalistic. Building allegiance by building patronage. In doing so, it takes money out of a state budget that's needed for all sorts of other things. Stealing from Peter to pay Paul, essentially.

"Why should you have to take care of it?" I asked Sargsyan. "In the Western world, orchestras get funded by corporate sponsorships or rich benefactors. You've got lots of wealthy friends; why don't you get one of them to pitch in?"

It didn't occur to me until later that evening that he might've found my response a little offensive. Rich oligarchs generally don't like to be called out as rich oligarchs. He was diplomatic, though, and didn't appear bothered by it at the time. He wished me luck on the concert and left.

The show went well. There were so many people there that the sound system could barely reach those in the back, but they seemed happy to be there just the same, enjoying the vibe. At the end of the set, right before the encore, I walked offstage for a moment, and my manager George was there with a message.

"Dude, I don't know how to tell you this and I hate to do this to you, but the promoter is asking if you can announce President Sargsyan from the stage," he told me.

This was the quid pro quo, I guess. He'll let me play a show in his country, he'll be polite as I tell him how to fund his orchestra, but in return, he wants to soak up a little of the reflected glow of my popularity with ordinary Armenians. This was the trade-off.

Obviously, I didn't want to do it. It was one thing to meet with him in private, but I didn't want to come off as endorsing him in any way, shape, or form. It felt cheesy. On the flipside, Armenia, though a democracy, was still under the yoke of oligarchic rule. I didn't feel like defying the president's wishes would put me in any danger, but it might make the rest of my stay in Armenia and any other efforts to play there or to be effective politically or socially within the country more complicated. Either way, I had about thirty seconds to make a decision.

I got back onstage and said quietly into the microphone, "My name is Serj Tankian and there is another Serzh in the audience tonight who happens to be president of this country." There was very little reaction from the crowd, probably because I'd delivered the lukewarm announcement in English, rather than in the Armenian I'd been speaking to the crowd in for most of the night. I delivered on my half of the bargain, but did so quietly, unenthusiastically, and in a language most in the audience wouldn't actually understand.

Later, just after the show had ended, I was in a tent backstage, when I heard the emcee say, in Armenian, "Let's hear it for Serj Tankian and the Armenian Opera Orchestra!" The crowd roared in response.

"Now, let's give it up for Armenian president Serzh Sargsyan!" This time his name got a reaction. Choruses of boos rained down.

I looked at George and Sam Simonian and said, "I should probably get the fuck out of here."

———

My relationship with Sargsyan didn't end there. Two years later, there was another presidential election in Armenia, and the result was largely a replay of the previous one. Sargsyan declared victory; his opponent, Raffi Hovannisian, declared fraud; and the people took to the streets to voice their disapproval. Fortunately, this time no one died, but hundreds were arrested.

About a week after the election, I wrote an open letter to the president. "Based on the overwhelming reported fraud from many NGOs," I wrote, "it seems like it would be scientifically impossible for even you, Mr. President, to know whether you actually won the majority of votes. That's quite funny, isn't it? That you, the President of Armenia, are not really sure deep inside whether you are the true chosen leader of your people or not."

Then, I pivoted. "You took an oath to the constitution of Armenia to protect the country from enemies foreign and domestic. Those who steal elections from my people are domestic enemies that need to be prosecuted. It should be your duty to enforce that." I urged him, even under the cloud of a disputed election, to stand up for the rule of law.

What happened next, I did not expect. My old friend Serzh wrote me back. His reply was polite but in the same paternalistic tone he'd taken with me backstage at the TUMO Center. His letter actually referenced several of my lyrics, as well as "Bari Arakeel." Mostly, it was a lot of flowery words that a friend of mine compared to Russian romantic literature. He never responded to my accusations, and concluded his letter with a proverbial, patronizing pat on the head, essentially saying, "We know what we're doing and everything will be fine." I have no doubt the letter was written by an aide, but I figured I'd keep this correspondence going while I had his attention.

I penned a second letter to Sargsyan, thanking him for his response but noting, "You have not answered any of my questions nor addressed any of the issues I brought up directly. I think you have done a great job at securing Armenia's borders," I wrote, giving him some credit even though he'd largely done so by sucking up to Russia, "but security cannot be the scapegoat to distract attention from the inequalities and injustices in our homeland."

I didn't get another written response this time, just Sargsyan's spokesman acknowledging my letter in an interview with *News.am* and noting that the president "agrees with Mr. Tankian on the vast majority of the issues that have been raised." I figured that was that.

Later that year, System Of A Down had a three-week European tour scheduled during which I hoped the band could play its first-ever show in Armenia. Having performed there twice as a solo artist, I felt like I'd cracked the code. I'd found promoters and agents who could help with equipment, ticketing, a venue, and all the other minutiae that goes into a show.

We had a tentative plan to play at a big stadium in Yerevan, where the Armenian national soccer team often plays. Suddenly, just before we were getting ready to announce the tour, we received a call informing us that we couldn't perform in the middle of the stadium, because it would damage the grass. It was puzzling. The stadium had hosted plenty of concerts in the past, and it's not as if there was any other place to set up a stage in a stadium. We couldn't very well play in the stands.

I asked the promoter what other options we had and he said that there was another stadium we could try. Two weeks later, we got the same message back about this other venue: we couldn't play on the grass. I called the Armenian promoter, a guy named Armen, who is the brother of a friend of mine.

"Armen, what's going on here? And don't tell me anything about the fucking grass. What's the real deal?"

"Well," he took a deep breath, "I talked to the president's chief of staff, and he wanted to know if you were going to play ball, or if you were likely to get onstage and criticize the president."

The president's chief of staff was a man named Vigen Sargsyan— no relation to Serzh. I'd never met him, but he was a well-known political figure in Armenia who later became the country's defense minister.

"What did you tell him?" I asked.

"I just said, 'You're asking me if the lead singer of System Of A Down is going to speak his mind onstage? How would I know? How could I possibly have any control over him?' And I can only guess they didn't like that answer."

I appreciated Armen's honesty. I was never going to agree to shut up and sing, and the price for that, in this case, was that System wasn't going to be allowed to play in Armenia. I was frustrated and sad but didn't really see any other way to work it out, at least not at that point.

Two years later, it appeared the Sargsyan regime's view had softened. It feels incredibly immodest of me to say so, but at this point, System Of A Down were kind of the Beatles of Armenia. There were more famous diaspora Armenians in the world—after all, the Kardashians are Armenian-Americans—but I think we held a special place in the country's consciousness. It wasn't just that we were a famous band with Armenian roots; it was the fact that we'd made those Armenian roots—and the Genocide, in particular—such an integral part of our music and our message. As plans were being put together to commemorate the hundredth anniversary of the Genocide, Sargsyan's government sent me a letter inviting System Of A Down to play in Yerevan as part of the ceremonies.

I asked that the government send each member of the band a letter of invitation before we'd commit to doing it. In part, I wanted everyone to feel special, but I was also just heading off any angst or jealousy Daron would likely have if he knew the official invite had come only to me.

Once the show was confirmed, we arranged a short tour, mostly through Europe, to precede the Yerevan show. We titled it the "Wake Up the Souls Tour," and the idea was to focus more attention on the centennial anniversary and rally for recognition of the Genocide. I asked our London-based booking agent to look into including a show in Turkey on the itinerary.

Seventeen years earlier, on that first European tour with Slayer, the band had refused to perform in Turkey. I'd thought a lot about that decision in the intervening years. At the time, it was the right thing to do; I still stand behind that. As a support act that no one had really heard of, we wouldn't have had a platform to make our voices heard. But since then, I'd met quite a lot of Turkish System Of A Down fans. A few had said that they hadn't known much of anything about the Genocide until they heard us talking about it. Many more had heard about the events but had been taught that it wasn't a genocide, but rather something that happened in a war to people on all sides of the conflict. In Erdoğan's Turkey, the Genocide is rarely spoken about honestly, and certainly never taught about in schools. If we might have a chance to educate people about something they'd otherwise never get a chance to learn about without leaving the country, that seemed like a pretty powerful argument for engagement. And what better time to do it than on a tour specifically designed to spotlight the Genocide the Turks had perpetrated? It felt audacious. Going to Turkey to play in 2015, at the centennial of the Genocide, was daring the children of the perpetrators and all of the denialists, daring the Turkish government, to react, as the grandchildren of their horrible ethnic cleansing would be in their face, screaming our brutal truths.

Our booking agent had arranged big tours in Turkey before with bands like the Red Hot Chili Peppers and Metallica, but she also knew that this was not just another rock show. She told me that the local promoter was going to have to get approval directly from Erdoğan's office. In the meantime, I had to convince Daron and Shavo that this was a show worth playing. They were both dead set against going to Turkey. I don't think it was an ethical issue for either of them; it was a safety issue. I suggested that we could fly in on a private charter and hire American security contractors to flank us wherever we went. Plus, we wouldn't even need to stay there over-night. Daron and Shavo were not convinced. As it turned out, neither were the Turks: we never got the required permissions from the gov-ernment, so it was a moot point. The Turkey show wasn't happening.

Daron wasn't even that keen on playing Armenia. He'd never been to the country before, and to him, it just seemed like a huge hassle. Other issues lingered beneath the surface. There had long been a feeling that I used the band when it suited my activism, when I wanted it to give me a bigger megaphone than I'd have on my own. If I'm being hon-est, this is a fair criticism—albeit not one I'd apologize for. I don't want my bandmates to feel used, but I genuinely believe that some things are more important than music, or the band, and this was one of them.

At any rate, I could see that if we wanted to arrive at a deal, we'd need to make some compromises. As was always the case, the rest of the band really wanted to tour more extensively than I did, so I agreed to play two weeks of unrelated shows in Latin America later in the year in order to get Daron to agree to the show in Yerevan.

That trip to Armenia in 2015 was unlike any before or since. The day before we were set to perform, the president's chief of staff,

Vigen, asked if he could come meet me in my hotel suite. He wanted to talk. This was the same guy who wouldn't let System play on the grass two years earlier, so I was skeptical. As much as the band was loved within Armenia, this was still a country ruled by a fairly lawless, oligarchic regime who I'd talked a lot of shit about. Now I was on their turf. It all felt a little dicey. Still, it might be worse if I refused to see him. So, I invited Vigen upstairs, and told my security guy I wanted him in the suite with us.

Perhaps unsurprisingly, Vigen was incredibly gracious and diplomatic; after all, he was a graduate of Tufts's esteemed Fletcher School of Law and Diplomacy. He came in, we shook hands, and then we sat down across from each other. After some polite chitchat, he paused.

"Let's clear the air between us," he said, getting straight to the point. "I know you know that it's me that made it hard for you to come with System in the past, but you should know that it's also me that insisted that you come now. There were people around the president who said, 'No, we can't trust Serj. He'll criticize and embarrass the president.' I told them that you were a real patriot, that you had fought to tell your grandfather's story for your whole life, that we're all on the same team when it came to commemoration of the Genocide."

I replied that I appreciated his advocating for me and the band. But deep down, I also recognized he was buttering me up for something. In part, I'm sure he just wanted to establish that we were, as he put it, "all on the same team," to defuse any criticism of the government I might want to blurt out from the stage. But it still seemed like he wanted something more than just that. When you're talking to politicians, compliments and favors rarely come without strings attached. They're almost *always* followed by an ask.

"The day after your show, we'll be having the big commemoration ceremony for international media," he said. "The president will be speaking, as will Russian president Putin. After Putin finishes his remarks, we'd like you to say a few words and then maybe even play 'Bari Arakeel' with your father."

There it was: the ask. It was a lot bigger than I'd even anticipated. I could feel my heart beating quicker and heavier in my chest. Even on a logistical level, what Vigen was talking about would be difficult to pull off.

"My father isn't even here," I told him.

"That's okay; we can fly him in."

"All I brought with me are jeans and t-shirts," I pushed back again. "I'd feel strange being at such a somber ceremony dressed like that."

"That's no problem," Vigen said, waving his hand in the air. "We'll get you a suit."

Whatever issues I raised, he had a solution. I was flustered.

"Look, your offer is extremely gracious," I told him, pausing briefly. "I need to think about it."

That night, I tossed and turned in my hotel bed. There was nothing wrong with the bed, but the situation didn't feel right. For hours that night, I was having trouble putting my finger on what was really bothering me about the offer. Was it the idea of flying my eighty-year-old father halfway across the world to perform alongside me, with Vladimir Putin and Serzh Sargsyan as our opening act? I mean, yeah, that *would* be odd, but that wasn't quite it. Was it that they were just using me to tacitly endorse these men that I found rather loathsome? Sure, that was part of it but not even the whole thing. After all, I could say whatever I wanted up there.

Then, it hit me: I wasn't, and had never been, a politician. If I had something important to say, something I wanted the people of Armenia to hear, I already had a platform for that. We were going to play a concert the night before this ceremony. I would have a microphone in my hand, fifty thousand people in front of me, and millions more watching on TV and the internet. *That* was where I was supposed to deliver my message, as an artist—not among the forever-compromised men with their dark suits and even darker objectives.

Once I'd worked this out in my mind, my heart rate slowed, my mind eased, and I finally drifted off to sleep.

———

The next day, it was raining. I mean, *really* raining. In Armenia, people say it always rains on Genocide Remembrance Day, a symbolic representation of the tears of our ancestors, of their grieving descendants, of God himself. On the hundredth anniversary, the downpour started a day early. The cold rain was lashing down in sheets, soaking the fifty thousand or so assembled in front of the stage in Republic Square, a sprawling, picturesque piazza in central Yerevan.

As the band huddled together backstage, something felt different between us. Since we'd started performing again in 2011, we'd played dozens of shows, and some had gone really well. But it had all felt a little, well, empty. Or if not empty, just kind of directionless. Standing there, looking into the faces of my bandmates as we listened to the crowd in the square rumbling in anticipation, it was as if we'd found our purpose. All the grinding, all the struggle, all the arguments, all the endless tours, all the months away from home, all the death threats, all the hours in studios and rehearsal spaces—it had all been for this.

We could all feel it.

Daron smiled widely. There was a lightness to him I'd rarely seen before.

"This is incredible," he said. Even though he'd been unenthusiastic about coming here in the first place, once he'd arrived, I'd seen a change come over him. In fact, he even delayed his return flight to extend his stay in Armenia. "This is such an amazing moment."

When we walked out onstage and the eerie opening notes of "Holy Mountains" gave way to big, loud guitar riffs and the crash of John's drums, the stage lights lit the audience and the square erupted. Although Genocide Remembrance is typically a somber occasion, that show felt like a heaving, joyous, defiant communion. The crowd that night *got* the music in a way few crowds we'd played for ever had. The subtle nods in the performance—an Armenian folk melody here, a traditional dance step there—felt as if they were being absorbed on a molecular level. We'd grown up an ocean apart from most of the people in the square that night, but there was no mistaking that we were one with them. These were our people.

Nearly two hours into the show, as Daron picked out a mournful melody on the guitar, I thought about the offer I'd turned down to speak alongside world leaders. I looked out over the jubilant, dancing, soggy throng in front of the stage, and realized that if I had anything to say, now was the time to say it.

"For the last few days, I haven't been able to sleep well," I said, pacing the stage. "All I can think about is my grandparents." I explained how my grandmother was just a little girl when she was sent on the death march with her grandmother. "It was a Turkish mayor that saved my grandmother. The government of Turkey should be hailing these saviors as heroes, instead of denying the obvious history.

"My grandfather was five years old when he saw his own father die. He lost his sight from hunger. He ended up in an American orphanage in Greece. . . . So, the fact that the US government uses the wrong word to recognize what we *know* is genocide is not only appalling to us, it's appalling to *all* Americans."

I took a minute to acknowledge Russia for recognizing the Genocide and being Armenia's ally, while reminding them that Armenia should be treated as an equal, not a client state. I saved perhaps my most scathing words for the Armenian government itself. "In twenty years of independence, we've come a long way, but there's still a lot of fucking work to do. It is the responsibility of the government of the Republic of Armenia to bring in the principles of egalitarian civic society, get rid of institutional injustice, and stop the depopulation that is occurring. We are System Of A Down, and it is our responsibility to tell you these things, and to rock you at the same time."

Whenever I speak from the stage, I never script exactly what I want to say. I always trust that if I'm in the moment, if I'm connected to my truest self, if I allow the music to flow through me, it has a way of bringing out a truth I otherwise may not be able to access. In Republic Square, it wasn't just the speech—the whole show felt like that.

The concert was, in many ways, an act of persistence and defiance. Not just against Sargsyan's kleptocratic Armenian regime, but against that version of me who'd once backed down from fights, who'd shied away from confrontation. I felt empowered. I felt whole.

Whatever courage I'd mustered had not come naturally to me. It had been painstakingly learned.

At the end of our performance, Daron, Shavo, John, and I huddled up onstage, just the four of us, our arms around each other's shoulders, our heads pressed together, a tight circle of brotherhood. It was as if the entire band had existed just for this show, for this moment. It's rare in life to feel like you're exactly where you're supposed to be, where the universe needs you to be, but there we were, rain still pouring down, all four of us living out a cold, wet fever dream that felt like our shared destiny.

It was the only time System Of A Down would ever play in Armenia, and it was perfect.

CHAPTER 17

What is a band? Is it simply a bunch of people who get together to create music? If you don't have any gigs, are you still a band? What if you only play shows, but you don't create any new music? Are you still a real band, or are you just a glorified cover band? And is there anything wrong with that?

When I decided to quit the jewelry business and then shrug off the idea of law school, the band I was playing in had never played a show or released any music. We didn't have any fans, at least none we weren't related to or didn't know personally. But that band felt real to me because we had a vision. It had vitality. That was more important than recordings or concerts.

In the year or two after playing in Yerevan, System Of A Down felt like it was largely on cruise control. We did those Latin American tour dates, we played some festivals in the US, and then a run of more than twenty European tour dates in the summer of 2017. Ultimately, for me, it felt like just a part-time job, albeit one that paid significantly better than most people's full-time gigs. In fact, it paid better than what was essentially *my* full-time gig.

At that point, much more of my time was being split between two main ventures: film and video game composing, and painting. I'd written the scores for a few independent films and a documentary, and was taking meetings with studios like Fox, Disney, and Lionsgate for bigger projects. A few years earlier, I'd also started painting, and matching each work with a musical composition unique to that painting. I wanted people to experience something truly synesthetic—to see my music and hear my art, all at the same time. I'd had my first exhibition of this sort of multimedia art in 2013. I later partnered with an Armenian tech company, Arloopa, that offered optical recognition software for your smartphone that would unlock the composition associated with each painting. All this stuff gave me that same liberating feeling of discovery that I'd gotten when I'd first started making music decades earlier.

Daron, Shavo, and John were always pushing to do more with System Of A Down. I'd been the one holding them back, mostly because I didn't really want to tour. I'd never loved life on the road much before, and now I had a wife and a young child at home. To make things worse, on that European run in 2017, I messed up my back pretty badly. After a rough flight and who knows how many different soft hotel beds, I woke up one morning in Belgium in extreme agony, barely able to walk. I saw a chiropractor backstage who worked on me for a while, but I had to Tiger Balm my way through the rest of the tour. Even after getting home, I was in serious pain for three or four months. My back has never really been the same since, and the constant travel that comes with being on the road always seems to aggravate it.

Even when the band was making new music, I didn't find the life cycle of a major-label artist particularly satisfying. We'd typically spend six months writing, six months recording, and then two to three years touring and promoting. That means that two-thirds to three-quarters of your time as a signed artist is spent doing things that didn't feel very artistically fulfilling or creative.

The obvious riposte to all this is that if you're successful, you get paid quite well for your trouble. System is lucky enough to make royalties from selling music, and that income is reasonably consistent. If you outspend that income, you can always refill the coffers with big checks from touring. Playing live can become a bit like visiting the world's most generous ATM.

But remember: I'd *never* wanted to be someone who made decisions because of money. I recognize it's a tremendous privilege to be in a position to not have to do exactly that, but I can't ignore the fact that *not* making decisions based on money was what had led me to that privilege in the first place. As it happened, I was pretty good at staying within my budget anyway, so the financial lure of touring was never going to outweigh all the negatives. With music, I've never made compromises and it's always worked out, so why start now?

Toward the end of 2017, we had a band meeting at Beno's office. When I arrived, I told everyone that I had an item I wanted to add to the agenda. We went through the rigamarole of regular business discussions, and then it came time for my item.

"So, who's going to throw me a going-away party?" I asked the group. "Do one of you guys want to be the master of ceremonies?" I laughed a little, but I was serious. "Look guys, I've been very clear that I'm no longer interested in touring both due to my back and because it's just no longer something within my vision.

"The thing is, though," I continued, "I don't want to hold you guys back. This is your dream. This is what you've worked for your whole life. You deserve to have this." I looked at Daron, Shavo, and John, knowing what I said next would hit hard.

"I think you guys should find a new singer."

For the longest time, System Of A Down was about the four of us. We'd built it up from nothing, we'd been through all the battles together along the way, and if any one of us left, it simply wouldn't be the same thing anymore. A couple of years earlier, I'd even tried to codify this with a legal document that stated that if someone left the band for any reason—other than, God forbid, dying—that the remaining members couldn't use the band name without him. Everyone else resisted that idea, probably because they sensed I was looking for a way out of the band at the time, and they weren't ready to kiss it goodbye. I'd initially been upset that they didn't see System the same way I did, but after a while, I stopped being so precious about it, and just thought of these three guys not as my bandmates but as my close friends.

That's who they are to me still. Shavo is one of the nicest, happy-go-lucky guys I've ever met in my life. He gets along with everyone, even at the worst of times. I can remember riding in the back of a bumpy camper van once with a bad flu, and as soon as I started to feel sick, he insisted on giving me his seat on another band's more comfortable bus so I could recover. That's Shavo: joyful, hopeful, helpful.

When I first met John, we got along due to our mutual sensibilities. We both appreciated reading and reason. By the time we all sat down together in Beno's office in 2017, John and I weren't just friends and bandmates; we were brothers-in-law. In a fairly unlikely turn of events, he'd married Ange's sister, Diana. In a somewhat more concerning development, he'd also grown into a fervent Trump supporter. Yet even though I was at the far opposite end of the political spectrum, backing Bernie Sanders at the time, we could always sit at the dinner table and laugh with each other. No matter what happened, John always had my back, and I had his.

And Daron and I . . . well, we have always had a long, complicated relationship. The love of music welded our unique friendship early on despite our age difference. Artistically and even politically, we were like-minded partners at first. We both had a punk-rock ethos from different sources and experiences. Musically, we'd often finish each other's sentences and had this incredible harmonic resonance in our voices. But it was almost impossible to separate our personal relationship from our creative one. It got messy at times, though neither of us ever let it fall apart. He had a possessiveness I didn't always understand or appreciate, especially when it started affecting my relationships with others. I think he viewed me like an older brother, and I was protective of him, as I felt he was emotionally vulnerable. He has always made music the priority in his life and remains stubbornly true to his own artistic vision. Even though that has sometimes put us at odds, I have a lot of respect and love for him.

So, what did I want for these three people whom I was closer with than anyone outside my own family? I wanted them to be happy. I wanted them not to have to depend on my health, my back, or my willingness to spend months on the road each year for them to have this band that they wanted so much. These three guys meant more to me than System Of A Down had ever meant—and they still do.

Of course, I wanted *me* to be happy, too. It seemed like the solution was to ease myself out of the band while they invited in a replacement. I told them I'd even help train a new singer.

"Think about it," I said. "We can be the unique band that's able to make this transition amicably, where the member of the band who's leaving is 100 percent on-board with the new direction. I'll do press and talk about it positively. I'll make it clear that I support you guys."

I don't think the guys were totally shocked by my announcement. In fact, I almost sensed they'd expected it, or at least something like it. They didn't dismiss the idea outright, but their collective response at the time was for me to essentially pump the brakes. They asked me not to announce that I was leaving the band. They promised not to pressure me into touring anymore. Management would merely present show offers as they came up. If I said yes, we'd do them. If I said no, we wouldn't. End of story.

It sounded reasonable enough to me.

I sort of thought they'd forgotten about the whole idea of hiring a new singer, but a year or so later, John, Shavo, and I were at a fundraiser in Glendale, and this singer I knew got up and sang this beautiful Armenian song. Shavo was sitting next to me at the table. He leaned over and tapped me on the shoulder.

"By the way," he nodded toward the singer, "we tried this guy out as a singer. The only problem was that he couldn't scream and growl."

I was taken aback. Not that they had been auditioning replacements, but that they'd kept it a secret.

"Why didn't you guys ever tell me?" I whispered.

Shavo shrugged. "I dunno."

I turned toward Shavo, now looking directly at him. "Listen, he's a good singer," I said. "I can literally take him in the parking lot right now and teach him how to growl. You should really consider him."

In more recent years, I pitched another friend to them as a potential replacement that they ought to seriously consider. But I don't think they ever did.

———

If touring was always going to be a challenge, I did hold out hope that maybe we could find our way back to being a functioning creative unit. Again, I'd been the one who'd been reluctant to start making music together. The year before we played in Yerevan, though, I tried to test the waters.

I had a song called "Justice Shines" that I'd written about my grandparents' experience during the Genocide. Since the hundredth anniversary of the Genocide was fast approaching, I thought that maybe we could record this song as a benefit single to raise money and visibility for the recognition campaign. When I proposed it to the band, Daron mentioned that he also had written a song, "Lives," about the Genocide. I suggested we record them both and release them as a double-sided single.

We worked on both songs, and if I'm being honest, some of the changes Daron made to the arrangement on the one I'd written didn't thrill me. This felt like déjà vu all over again, since this sort of thing had happened a fair bit during previous System sessions. I'd bring in a song, and by the time the band was finished with it, I didn't even like it anymore. Nonetheless, at this point, I was excited that things were moving forward and didn't want to derail them.

Rick Rubin heard the two songs and offered his input. Basically: after so long without releasing new music, he didn't think these should be the first things people heard from the band.

I love Rick's honesty but that doesn't mean I always agree with him. In this case, I certainly didn't. I felt like this should be an artistic decision, not a business decision. This was for a cause that was way more important than whether these were the exact kind of songs System fans would want to hear after nearly a decade without any new music. I don't think Rick was even that adamant, but his lack of enthusiasm dissuaded the other guys from finishing and releasing the songs.

———

Around 2018, after coming back from New Zealand, Daron and I had started getting together, just the two of us, to hang out, to talk, to eat, and to play music for each other—almost like we had when we'd first met. On some level, I think I was trying to rebuild that creative partnership in a way that felt more like an actual partnership. Instead of being passive, and letting the relationship take whatever course it would, I was being intentional.

I'd continued to write and record music on a near-daily basis, and although a lot of it was instrumental stuff I channeled into my scoring work, I'd recently written a handful of rock songs that felt like something that would work for System. I played some for Daron and asked him to play me what he'd been working on. He was reluctant at first but eventually started loosening up. Unsurprisingly, he had some great songs. It felt like between these two batches of music,

I could finally see a path toward something I hadn't even been looking for in more than a decade: a new System Of A Down album.

I wanted to tread carefully. I started talking to Daron about what it might take for me to start making music again with the band. I wasn't willing to just bring my new songs into System and feed them to the same old beast that had made my previous experiences so unsatisfying. He thought, not unreasonably, that this was a discussion we needed to have with the whole band, not just the two of us.

With that in mind, I started jotting down ideas by myself. When I was done, what I had looked like a bullet-pointed manifesto, mapping out a creative future for System Of A Down:

1. **Equal creative input**: Daron and I will both contribute equal numbers of songs. If Shavo has riffs to contribute, we'll work them into songs too. Everyone in the band has veto power over any song. If anyone doesn't like a song, we'll set it aside.

2. **Equal publishing splits**: Regardless of who wrote the song, the publishing should be split evenly among all four of us. Our current model has created serious financial disparities within the band, which cause all sorts of other problems. This will address that.

3. **Director's Cut**: Whoever wrote the song makes the final decision on it. We should exhaust all the ideas from everybody in the group, but in the end, no one should have to live with a version of a song they brought in that they're not happy with.

4. **Develop new concepts for releasing music**: Instead of simply putting out albums and touring, let's find other visual and creative formats to launch our music into the world. Let's create experiences just as engaging as the music itself.

Those were the four big points. In my mind, this was a way to not only create an egalitarian atmosphere in the band but to revitalize it artistically. It had been two decades since System first got together, and the music industry had changed in that time. I didn't want System to just be some dinosaur that kept doing things the same way until it went extinct. I was imagining ways of transforming the release of new music into an event, not just a digital file that shows up one day on Spotify.

I sent my little manifesto around to the other guys, and not too long after, the four of us met up at John's office, ordered a whole bunch of food, and got into it. *Way* into it.

Shavo, who it's worth noting had gotten sober by this point in his life, seemed open to the ideas I'd raised. Daron and John, not so much. I understood some of their reluctance. With the new publishing splits, Daron stood to lose the most since he was currently taking home the lion's share of that money. John stood to gain financially, but he felt like I was dictating terms to the band. He likes being in charge and doesn't take well to being told what to do. For Daron though, it was the creative changes that seemed to rile him up the most.

I suggested that we each bring six songs into the sessions for a new album. If everyone in the group didn't agree on one of the songs we'd brought in, we'd have to write another one until we got to that unanimous approval. On previous albums, Daron had always controlled the creative process and seemed to feel like this new method was not only a challenge to his control, but it was also an attack on his songwriting. Obviously, that wasn't my intention.

I insisted that this was a way for us to both grow artistically. As he'd gotten more confident as a lyricist, I'd always encouraged him to write more, but as I'd grown more confident writing music, all the avenues within the band to express that felt blocked for me. This was a way for everyone to have a creative stake in the band's output.

Daron and John weren't convinced. The more we debated, the more frustrated they grew.

"Damn it!" Daron said finally, standing up from the table. "I'm a great songwriter! Why are you trying to stop me from writing songs for the band?"

"Daron, you're an amazing songwriter," I agreed. "But that doesn't mean I'm not. Both things can be true. We can both be good songwriters. We're even *better* together."

This discussion went round and round, getting more and more heated. Finally, John stood up and slammed his meaty hand against the table in his typical Tarzan fashion. "Enough of this bullshit!" he thundered. "You write the music," he yelled, pointing at Daron, then turned to me. "You write the lyrics! I play the drums! He plays the bass! That's the way the band *works*. That's the way it has always worked! Why do you have to make this more complicated than it is?"

"John, please sit down," I said quietly.

"No!" he continued. "This is System Of A Down! This is how we do things! You don't tell us what to do!"

"I'm not telling you what to do," I replied. "I'm just saying that if I'm going to be involved with this, *this* is what will make it work for me. If that doesn't work for you guys, I understand and respect that, but I can't be a part of this project otherwise."

The meeting went on like this for something like six hours, but it felt much longer than that. We never really reached an agreement about it, but we didn't give up on the idea of recording together either. In fact, they wanted to get in the studio right away and start working. But I knew if we did that, nothing would change. People don't usually change unless they're forced to.

As we tried to plow forward, some of the issues we were up against were purely logistical. I'd started living part of the year in New Zealand. Even when I was in California, Daron tended to wake up mid-afternoon most days. He wanted to be in studios and practice spaces banging out songs late at night like we had in the band's early days. I didn't want to live like that, and I don't think Shavo or John did either. We had wives and kids. I liked to have breakfast with my son before school and go to sleep alongside my wife at night.

I suggested that we consider working remotely at times, as I had on many other projects from my studio. There wasn't a ton of enthusiasm from the guys for that idea, but nonetheless, once I was in New Zealand, there was very little other choice. I sent them some of my songs to work on alongside Daron's. I asked them to send me whatever they came up with together in the rehearsal space, then I'd offer feedback or add my own parts. I felt that Daron, like most artists, often had an insecurity when bringing in the songs he wrote, at least initially, and got weird about sending the stuff they were working on to me. He and John weren't on great terms at the time anyway—they had their own personal squabbles—and when John and Beno finally sent me the music anyway, John and Daron ended up having a major falling out.

The demos they sent weren't thrilling anyway, to be honest. I wasn't crazy about the changes they'd made to my music, and a lot of those songs I loved that Daron had played for me months earlier were not the ones they were actively working on. Daron liked the band to work on *all* his songs—the good ones *and* the not-so-good ones—and then at the end of all that, we'd pick which ones sounded best. His contention was that the songs sometimes got better with time, effort, and lots of discussion. He may have been right about that, but to me, it just felt inefficient and unfocused, which was what I'd been hoping to avoid when I wrote the manifesto.

I'd hoped my vision for a more egalitarian existence within the band would solve our problems or at least point us in the right direction. I really thought it would light this creative path forward. Instead, it just became a giant mess. The sessions broke down. Hopes for another System Of A Down album withered. I took my songs back, recorded them myself, and eventually released them as the EP *Elasticity*.

I love those songs. "Elasticity" is a crazy mix of punk, metal, progressive and alternative rock. It's got funny verses inspired by my son's ramblings, singalong pre-choruses, a dark, gothic breakdown, and a strong anthemic chorus. "Electric Yerevan" was written about the 2016 protests in Armenia. "Your Mom" was originally written about the terrorist group ISIS, but was later converted into a Dada-esque jaunt about, well, your mom. And then there was "Rumi," a piano ballad and a message from a father to a son. I really laid a lot out in the song's chorus: "When you grow up in your prime / Stay away from God and crime / Embody justice for this tormenting and tormented world / You will learn something every day / Don't dip your toes, go all the way / Be the change you wanna see / And be the man you want to be."

The rest of the band really liked a few of my songs, but "Rumi" was too sentimental for them. For me, an artist's sentimentality is a strength. In System, it was seen as a weakness. The fact that the guys didn't like this song made me realize that we just weren't on the same page creatively anymore. I had been waiting for them to change but I couldn't wait forever. Although I wished these could've been System songs, the fact that I stood up for them and for my own artistic vision makes me love them even more.

As for my manifesto, it was the most valiant attempt I could make to fix the unfixable. As we've seen all over the globe in one geopolitical morass after another, you can't force rules on people and expect democracy to break out. I guess that's true whether you're talking about a nation of forty million or a group of four. While I certainly believe in the virtues of equal rights and democracy, maybe that doesn't work in a band. At least, not this one.

CHAPTER 18

In late 2015, Serzh Sargsyan proposed a constitutional referendum in Armenia to transform the country into a parliamentary republic. It was perceived as a sinister move, and was referred to by his critics as "Sargsyan's project," because beneath the sheen of democratic empowerment, it was seen as designed to achieve the opposite by enabling him to hold on to power past his term-limited ten years as president. Rather than abolish the term limits, the referendum would essentially rejigger the system to make the prime minister the de facto head of state, a position to which Sargsyan planned to transition. It was a game of political musical chairs that Sargsyan had already seen Vladimir Putin pull off in Russia. In the case of the Armenian referendum, the vote itself was marred by charges of ballot-stuffing, bribery, violence, and voter intimidation. Unfortunately, it passed, nonetheless.

Three years later, the Armenian parliament was getting ready to rubber-stamp Sargsyan's ascent to prime minister, cementing the country's slow-motion slide toward authoritarianism. It was alarming and a little surreal to see such an obvious power grab, though I wasn't surprised. Sargsyan never came across to me as a monster but more of a paternalistic, corrupt, but otherwise fairly ordinary opportunist politician. It's a pattern that repeats itself around the globe, regardless of what sort of political system a country is operating under. Give someone a taste of power and money, and they'll do everything they can to acquire more of it. Exceptions are rare.

Seventeen days before parliament was scheduled to anoint Sargsyan, Nikol Pashinyan began walking to Yerevan from Gyumri, Armenia's second-largest city, to build a movement against the burgeoning autocracy. Pashinyan was a crusading journalist-turned-parliamentarian who had opposed Sargsyan for a long time. Back in 2008, he led the protests against Sargsyan's election. When the police opened fire on protestors on March 1, killing ten of them, Pashinyan was forced to go into hiding. After more than a year on the run, he surrendered to authorities in 2009, and spent nearly two years as a political prisoner. Following Sargsyan's second disputed election in 2013, Pashinyan was back in the streets, calling for a peaceful, bloodless revolution. By 2018, he'd been elected to parliament, and hoped his two-week walk to Yerevan, which he streamed live on Facebook, would rally hundreds of thousands of Armenians against Sargsyan's regime.

Throughout the decade Sargsyan had been in power, I'd become ever more enmeshed in domestic politics in Armenia. It wasn't just meetings with the president and his chief of staff, open letters, or speeches from the stage in Republic Square. I'd also become close with a lot of the country's most prominent political figures. Garin Hovannisian, an Armenian-American writer and director who I knew from AYF circles in LA, had hired me to score his first film, the Genocide-themed thriller *1915*. His father, Raffi Hovannisian, had been Sargsyan's main rival in the contested 2013 election. Following reports of vote-rigging, Raffi led protests and went on a hunger strike.

As a well-known, politically connected member of the diaspora, I was acutely aware of the stature I had within Armenia and very careful about how I deployed it. As one political crisis cascaded into the next, I'd inevitably get calls to join one movement or another against the oligarchy. Political candidates would reach out asking if I might come to a rally, declare my support, or speak at an event. Each time, I'd ask my inquisitor some version of the same question: "Are we at a tipping point? Are people truly ready for a change?"

Strange as it may sound, I didn't want to be seen as the leader of any kind of revolution; I wanted to be a follower of the people's true wishes, which by most every indication was supporting Pashinyan and his insistence on real, substantive democratic change. The truth is that despite the fact that I considered Armenia my homeland, I was an outsider. Any movement I led was going to be tarred as a Western, George Soros–hatched plot led by a rich, famous interloper. That's not fair and it's not accurate, but that's bare-knuckle politics. Even more to the point, if I put my thumb on the scale of some candidate or some movement, and my influence led people into the streets only to be shot by police, that's an awful responsibility to take on. If I encouraged a protest that ended with hundreds arrested and no real progress made, what good would I have done? Ultimately, I wanted to support change, but not be the instigator of it.

It was a delicate balancing act.

Throughout Pashinyan's two-week walk to Yerevan, I followed along on social media like a lot of other Armenians. He called the endeavor "My Step" and even wrote lyrics to a song of the same name that he and his compatriots sang during their trek. He didn't mince words as to the purpose. One of his movement's enduring slogans summed it up simply: "Reject Serzh."

When Pashinyan arrived in Yerevan, his support was still spotty. A rally in Freedom Square attracted only hundreds. It appeared his two-week stunt had failed, but Pashinyan was in this for the long run—he wasn't so easily discouraged.

Reading Gandhi had convinced Pashinyan that nonviolent civil disobedience was the only logical path forward. He stumbled on his own twist when he and a few supporters decided to sit down in front of a city bus on a crowded street in Yerevan, stopping traffic. It was disruptive, it was attention-grabbing, *and* it was peaceful. He began urging supporters to do the same all over the country. Suddenly, pockets of activists with nothing more than their bodies and a willingness to put them in front of traffic had ground the entire country to a halt.

The beauty of this tactic was manifold. It required few people, could be done anywhere, needed very little strategizing or leadership, and was entirely portable. If the police arrived, activists would simply get up and sprint off somewhere else. It became a cat-and-mouse game in which the authorities simply couldn't keep up.

This sort of decentralized civil disobedience also dovetailed with the larger message of the movement: the oligarchs and despots don't have the power in Armenia anymore, the people do. It was a stroke of accidental genius.

As the movement gathered momentum and supporters, the answer to that question that I always asked my friends and political contacts in Armenia—*Was this the tipping point?*—finally seemed to be "yes." Pashinyan was demanding Sargsyan resign and urging those in the diaspora to come join the revolution. It was important for Armenians in the homeland to feel that they had the support of the much larger diaspora. At one point, he mentioned me by name. It was clear I had to make a decision.

At the end of April, a mutual friend put me on the phone with Pashinyan and his wife, who was leading the demonstrations alongside her husband. We'd never spoken before, but Pashinyan appealed to me personally.

"You need to be here," he urged me. "This is your country, too. This is your revolution, too."

At the time, I happened to be sick as a dog: cough, fever, runny nose, the whole deal. I felt awful. But I knew he was right. I took a cocktail of potent antihistamines and headed for LAX. By the time I landed in Yerevan, it was already a victory party. Sargsyan *had* resigned. He'd been toppled without anyone firing a shot. It was a true Velvet Revolution, very much in the tradition of the one that had toppled the Communist government in Czechoslovakia in 1989: a nonviolent popular uprising and transition of power.

When I arrived at the main airport terminal, Pashinyan was there to greet me, wrapping me up in a bear hug as I kissed him on the cheek. We did an impromptu press conference in the street outside the terminal, and then as we exited the airport, we were mobbed by a crowd of thousands. I was undeservedly being treated like a hero, even though it was these people, not me, who'd ousted an autocrat. One woman presented us with a cake that had my photo alongside Pashinyan's on it, depicted in frosting. Another handed me flowers. Others just wanted to reach out to shake my hand or take a photo. Pashinyan took out his trademark bullhorn, the kind he'd used to direct crowds during protests, and tried to clear a path for us. We climbed into the back seat of a sedan and began inching toward a rally in Republic Square.

Even though Sargsyan had resigned, his party still controlled Parliament and had initially blocked Pashinyan from becoming prime minister. In response, Pashinyan had rallied people back into the streets, and called for a general strike. The message was again unequivocal: the people rule Armenia, not the oligarchs. There was another parliamentary vote set for the day after I'd arrived, and it seemed unlikely that anybody would dare try to block Pashinyan again. Now, he had the country behind him.

As we drove, the streets were so packed with revelers we could barely move. We'd inch a few hundred feet forward, stop the car, get out, and people would hand us gifts, Armenian brandy, or offer slices of cake. We'd dance and hug, get back in the car, drive a few hundred more feet, then do it all again.

All around, people were celebrating, waving Armenian flags, honking car horns, blasting music. I've seen happy faces before. I've been to Rock in Rio with 150,000 people partying. But I've never in my life seen anything like the kind of elation I saw on the streets of Yerevan that day in 2018. It was more than just happiness on those faces; it was liberation. And it was fucking beautiful.

I was still getting over my cold, and as I sat in the car, Pashinyan admitted that he was sick, too. It turns out that leading protests, facing down an authoritarian regime, getting battered by police, and sleeping outside is not great for your health. To look at him, he was an unlikely revolutionary leader: short, balding, and kind of paunchy. The overall effect was more middle-aged history teacher than charismatic states-man. But he had genuine courage and a stubborn idealism that hadn't been ground out of him by the years he'd spent in prison, in hiding, and trying to incite a sometimes-feckless opposition.

"I am so glad you came," he told me.

"I am as well," I smiled. "I can't believe what you all have achieved here."

"It's not just us," he said. "It's time."

As we finally approached Republic Square, a video of System Of A Down's performance from that same square in 2015 was being projected onto screens flanking the stage. Pashinyan told me he'd been among the wet, wind-whipped crowd that night three years earlier. "Seeing all those young people, I knew this day was coming," he insisted. "If you could bring fifty thousand people into the square for a concert, that gave me hope that we could do the same to rally for justice against Serzh Sargsyan."

When we finally wove our way through the crowds, Pashinyan and I walked out onstage arm in arm, and the audience in front of the stage exploded. There must have been close to two hundred thou-sand people out there. I'd written a speech, and as I stepped up to the microphone, I thought about everything that had happened in my life to lead me to this place—the bombs shaking our Beirut apart-ment, the AYF shows, the reams of hate after 9/11, the creative strug-gles within the band, the joyful communion in this very square a few years earlier. I'd been an artist and an activist for most of my adult life, and now I had a chance to speak to a country, *for* a country, on the brink of a peaceful, democratic revolution. It was transcendent.

I'd previously avoided giving political speeches, but this was different. It was important for me, almost critical, to congratulate the Armenian people, *my* people, on their victory over the hopeless years of oligarchy and injustice. Although I loved what the young revolutionaries had accomplished and respected their courage greatly, it was the everyday people who made this happen. I was supporting them, not a random candidate for office.

The speech went by in a flash. In the car beforehand, Pashinyan had asked me if I was going to play anything for the crowd. I wasn't prepared to perform and was still feeling the effects of whatever illness I'd been battling. But the minute I finished that speech, I was overcome by a desire to sing.

People have been singing since pretty much the beginning of human history. We do it to mourn, to celebrate, to connect. We do it, sometimes, just because the very act of singing makes us feel alive. That night, I reached back to the song that in many ways had been my first connection to this place and these people, "Bari Arakeel," the story of the white stork that would always return home. I sang it, a cappella, leading the crowd in a sing-along.

As I sang the song I used to sing with my dad when I was a child, waving my arm as if to conduct the two hundred thousand of my compatriots in the square singing along with me, waving flags, hoisting their arms toward the heavens, I felt metaphysically at one with my people and their past, present, and future. I felt at one with my grandparents, completely out of time and space. Looking out into the sea of people, the lights from their phones illuminating the night, their voices seemed to speak as one, celebrating the prospects of a new and, for once, hopeful Armenia that they themselves had willed into existence. I've given more accomplished performances in my life but never one that was more meaningful.

The following day, parliament voted Pashinyan in as the next prime minister. I was there as he was sworn in. A couple of days later, he invited me to have coffee with him in his new office. It was a peculiar scene: this former journalist who'd been sleeping in tents on the side of the road a month earlier was now ensconced in this gleaming, cavernous office. As we sat down, an older man shuffled in and out of the office, making coffee.

For all the support Pashinyan had in Armenia, I remember thinking at that moment how exposed he was, how vulnerable. Weeks earlier, a friend of mine who'd provided security for me in Armenia had reached out and asked if I thought he should go and help protect him. At the time, Pashinyan was on the streets constantly—walking, sleeping, protesting. He had the people on his side, but much of the apparatus of the government against him, and he had no security whatsoever. I told my friend that he should *definitely* get out there and help him. Even now that he was prime minister, perhaps *especially* now, there were real dangers for him. The Armenian version of the Secret Service was supposed to be nonpartisan but had, like most everything else in the country, been corrupted by years of bribes and handouts from the oligarchs. I asked Pashinyan if he was being careful, if he had protection.

"I'm not worried," he brushed it off.

The man who'd brought the coffee was now in the corner of the office, scribbling into a notebook. As I walked by him, I could see his notes weren't in Armenian script, but in Russian. I nodded toward Pashinyan and then motioned toward the man with the notebook. "Doesn't that worry you, people listening?" I asked.

He smiled again. "It's all good. I've got nothing to hide." He waved his hand toward the walls of his office. "You know what the weirdest thing is, Serj? There's no Wi-Fi or internet in this entire building." He laughed. Apparently, his predecessor didn't use a computer.

Pashinyan wanted to show me something else. We walked into a room next door to his office. There was a huge conference table and on the floor beneath it, all these big plastic bags. "What's in the bags?" I asked.

"Go have a look," he nudged me forward.

Inside each were Armenian Army uniforms, boots, and other equipment. The oligarch class had funneled so much money from the state's coffers, that there was no longer even enough to outfit and equip the military properly. That was the first moment when it dawned on me the size of the task Pashinyan had in front of him. The state and its institutions were in complete shambles. Getting into office, it would turn out, was the easy part.

Nonetheless, it had already been an incredible journey for him, and for Armenia. I told him, "Somebody should make a documentary film about the revolution, otherwise no one will believe what really happened."

"You're right," he agreed. "Go make it!"

"I'm not a filmmaker," I protested. But immediately, I realized that I knew people who were. In fact, my friend Garin had been in the streets filming the revolution nearly from the beginning. I called him and told him my idea, which—as it turned out—mirrored something that had been on his mind as well.

That was the germination of the first film I ever produced, *I Am Not Alone*.

Garin did a stunning job with it. It follows Pashinyan from the beginning of his walk to Yerevan through his ascension to prime minister. It's filled with on-the-ground footage of him facing down the police in the streets and laying in front of traffic. Garin also managed to convince the police chief, opposition politicians, and Serzh Sargsyan himself to be interviewed. It's a remarkable piece of storytelling. I mostly helped to bring in other producers, distributors, and financiers. Of course, I also composed the score. The response to the documentary was incredible. It won a slew of awards at film festivals, and we eventually sold it to Netflix.

Political documentaries are a fickle business, though. Not too long after Netflix bought *I Am Not Alone*, the domestic political situation in Armenia turned—for reasons I'll get into in a minute—and Pashinyan became *very* unpopular. The streaming company decided they didn't want to release the film anymore. Netflix paid us under contract and reverted the rights. After all that praise and buildup, *I Am Not Alone* got a relatively muted virtual release. It was a strange conclusion to what had been one of the most amazing journeys of my life, but not one that made me regret a moment of it. After all, I'd fully embraced the idea that I'd learned from those Buddhist sand mandalas all those years ago: the art is in the making of it, not in how it's received.

———

Activists rarely live to see the fruits of their labors come into full bloom. The best you can hope for is to hack away at injustice and have faith that your efforts will make it easier for future generations to get their arms around it. Whatever causes you take up—nuclear proliferation, climate change, gun control, immigration, world peace—as an activist, you learn to celebrate the little victories, because the big ones always seem far out of reach. Even minor gains sometimes evaporate before you have a chance to revel in them. Often, you feel like Sisyphus, forever rolling your boulder up the side of a mountain. Each time you break through the clouds and expect to see the summit, you only find more mountain and more clouds as the boulder rolls back down and you have to start again. To shift to a different rock-based metaphor, activists must be prepared for the fact that all of their work may amount to no more than a pebble tossed into a giant pond. You trust that the ripples will continue to have an impact long after your stone has sunk to the bottom.

For much of the past century, Genocide deniers like Turkey have been abetted by other nations, including the United States, who've turned a blind eye to this historical atrocity for reasons of cynical diplomatic convenience. However, in 2019, both houses of the US Congress passed a resolution making recognition of the Armenian Genocide official US policy. On April 24, 2021, Joe Biden became the first American president to formally acknowledge the Genocide while in office. While the US is only one country, it's also the one country where I'd spent more time pushing for Genocide recognition than any other. From my earliest days at the AYF, to the "Souls" shows, to the songs we wrote and performed with System Of A Down, to the protest outside Dennis Hastert's office, to the trip I made to Congress, to my confrontation with Ahmet Ertegun—this had been the animating political issue of my entire life.

It wasn't as if this milestone was something I achieved on my own, or that System did, but we were a part of it. I was a part of it.

When I began agitating for Genocide recognition, I don't think most people in the US knew much of anything about it. I can look back at what I did and what we did with the band and know that we made a difference. The protests, the shows, the songs, all the interviews, the relentless campaigning—all that stuff moved the needle. We'd tossed our pebble into the pond.

I can say all that while still knowing that the reason why Congress finally passed the resolution wasn't because we finally convinced enough senators and congressional representatives of the truth. It wasn't even because we finally had enough political capital to force the issue. No, the reason why that resolution passed is in many ways the same reason why it had never passed for decades before that: cynical geopolitical reality.

At that moment, Turkey had fallen afoul of the US's greater foreign policy agenda. Despite being a NATO member, in 2019, Turkey completed a purchase of two S-400 anti-aircraft missile systems from Russia rather than buying the Patriot missile systems the US had been angling to sell them. The US sees the S-400 not only as incompatible with NATO air defenses, but also as an intelligence problem, as the system could potentially collect information on US military hardware operating in close proximity. Additionally, in neighboring Syria, the Turks had been attacking the YPG, a militia composed mostly of Kurds, a longtime US ally. The passage of the Genocide resolution was part of a package of retaliatory actions by Congress against Turkey.

That doesn't mean it wasn't a special moment. When the resolution passed, there were congratulatory phone calls and celebrations among activists, among close friends. No matter what happens next, the resolution is permanent. The US formally recognizes the Genocide. Whatever the impetus for it, that is now a hard fact. At the very least, the resolution was a long-overdue acknowledgment of my grandparents' legacy, and the legacy of millions like them.

It's also an acknowledgment of America's own history. It's in part due to the diligent work of Henry Morgenthau, the American ambassador to the Ottoman Empire during World War I, that the world knows about the Genocide, that there is a precise record of it. Morgenthau pressed the US to intervene, he warned Talaat Pasha, the Ottoman interior minister and one of the Genocide's architects, that "our people will never forget these massacres," and he eventually helped form the Committee on Armenian Atrocities, later renamed the Near East Relief Foundation, which saved tens of thousands of Armenian orphans, including my grandfather Stepan. That legacy makes me prouder of the resolution as an American than as an Armenian.

Ultimately though, the impact of the US's recognition of the Genocide is mostly symbolic. It's one of only thirty-four countries where recognition is official policy. The UK, Australia, and New Zealand are among the many where it's not. So, US recognition—while important and necessary—is only another step, a small win to savor before rolling up our sleeves to continue the hard work. In real-world terms, it doesn't change much. It certainly doesn't change Armenia's relationship with Turkey or Turkey's belligerent foreign policy or its fascist domestic policies.

The hard truth is that the one country whose recognition of the Genocide could be more than symbolic, the only one that would have monumental practical impact, is the country that perpetrated it. But until that society opens up, until real democracy flowers there, until the Turks themselves are willing to come to grips with the realities of their own history and make amends for them, I will have to somehow content myself to be Sisyphus pushing that boulder up the mountain.

———

If I needed a demonstration of the lack of real-world impact of the congressional resolution, it came less than a year later, on September 27, 2020, when Azerbaijan launched artillery and air strikes on civilian populations in Nagorno-Karabakh, including around the capital of Stepanakert. From 1988 to 1994, Armenia and Azerbaijan had fought a brutal war over Nagorno-Karabakh, an autonomous region populated for millennia by Armenians but surrounded on all sides by Azerbaijan. Since then, the territory, also known as Artsakh in Armenian, had been a fledgling second Armenian republic, but the Azeris had never relinquished their claims to it. It was a conflict frozen in time but never forgotten. Now, Azerbaijan had reignited the war with the full participation and support of Erdoğan and Turkey.

The Second Nagorno-Karabakh War wasn't simply a continuation of the first one. It carried the legacy of the Genocide too. Turkey and Azerbaijan are more than just allies. They refer to their relationship as "two states, one nation." While many countries fail to recognize the Genocide, Azerbaijan is one of only three, along with Turkey and Pakistan, that actively denies it took place. The country is ruled by a racist, fascist, authoritarian oligarch, Ilham Aliyev, who has claimed that Yerevan is historically part of Azerbaijan and that his goal is to see it and the rest of Armenia under

Azerbaijan's control. Officials in his government have stated that Armenians "have no right to live in this region," and that Azerbaijan's aim "is the complete elimination of Armenians." As Aliyev himself put it, "One day, they may wake up to see the Azerbaijan flag above their heads."

This sort of bellicosity would be concerning to Armenians regardless of its source, but the fact that Azerbaijan sees itself as an extension of the Turkish state makes it all the more frightening. The Turks helped provide arms and tactical expertise to Azerbaijan in their brutal campaign of aggression into Artsakh that began in the fall of 2020. The military action was augmented by a sophisticated misinformation operation by the Azeris and the Turks to falsely portray the Armenians as the aggressors. As the Armenians in Artsakh were coming under fire, few around the world were noticing, and none were rising to their defense.

When we read history, particularly the history of human rights atrocities, it's easy to judge harshly those who failed to answer the moment. Bill Clinton famously expressed his profound regret for failing to do anything to stop the genocide in Rwanda. George W. Bush allowed the slaughter in Darfur to go on unabated because he viewed the Sudanese president Omar al-Bashir as a useful ally in the so-called war on terror.

But it's not just world leaders who have a responsibility. What about all the ordinary people who stand by and do nothing? As I watched the tragedy slowly unfolding in Artsakh, I couldn't live with the idea of standing on the sidelines. But what could *I* do?

After making substantial donations to the Armenia Fund for humanitarian aid to Artsakh, I initially suggested to my brothers in System that we release a statement together, standing against Azerbaijan's aggression and pushing back against the false narrative they'd manufactured with the Turks. We did that. Then, John dropped a suggestion into our group text. It had been so long since we'd released any music together, he wrote. Imagine how much of a spotlight we could draw to the situation if we were to break that streak by putting out a song together.

Even with all we'd been through as a band, I didn't hesitate. I was totally in. At the time, I was in New Zealand, but I'd be back in LA in a week or so and we could record it then. As excited messages zipped around the band's group text, I suggested that we write something specifically about what was going on in Artsakh. The next text in the long chain came from Daron: "Fuck this. I'm out. I don't want to do this."

Huh? I was stunned and confused. After all these years of wanting to make music together again, now that I'd finally agreed to it, *Daron* was the one bailing? It felt like I was missing something. I started scrolling back through the group text. Because I was in New Zealand, in a different time zone, I'd only skimmed through the chain of messages when I woke up that day. As I reviewed what I'd missed, I found a text from Daron saying that he had a song he'd already written that would work. He'd assumed that when I suggested writing something fresh, it was my passive-aggressive way of telling him I didn't want to record his song. In fact, I simply hadn't known it existed. We eventually ironed out the misunderstanding, but the hypersensitivity didn't exactly bode well for the process of recording our first music in fifteen years.

I really liked what Daron had written, a Sabbath-y rock song called "Protect the Land." Management thought we should put out two songs, though, and Daron volunteered that he had a second one, "Genocidal Humanoidz," ready to go as well. I didn't love that one as much, but realized I had to put those feelings on the shelf. The point was to put out music and do it quickly to raise money and awareness for the humanitarian suffering in Artsakh. The longer we spent trying to resolve creative differences that we'd failed to resolve for the previous fifteen years, the worse the outcome would be for our people.

When we got in the studio to record, Daron micromanaged every aspect of the recording—even more than before. He'd written the music and lyrics to both songs and had already recorded demos himself. He wanted John to play the drums exactly as he heard them in his head and wanted me to sing my vocal parts exactly as he'd sung them on the demo. This was the kind of stuff I'd sworn I wasn't going to stand for anymore, but again, I decided to suck it up. After all, people were dying. Azerbaijan was shelling homes in Artsakh with cluster bombs. There were videos of the Azeri military decapitating Armenian soldiers and civilians. They were doing all this with impunity. I was looking at these songs as weapons of soft power that needed to be deployed as soon as possible. If I had to swallow my pride to make that happen, that was a pretty minor sacrifice to make in the scheme of things.

When the songs came out in the fall of 2020, I did as many interviews as I could, during which I tried to focus public attention in the US and Europe on the war and dismantle the misinformation Turkey and Azerbaijan had been disseminating. Our campaign made a tangible difference. The songs raised something like $700,000, which we donated directly to benefit soldiers and veterans who'd been injured or needed protective gear. Perhaps even more importantly, we began to rewrite the public narrative about what was happening there. An analysis of the stories that appeared in the international press showed that the tide began to turn after the release of the songs and the campaign behind them.

Unfortunately, it was not enough to alter the military facts on the ground. Azerbaijan, rich with oil money, had a big advantage in military hardware and technology, which they had purchased from Russia, Turkey, Europe, and Israel. They had the backing of the Turkish state and thousands of Syrian mercenaries and jihadists at their disposal. At one point, Turkish generals took over the campaign due to the ineffectiveness of Azerbaijan's attack.

The Armenian military, on the other hand, had been gutted by decades of corruption and an overreliance on Russia and the CSTO, a military alliance of post-Soviet states, as protectors. Putin also hated the Velvet Revolution and Nikol Pashinyan. Although he didn't physically intervene in 2018, he allowed the Azeris and Turks to start a war during the COVID pandemic in their region of influence, their geopolitical backyard, just two years later. He was afraid of the same thing in Armenia that he feared in Ukraine—a pivot to the West.

The war went badly for Armenia and Artsakh, and after forty-four days, nearly seven thousand deaths, and tens of thousands displaced, Pashinyan agreed to crippling terms for a ceasefire, ceding most of the territory in Nagorno-Karabakh to Azerbaijan.

It was a humbling defeat that did not go down well in Armenia. Pashinyan, who'd come to power on the back of massive protests, now became the target of such protests. Some of the domestic chaos was the work of his opportunistic political enemies. The day after the signing of the ceasefire, Parliament was ransacked by thugs close to the former leaders—just a few months before the January 6 attack against Congress in the US. Pashinyan was tarred as a traitor who'd badly mismanaged the war. There were calls for his resignation.

Pashinyan agreed to resign and called for early elections. Such was the lingering enmity toward the oligarchs who'd ruled Armenia before him that Pashinyan won back his seat in the free and fair elections that followed and remained prime minister. But public opinion had turned against him, which was why Netflix no longer wanted to release *I Am Not Alone*, the documentary we'd made chronicling his heroic rise. At the time I asked to get on a separate call with the executive at Netflix and our producers, without the creatives, and point blank asked if pressure from Turkey was really the reason they are refusing to release the film. The executive denied it. I couldn't help but to think that to be the reason since so many films dealing with recognition of the Armenian Genocide had been shelved for distribution due to Turkish pressure in the past. My tight connection to Pashinyan also made me a target of social media attacks by fellow Armenians. The beautiful unity of 2018 was in tatters.

As of this writing, Pashinyan remains the country's prime minister, though he's still generally unpopular among huge parts of the population. There is an old adage in politics that you campaign in poetry but govern in prose. In this case, that adage seemed even more pointed.

Assaults by Azeri military units on Armenian civilians and soldiers continued intermittently after the ceasefire. They shelled villages and made further incursions into sovereign Armenian territory, where, the Columbia University Institute of the Study of Human Rights reported, they took dozens of POWs, and even executed a group of Armenian soldiers who'd surrendered, a clear violation of the Geneva Conventions. There were reports of torture and indiscriminate killing of Armenians in and around Artsakh. In late 2022, Azeris began blockading the Lachin Corridor, the only road connecting Armenia to Artsakh, cutting off deliveries of food, medical supplies, gas, electricity, water, and internet service to the 120,000 Armenians living in the region.

Azeri government officials also stepped up their dehumanizing portrayals of Armenians, calling them "dogs" and a "cancer." Aliyev, the fascist billionaire oligarch whose ex-KGB father had essentially passed the country to him as a family inheritance, instituted a policy of ethnic hatred toward Armenians that often begins for Azeris as early as kindergarten. In a particularly ominous development, the government in Azerbaijan minted a stamp commemorating the Second Nagorno-Karabakh War with a picture of a person in a hazmat suit cleansing the region. All this prompted nonprofits Genocide Watch and the Lemkin Institute (named after Raphael Lemkin, who coined the word "genocide") to issue a warning in late 2022, that the Armenians in the region were increasingly under threat of a potential genocide at the hands of the Turkish-backed Azerbaijan government.

For nine months, Azerbaijan starved the population of Nagorno-Karabakh with this illegal blockade of essential goods and services along what became known as "the corridor of life." Luis Moreno Ocampo, the former prosecutor of the International

Criminal Court, called it an act of genocide. Despite condemnations by the international community, including two UN International Court of Justice decrees to open the Lachin Corridor and pleas from the European Court of Human Rights, Amnesty International, Human Rights Watch, and the leaders of many countries, Azerbaijan refused to comply or even allow in international observers or journalists. All the while, the Azeris used their oil money and its accompanying geopolitical influence to muddy the waters as to what was really happening in Artsakh. After I did an interview with the BBC to draw attention to the unfolding humanitarian disaster, the Azeris threatened to take the BBC off the airwaves in Azerbaijan unless they got equal time for their genocide apologists. Sadly, the BBC folded and gave them that airtime.

In September 2023, the Azeris launched a full-scale military assault against Artsakh, complete with indiscriminate bombings, causing the death of at least four hundred people including civilians and children. There were also eyewitness reports and video evidence of massacres in the northern part of Artsakh by the approaching Azeri army. As a result, Artsakh's much smaller defenses collapsed, and the government was dissolved. More than one hundred thousand Armenians living in Artsakh immediately grabbed what little they could carry and fled across the border to Armenia, driven from their homes much as their ancestors had been before them, leaving behind their indigenous homeland of three thousand years and creating a huge humanitarian catastrophe.

Throughout the invasion and the illegal blockade that precipitated it, the international community repeatedly condemned the Azeri aggression but otherwise largely sat on their hands, refusing to take concrete actions. Even the Russian peacekeeping troops who were already stationed in Artsakh to enforce the supposed cease-fire did nothing. In short, the world failed us once again. Because of the war in Ukraine, Russia realigned its geopolitical priorities and allied with Azerbaijan and Turkey, throwing Armenia under the bus again, and causing us to lose our historic homeland, as it had nearly a century earlier. The West promised support and criticized the aggressors but didn't back up their words with actions like sanctions or military support. The UN, which had not visited Artsakh for thirty years, arrived after the invasion was all over and twenty-four hours later released a whitewashed statement to blur its own complicity. Armenians, meanwhile, were left with the same pains from 108 years earlier, as well as the same results.

What's worse, Aliyev has given every indication that the ethnic cleansing of Artsakh will not satisfy his territorial ambitions, and that his next target is Armenia itself. More than a century on from 1915, this is where Armenians find themselves today: staring down the barrel of the same terror our grandparents and great-grandparents once faced, at the hands of essentially the same oppressors. History repeats itself and that frequently uttered mantra about genocide, "never again," is just a self-satisfying crock of shit so long as we continue to choose profits over people. Russia, the EU, and the US all chose the genocidal dictatorship of Azerbaijan over democratic Artsakh and Armenia because of oil and gas. *Again.*

On one hand, this full-circle moment is monumentally disturbing. All the work that's been done—by me, by many, many others—to bring the events of 1915 to light, and here we are again.

On the other hand, it only makes the mission and the work more urgent and vital. It reaffirms to me the existential importance of the cause. If we don't tell these stories, whether they're in Artsakh or in Efkere or in Auschwitz or in Rwanda or in East Timor or in Darfur, if we don't demand accountability for the victims and fight for justice, we are doomed to see these stories repeat themselves again and again, all over the globe in years to come. What else can we possibly do anyway other than keep pushing our boulder up the mountain, hoping against hope that it doesn't one day roll back down and flatten us?

CHAPTER 19

In the fall of 2017, I took Anthony Bourdain to Armenia for his CNN food and travel show, *Parts Unknown*. Earlier that year, while Ange and I were watching the show, she'd remarked that it would be amazing to have Bourdain visit Armenia. We knew he was a huge music fan and she suggested I reach out to him.

I laughed. "Yeah, I'm just gonna hit the guy up and say I'm this singer from this band, and he should go to Armenia." But that's basically what I did. I got his email from a well-connected agent friend of mine, then emailed him explaining who I was and what I liked about him, specifically his authenticity and search for truth behind cultures, politics, and world events. I told him, "If you decide to go to Armenia, I've got your back." I didn't know him at all, but to my surprise, he responded immediately: "You're on." As it turned out, he'd been looking for an angle for visiting Armenia and I had just given him one.

My week with Tony in Armenia was unforgettable. I got a chance to show him this unique place that was so important to me through *my* eyes. He was boundlessly curious about what made people tick, what made a whole nation tick. Once he learned about what had been happening in Nagorno-Karabakh, he insisted on going, even though CNN's lawyers weren't thrilled with the idea. When I warned him that Azerbaijan would blacklist him if he visited the region, I remember exactly what he told me: "I don't give a fuck. I'm tired of petty dictators." He wasn't just referring to Aliyev but also Erdoğan and Putin. I loved his determination, his courage.

Our first night together in Yerevan set the tone for the whole trip. We went to one of my favorite restaurants there, Dolmama. At the time, I'd only just met Tony. He sat down across from me, thanked me for joining him, and then someone on the crew counted down, "5, 4, 3 . . ." and we were rolling. Tony had a question loaded up for me.

"You were born in Beirut, you live in California and New Zealand, yet you call yourself Armenian," he started. "So, how Armenian are you?"

I was floored. When I peeled back the layers, his question wasn't just about my Armenian identity. What he was really asking was not just "Where is home for you?" but also, more deeply, "*Who* are you?" So much for the small talk, I guess.

Those are questions I've been chasing answers to since, well, forever. Yes, I was born in Lebanon, but I always had a sense that I was just passing through. Lebanon is where my grandparents Stepan and Varsenig found each other after losing most of their family in the Genocide. It's where my dad met my mom, but it's not where we were from nor where we were headed. It felt like an important place for us, yes—but not really home.

After all these years, in many ways the United States *is* a home for me, but it doesn't always *feel* like home. It's where my friends, my work, and most of my extended family are based. My life in the US is exciting, it's full of hustle and action, but my soul doesn't feel settled there. Much of this is personal, but some is, sadly, political. The US is turning into its own mortal enemy. It's a country that doesn't need external enemies because the obfuscation of personal relationships, coupled with the abomination of partisan politics, has caused unparalleled fear and paranoia of one another. All this breaks down the cohesive cement of national unity. So, even though I technically reside here, I wouldn't necessarily call the US my one true "home" either.

When I started living part of the year in New Zealand, my physical being immediately felt different. The land, the air, the water, the trees, the people—it all made my body comfortable in a way I'd rarely experienced before. I felt an intuitive sense of belonging when I first landed on her shores. I feel healthier there, calmer.

But even though I feel physically at home in New Zealand, it's only been during my extended stays in Armenia that my spirit itself begins to feel untethered. It's the place where my life, my history, my very existence makes total sense. Yet, I've never actually *lived* there. Even with the good fortune I've had and the resources at my disposal, it's as if I've been cobbling this fractured idea of home together from various points on the globe, unable to settle myself definitively in just one place.

I suppose this is the original trauma of any displaced people. If you're chased out of your homeland, a part of you is always trying to get back there, even generations later. This is particularly stark for Armenians like me who trace their roots to lands in a country that still denies responsibility for driving us out. One day, I'd love nothing more than to visit my grandfather's village, feel the sun there on my face, smell the air, and touch the land. But that can only happen when Turkey's face changes to a more humanitarian one honoring their own history and ours. I don't know when that day will come. And if you can't get back to the physical land your ancestors lived and worked and loved and died on, you find yourself searching the world for a feeling you can't quite put your finger on, a sense of contentment that always seems just beyond your reach.

———

I recognize how lucky I am today and am filled with gratitude. Even if my home address has never been as spiritually fixed as I'd like, I live a life where I can afford to hop between continents, spending my days working on projects that nourish my soul. I wake up these days, see my son off to school, then usually spend my time painting or making music or writing.

My creative life also looks very different than it did twenty years ago, something for which I'm extremely thankful. I've composed music for multiple films and TV series, even produced a handful. I regularly release albums of classical compositions, and still occasionally crank out my own brand of rock music. I don't sit down with the idea of making rock or jazz or classical music or anything else. The music comes in whatever form it comes in and I let it. I find that I'm not as interested as I once was in being a vocalist, a lyricist, or a performer. Nowadays, most of the time, I prefer to be a composer, building the full scope of musical architecture's emotional depth from the ground up, with or without words, and sometimes watching others bring that truth to life. It's quite a different feeling—an honor, really—seeing and hearing sixty to seventy musicians playing your music without you. I still like to sing sometimes, and if I have something urgent to say, I'll write it down—but mostly in prose.

I've also had dozens of exhibitions of my paintings with music over the past decade, in both the US and New Zealand. I've created an immersive experience where people can hear the art and see the music. Giving people the chance to interact with multiple senses amplifies the artistic potency of each painting and associated message. Whether it's through music, painting, or any art form, my intention is always to move people. I don't do neutral well. I enjoy art that changes me and, as grandiose as it might sound, I want to try to change the world around me with art. That to me is success, not how much royalty your music has earned.

———

In 2023, System played only one show, in Las Vegas, at a big festival called Sick New World. In the lead-up to the show, I was thinking it would be my final show with the band. I'd been stuck in a pattern over the previous few years, where the rest of the band would press me to do shows each year, I'd resist, they'd push me a little more, I'd feel guilty that I was standing in the way of these guys doing what they really loved (and getting well paid for it), so I'd buckle and agree to do a handful of gigs. It isn't an emotionally healthy cycle, and I was ready for it to be over. I told the guys that we could announce in the press that it was my last show and make a big deal of it. As had been the case in the past, they didn't want to.

A week before Sick New World, my attitude was very much "Let's get this over with." I mean, I knew being onstage, seeing excited fans, and performing would all be a lot of fun, but artistically, it just feels redundant. Then when I showed up for rehearsals, something happened that I didn't totally expect: I *enjoyed* it.

The afternoon before the show, I was there in Vegas on the big outdoor stage, surrounded by my bandmates, as we ran through a final rehearsal. In the pit in front of the stage, I could see Rumi, along with John's daughters and Shavo's kids, jumping around, dancing, and rocking out to our music. I almost had to catch my breath. It was so clear at that moment that System Of A Down is not just a band, it's a family—a dysfunctional one, no doubt—but a family, nonetheless.

The show the next day felt so comfortable, like we were playing in our living room to our friends and family. Maybe it was easy because there was no tour, no crazy schedule, no bus to climb on, no radio stations to go butter up. Maybe it was because we were just playing for the sake of playing. It was pure.

When you scrape away all the complications, it sometimes can be that simple. There was something about hanging out with these guys, being around our crew, sharing thoughts, and playing music that I really do love that felt *good*. It didn't change any of my feelings about touring and it didn't fix any of the creative issues in the band that were broken, but what I sometimes forget about Daron, Shavo, and John is how much I genuinely *like* them.

Over the years, I've probably spent more time with the three of them than anyone else in my life, outside my family. The fact that I still like being around them after all this time means something. Maybe it doesn't mean that we need to be on the road for one hundred shows a year, and maybe it doesn't mean that we need to hole up in the studio every eighteen months to bang out a new album, but it means something. Is it art? Are we a glorified cover band? I don't know. But I love those guys with all of my heart and want to keep them in my life—as friends, as brothers, and maybe one day again, as bandmates.

I wrote a poem once that had the line "Home is a place you can't walk away from in the end." I didn't write those words about System Of A Down, or at least I didn't think I did, but when I read it now, I wonder if maybe my subconscious knew something I didn't back then.

System, for me, *is* a kind of home—and it always has been. It's where I found a feeling of belonging and grew to understand important parts of myself. Ten or twenty years could go by before the next time the four of us get on a stage or walk into a studio together, but even if we never do either again, I'll always be a part of System Of A Down and it will always be a part of me. *That* is home. It may not be where I want to live anymore, but I can certainly imagine—and even look forward to—coming back to visit.

———

In math, coinciding angles are where two lines meet at a specific point. Coincidence is not a random chance. In 2008, I was at the Burbank airport, waiting to take a JetBlue flight to New York for a *Prometheus Bound* workshop. The flight was horribly delayed. As I sat there in the departures lounge, I was suddenly overcome by the feeling that I needed to leave, to not be there. And so, on a very uncharacteristic whim, I asked for a credit from the airline, grabbed my bag, and started to drive back home.

On the ride home, I got a call from a friend with an offer to join a few other artists to meet the Dalai Lama in Philadelphia a few days later for a documentary someone was making about music and spirituality. They were looking for four different artists to ask the Dalai Lama questions. Three of the spots were already taken by Moby, Joss Stone, and KT Tunstall. They needed a fourth. I quickly and enthusiastically agreed.

It occurred to me afterwards that if I'd been on that JetBlue flight, I may not have gotten that call. It would've gone to my voicemail, and my friend could've moved on to whoever was next on his list. But I don't think it was luck or chance or coincidence that put me in the car to take that call. I think it was where I was meant to be. There were two lines destined to meet at a specific point.

A few days later, I was in a conference room at the Four Seasons in Philadelphia, about to come face-to-face with the Dalai Lama. The organizers had given each of us these beautiful Tibetan prayer shawls, and when the Dalai Lama walked in, we handed them to him. He nodded in appreciation and smiled. Then he approached me, saw my goatee, grabbed it, and started playing with it, like he was my friend's three-year-old child. I realized then that we were in the presence of someone whose spirit was truly uninhibited. His people might be in bondage, but his soul was totally free. He sat down and we began to ask him questions.

For years, I had thought hard about how justice and spirituality interacted, not just in my own life but life in general. I'd researched it academically as well as in the real world. In my life, this search for justice had come first, a perpetual hunger awakened by Genocide denial. Cognizant spirituality followed later, almost as its necessary antidote, because that road to justice is unpaved and painful at times. Meditation had the ability to soothe that pain and smooth out those bumps in the road. A holistic spiritual practice is great for relieving stress, but is the stress of injustice really something we should aim to alleviate? Shouldn't we feel as much of that pain and stress as we can bear so that we're moved to fix it? Isn't our complete emotional revulsion to particular injustices the reason we even react? The Dalai Lama had dealt with Chinese oppression of his people his whole life while walking a very spiritual path, so I figured there would be no better person to ask this question brewing in my head.

"What is the intersection of justice and spirituality?" I asked him.

The Dalai Lama thought about it for a few moments, then nodded and opened his mouth to answer. "To follow the path of injustice would be spiritually disconcerting."

At first, I thought his double-negative response didn't really lay out the reason why following a path of injustice would be disconcerting. But the more I reflected on it, the more I realized he was simply articulating something that I'd long felt: we are all eternally interconnected. We cannot harm others without causing harm to ourselves. We cannot love others without loving ourselves. As such, those of us who fight for justice do so because we can't live with ourselves if we don't. Injustice is spiritually disconcerting because it is an attack on ourselves and everything else around us, all at the same time.

Whatever you're fighting for, whatever struggle you're engaged in, putting positive energy out into the world is the only thing you can ever control. The results are out of your hands. As such, one of the main beneficiaries of any activism is the activist. Doing good *feels* good and right. That may sound self-indulgent, but it's not. It goes back to the Dalai Lama's answer to my question: we cannot love others without loving and honoring the truth in ourselves. If that feeling is what keeps me on the right path, if that's what brings balance to my universe, if that's what ensures I'm working to leave this place better than I found it, that could never be a bad thing. Making a gorgeous noise or a vibrant painting or an energetic protest aren't only a means toward something else—truth, beauty, justice—they are an end in and of themselves. In fact, these are the things we stay alive for. I think often about how my grandfather got to a point where his body no longer wanted nutrition. As human beings, when we no longer want to be nourished by art, by human connection, when we no longer want to be moved and inspired, that's when we know we are truly dying.

I can see now that my hunger for justice and my search for this idea of home have always been two sides of the same spiritual coin. I can't understand one without the other. I can't solve one before I find peace with the other. If I don't fight for the recognition of the Genocide, if I don't agitate for other just causes, if I don't work to create a more balanced world for all of us to live in, how can I ever hope to find that elusive feeling of home, that sense that I belong exactly where I am? I didn't need a Tibetan man in bright robes to tell me this, but sometimes it helps to have someone who is farther along on their path drop some breadcrumbs—or maybe brain-crumbs—for you, so you know which way to walk.

This has always been the way. My grandfather Stepan saw horrors in his life that I sometimes still have trouble even fathoming. He was forced from his home, he watched family members killed, and though he lived a long and fruitful life, he carried the weight of all that to his grave. Comparatively speaking, my journey has been charmed. The things I've spent my life longing for, searching out, and fighting for—home, identity, community, justice, creativity, connectivity—are all things that Stepan, and sometimes even my own parents, could only dream of. But they did dream, and they did strive, and they did search, and they did fight.

And in doing so, they created a world where I could not only live out that dream, I could transcend it—and then pass it on.

ACKNOWLEDGMENTS

My thanks for the help in creating this book to David Peisner; to my editors, Carrie Napolitano, Richard Roper, and Yvonne Jacobs; to my manager, George Tonikian; and to Max Edwards and Vanessa Kerr at Aevitas Creative Management.